IN SEARCH OF
WEALTH AND POWER

YEN FU AND THE WEST

IN SEARCH OF
WEALTH AND POWER

YEN FU AND THE WEST

Benjamin Schwartz

THE BELKNAP PRESS OF

HARVARD UNIVERSITY PRESS

CAMBRIDGE, MASSACHUSETTS

1 9 6 4

135956

Distributed in Great Britain by Oxford University Press, London
Library of Congress Catalog Card Number 64–16069
Printed in the United States of America

TO MY MOTHER AND FATHER
Jennie and Hyman Schwartz

ACKNOWLEDGMENTS

I N W R I T I N G this study I have benefited immeasurably from conversations with numerous people both at home and abroad. I should like particularly to thank Professor Chang Fo-ch'uan, who painstakingly scrutinized and corrected my translations from the Chinese. I should also like to thank Professor Ch'ü T'ung-tsu, who often helped me in my struggles with difficult passages.

I owe a particular debt of gratitude to Mrs. Elizabeth Matheson and other members of the East Asian Research Center at Harvard University for their editorial help. This volume, in fact, is number sixteen of the Harvard East Asian Series.

Finally, I should like to thank Professor Louis Hartz for his kind encouragement and his willingness to preface this book with his own observations.

Benjamin Schwartz
Cambridge, Mass.
January 1964

CONTENTS

INTRODUCTION

I T I S the genius of the foreign critic to bring to the surface aspects of thought implicit in the life of the nation he studies but explicit for him because of the contrasts supplied by his own culture. It is a shock of self-discovery which makes Halévy interesting to the English, Tocqueville to the Americans. In this work Professor Schwartz gives us a new foreign observer of Western thought as a whole, although a man centrally concerned with the texts of classical British liberalism—Yen Fu, who translated the European writers in the China of the turn of the century. And Yen Fu, from the angle of a culture which has not yet experienced modernity, seizes in their work on a theme of collective energy which, apart from anything they said about "individualism" or "laissez faire," reflected the movement of Europe into the modern world. That theme has not been a preoccupation of Western critics, precisely because it tended to use other ideas as channels for its expression. But the West has drifted into a new position now, where its involvement with nations overtly experiencing the issue of "modern history" cannot fail to inspire it to review that issue in its own intellectual past. It is likely that the perspective of Yen Fu will, in significant part, become in the end our own.

How does Yen Fu develop his view of the European theorists? It is a tribute to the patient care of Professor Schwartz that he manages to elicit from the writings of the Chinese critic a concept which, in Western terms, is almost endlessly elusive. There are at least two sides to the secret that Yen Fu finds in European thought, both of them necessary in his view to bring China out of its backwardness. One is the manifestation of sheer energy, the other is the public spirit which disciplines energy to collective ends. In the apparent formulations of the European thinkers themselves these ideas are distributed in terms of a well-known balance, recorded and enshrined in practically every textbook. The concept of energy is contained within the individualist ethic, and precisely because of the centrality of that ethic the notion of public interest is shoved out to the margins, serving as a kind of vague and benevolent end toward which free competition moves. What Yen Fu does is subtle enough. He thrusts forward the energy concept in its own right, and after having made individualism an instrument of it, he places public spirit at the very center of liberal thought. The result is that writers who in Western terms are ordinarily viewed as atomists subscribing to the notion of a natural harmony emerge as theorists of a titanic cultural drive leading to collective strength— "Faustian" figures, to use Professor Schwartz's own term.

Now we must not assume that this in itself is a distortion. When the submerged premises of an intellectual system are brought to light there is bound to be some disturbance, some reshuffling on the surface. Yen Fu would have no original meaning for us if he did not bewilder us in this way. On the other hand, the enthusiasm of the Chinese critic for wealth and power often leads him to actual mistakes. And Professor Schwartz, with a command of Eastern and Western sources that must be accounted rare in the field of scholarship, points these errors out. I do not refer here to Yen Fu's penchant for interpreting the most precious aspects of Western liberal morality in terms of the cultural strength they engender, as when he praises Montesquieu's concept of equal rights or Mill's notion of intellectual freedom for promoting Western national energy. Given his view, he has, as it were, a right to argue in this way. But there is no defense, on the basis of the actual texts themselves, for equating out of a common concern with both military and economic strength the industrial stage in the theory of Herbert Spencer with the military stage it presumably liquidates. There is no defense, either, for identifying, out of a concern with the national power that liberalism yields, the work of the liberal writers with the mercantilist ideas they tried to destroy. These are patent distortions of intellectual history, and they cannot be said to shed light upon it.

And yet we need not fear that the Western student, who has lived by the distinctions that Yen Fu obscures, will be seriously corrupted by these distortions. They are in fact a harmless price to pay for the force of a novel insight. I do not mean to imply that Western historiography has not itself at any time been concerned with the element of raw energy present in the modern ethos, or with the public spirit which suffused it. Actually the energy issue is one of the central themes of the study of the Renaissance, which is not surprising since this is the Western moment most analogous to that which Yen Fu is experiencing in China, when modernity is thrusting itself forward against the background of the traditionalist past. But it is the very triumph of energy, the very fading of the challenge of medieval quiescence, which means that this concern cannot last. By the time

Adam Smith has appeared, the concerns of Burckhardt seem irrelevant and the categories which emerge are those of individualism or mercantilism or collectivism, which presuppose, all of them, the drive and the energy of modern Western life. There is a curious principle of "combined development" here in which Yen Fu is viewing the latest manifestations of the Western modern spirit with the same fundamental wonder that we have confined to its origin. He is asking of those manifestations questions we have ceased to ask, not because they have been answered but because the medieval contrasts which make them vivid have receded into the distant background.

Nor could the uneven rate of development of the Western nations themselves provide a lasting enunciation of the Yen Fu perspective on liberal thought. There are, it is true, hints of his orientation in many places, due to the fact that the Western nations were unequally advanced, all of them "behind" England, in the manifestation of the peculiar virtues of wealth and power. France worshipped the capitalist energy and the civic spirit of the British, even though it itself provided the physiocratic inspiration for Adam Smith. Germany rejected the competitive individualism of classical economics, but in significant part only because it needed the "national economy" of List to compensate for its backwardness. The United States shared that need, and List as well, but after the Civil War it produced a group of Spencerians as passionate in their admiration of the master as Yen Fu himself. And yet none of these attitudes blossomed into the pattern of reactions that Professor Schwartz develops here, either in connection with cultural dynamism or collective purpose. And the reason was not merely that the Western nations shared a common cultural past but also that the unevenness of their growth and development was ironed out, in one degree or another, as history proceeded. All of them pursued the path of modernity. Indeed, this fact is registered in the outlook of Yen

Fu himself, which is another buried assumption he makes plain, for he seems unconcerned with the national differences that trouble the West and moves easily from a discussion of England to Europe as a whole. Where in Europe can one find a comparable perception of the common course that the European nations took? The truth is, one has to go at least as far East as Russian thought in order to find the "West."

In England itself, of course, the land where Yen Fu's major heroes live, the perspective he advances is least possible. For England, both in the realm of economic energy and liberal thought, is "first"—farthest away, as it were, from the contrasts of the Renaissance and without any more advanced nation to give it perspective on the duality of energy and community out of which the achievements of modernity arise. True enough, England carried with it, as it responded to the stimulus of Smith and Spencer, the weight of a Tory tradition, which is the miracle of its modern history. Actually it was this very Tory tradition, this lingering spirit of Burke, which accounted for much of the public spirit that Yen Fu, or even the French, found in the British liberals. The marginal notion of collective harmony, whether in the natural law of Smith or the Darwinism of Spencer, could not have acquired reality in the age of the Industrial Revolution in Britain without the actual nourishment that came from the more organic harmony of a medievalism that had not altogether disappeared. But in some ways it was this very collaboration between the middle ages and the modern world in Britain which mitigated the contrasts that might have produced an English analogue to the perspective that Professor Schwartz has studied. Sheer energy did not arise as a contrast to medieval quiescence because the medieval spirit, paradoxically, embraced it, as when the bourgeoisie became solid members of the British aristocracy. The collective ethos did not arise as a contrast to the undisciplined play of egotism, as it did in France, let alone China, precisely because a measure of the Burkean spirit suffused the old order and was implicitly assumed in the new. There is an ironic sense in which England, which produced Yen Fu's favorite theorists of wealth and power but did so within the framework of its traditionalist controls, exemplifies in its total cultural experience the ends toward which Yen Fu twisted the specific stream of liberal thought. Can it be that this is why, as Professor Schwartz keenly points out, Yen Fu himself seems unable to distinguish between England and Spencer, between Britain and the British thinkers?

Nor is the matter entirely one of the age of Smith and Mill and Spencer themselves. While Yen Fu was translating these writers in China, new battles were raging in England, replacing those of the early or the middle nineteenth century, and in the course of these battles the classical British thinkers were being revaluated. Smith and Spencer emerged increasingly, not as opponents of the old Toryism but as "reactionaries" themselves, opposing socialism and reform, and they were indeed absorbed into the ethos of the British Conservative Party. But the emergence of the socialist view did not, from its angle, give us the kind of perception that Professor Schwartz offers us so forcefully here out of the Chinese experience. To be sure, Marxism, in its doctrine of class struggle, showed a queer and angular appreciation of the energy displayed by the middle class in displacing the old feudal elites. Marx, no less than Yen Fu, admired the force of the bourgeoisie. But as the liberal writers became cast in collectivist terms, as Harold Laski arose to criticize them, this line of insight did not really flower; for the Marxian or the socialist admiration of capitalist energy remains an historical afterthought, not a central polemical concern. Indeed the polemical concern is that Smith and Mill and Spencer inhibit the fulfillment of their own productive drives by an individualism which, instead of serving collective ends, frustrates their attainment. The result is that the bourgeois heroes of Yen Fu become inadequate by both of his own standards: socialism becomes the true fulfillment of productivity and public spirit as well. This is not quite the Tory problem in reverse, but almost. In the earlier era British liberalism does not clearly enunciate the Yen Fu norms because the medieval ethos is ready to collaborate with it; in the later era socialism collaborates so well that liberalism ceases to be the distinctive champion of the norms. From Smith to Laski, by virtue of the rich continuities of English and Western ideological development, the Yen Fu perspective is kept in abeyance in British thought.

And yet the dimensions of energy and community that Yen Fu seized upon were always there. The Renaissance might recede into the distance, the Western nations might bury the matter by all of them proceeding along modern lines, Britain might becloud the issue by the character of its historic development, but the spirit of organized dynamism that Western thought expressed was vital to its character and its impact. That spirit revolutionized Western life—built its factories, altered its landscape, transformed its law. Here is a matter worth knowing, quite apart from world affairs. But it is of course the pressure of world affairs, in our time an "objective force" analogous to the pressure of the European middle class behind the capitalist ideas themselves, which assures our attention to the angle of vision that Yen Fu adopts. That angle, as Professor Schwartz notes, is very much like the one that other non-Western nations are bound to have. Nor is it this significant fact alone, the multiplication of foreign observers, as it were, which assures our concern. What does so as well is the fact that the West itself has become involved with the world for which Yen Fu speaks and therefore cannot, in terms of its own life, avoid the perspective he had. Usually in history comparative relationships are unilateral, as when Yen Fu himself admired England, or even Rousseau the

Indians. The admired party, the seat of virtue, does not need to put itself out. But in the case of the Western nations today, including those like the United States who caught up with England industrially, modernity is no exemption from involvement with nations less modern. It is this involvement which gives a sudden mutuality to East and West in their perception of the spirit of collective energy implicit in the philosophies of modern Europe.

This does not mean that we will ultimately hold to the prescriptive formulas that Yen Fu advanced. The critic who has watched Western thinkers twist the biological determinisms of Darwin into the channels of their ideological hope cannot fail, with a tired smile, to notice the way in which Yen Fu, from the distance of China, does so as well. Why was China backward? Because the struggle for survival had somehow been inhibited there. But it is not the perversion of evolution, a principle which was probably equally close to and equally remote from all of the social philosophies using it, that is the real issue here. What is significant is the fact that we may discover, as Professor Schwartz effectively suggests in his concluding remarks, that even Spencerian individualism is accidental to the energy, the national power, that Yen Fu worships. We may find that the atomistic ethic in modern times contained a substance which, in significant part, could do quite well without that ethic. The socialist movement, when it borrowed the notion of productive power from liberalism, already in Western terms suggested this possibility, and it is surely revealing that Yen Fu seems unaware of its dangers. But Western socialism did not force us to the stark finality of this observation, because it borrowed, together with power, a touch of the old individualist outlook. Even Spencer can live, somehow, with the Webbs or Laski. But that is not so easily true in the case of other collectivisms, energetic indeed, which have emerged in the world with which England and all of the Western nations are now entangled.

If this perception should become a central one, then the impact of Yen Fu's perspective upon us may take in the end an unexpected turn. It may be, after we have absorbed his elucidation of energy and community strength, that we will come to a larger appreciation of the moral formulas of individualism which contained them, and actually hid them, in modern thought. When the Faustian energies in Herbert Spencer are divorced from his ethic of private right, and go marching off on their own, that ethic is bound to be seen in a new and precious light. But this is an historical matter not only for the Orient but for the West itself. Yen Fu seems to foreshadow a China that has "bypassed" a truly liberal phase in its drive toward modernity, but in the West that phase was nourished by the fact that liberal values antedated all concern with modernity. The individualist norm did not arise with the classical economists, even with the Renaissance. It arose in Greece in the age of the Stoics, was absorbed by Roman Law and Christianity, and flourished for centuries during the medieval era. Its ethic is an ethic of the personal spirit which transcends quiescence and energy, poverty and national greatness. If Yen Fu's indifference to this ethic in his passionate search for wealth and power forces us back to the purity of its original meaning, then his insight may have accomplished its most significant result.

In any case, however the chips may fall in this matter, there is no doubt that Professor Schwartz has given us a fascinating new critic of the Western intellectual experience in modern times. Yen Fu was not the only Chinese commentator on the modern Western texts, nor did he have the precision of a Western scholar, an Élie Halévy for example, closer to the experience he examined. Professor Schwartz is balanced in his claims. But Yen Fu is nonethe-

less a figure of enormous distinctive impact, and if distance
dulls his precision it broadens the character of his insight.
The Western critics of Western thought tell us more of
what we already know about ourselves, but Yen Fu from
a farther point tells us something we do not know. And
yet Professor Schwartz could not have given us this result
if he were simply laying out the apparent effects of a foreign place upon a man, the dutiful record even of a distant
interchange. This book is not a study in "influence," that
graveyard where some of our most important historical
questions have been buried. It is a genuine work of comparative history, and on the broadest scale. I have spoken
of the fated involvement which has brought both Britain
and the West into the frame of reference that Yen Fu
exemplifies, but this is not merely a social or economic
matter. It is historiographical as well, and it must in the
end yield a perspective on the development of all the Western nations wider than any we have known. Professor
Schwartz is a pioneer of that perspective, his study of Yen
Fu a brilliant historical supplement to the work of Yen Fu
itself. The Western reader will be indebted to both for the
challenge they offer to the familiar view of Western
thought.

Cambridge, Massachusetts   Louis Hartz
November 4, 1963

IN SEARCH OF
WEALTH AND POWER

YEN FU AND THE WEST

CHAPTER I

The Setting

IN SPEAKING of the encounter between the West and the "non-West" we generally assume that the West is a known quantity. The metaphor of the "Western impact" suggests the image of a clearly perceived object impacting on an inert material. The recipient material may be somewhat amorphous and obscure, but we are all familiar with the impacting object. We know the West.

When we turn our attention back to the modern West itself, this deceptive clarity disappears. We are aware that the best minds of the nineteenth and twentieth centuries have been deeply divided in their agonizing efforts to grasp the inner meaning of modern Western development. We are certainly conscious of the enigmas and noisy controversies which surround words such as liberalism, democracy, socialism, nationalism, industrialism, and romanticism. Few would claim that the West which has emerged out of the eighteenth and nineteenth centuries forms an easily apprehended synthesis on any level—political, social, or intellectual. Yet when we turn our gaze outward to the non-Western world, that which has been obscure suddenly becomes clear. The West suddenly assumes the guise of a fixed, known quantity.

We are, of course, somewhat more aware that the non-Western world is not yet a completely known quantity—that we are still at an early stage of our exploration of non-Western societies and of the concrete historic situations of these societies at the time of their encounter with the West. Yet even here there are those who are convinced that they know enough. Having learned to employ a few fashionable categories, such as "pre-industrial society," "folk society," "traditional society," the "industrialization process," they are entirely convinced that anything which cannot be subsumed under these spuriously lucid concepts can be assigned to the dustbin of the inconsequential.

I would suggest that in dealing with the encounter between the West and any given non-Western society and culture, there can be no escape from the necessity of immersing ourselves as deeply as possible in the specificities of both worlds simultaneously. We are not dealing with a known and an unknown variable but with two vast, ever-changing, highly problematic areas of human experience. We undoubtedly "know" infinitely more about the West, but the West remains as problematic as ever. One may even hope that the ground of encounter may itself provide a new vantage point from which to take a fresh look at both worlds. No one can, of course, pretend to stand outside of any given culture. We are all "culture-bound." One may nevertheless hope that there does exist a realm of the universally human lying below and beyond culture which makes a certain degree of self-transcendence possible. Again, one cannot hope to be equally "expert" in all matters, but if fruitful inquiry is to proceed one must dare to pass judgment even on matters which lie outside one's "field" so long as they are relevant.

The encounter may be studied in an infinite variety of ways and from many different standpoints. In the following pages, I have chosen to look at it through a rather narrow focus—as narrow as the mind of one individual. I shall attempt to follow the conscious responses of this individual to the cultural and historic situation of China at the turn of the twentieth century. The individual in question has been chosen because he relates himself with peculiar directness to the confrontation of traditional China with the ideas of eighteenth and nineteenth century Europe. Like many of his predecessors and contemporaries he is profoundly concerned with the secrets of Western military, economic, and political power, but unlike them he is profoundly interested in what Western thinkers have thought about these matters. He is the first Chinese literatus who relates himself seriously, rigorously, and in a sustained fashion to modern Western thought.[1]

The limits of this approach are, of course, obvious. Yen Fu is not the voice of China incarnate. He belongs to a tiny literate elite within a vast illiterate society, and within that elite he belongs to the tiny segment which responds creatively to the situation of the time. It is by no means my intention to press the case of Yen Fu as a "representative individual," nor shall I concern myself overmuch with the measurement of his influence. As a matter of fact, his writings did exercise a considerable influence on his younger contemporaries and on the generation of Chinese intelligentsia and political elite now in their sixties and seventies. Liang Ch'i-ch'ao was profoundly influenced by him, while men as diverse as Hu Shih, Ts'ai Yüan-p'ei, Lu Hsün, and Mao Tse-tung all felt his influence in their youth. I would not maintain for a moment, however, that his ideas would not have come from other sources if he had never put pen to paper.

In the face of all these "methodological" limitations (to which many others could be added) I have one basic defense. I find his thought significant. Yen Fu's concerns are, it seems to me, significant concerns, and his efforts to cope with them are significant efforts. The problems he raises have profound and enduring implications for both China and the West. I cannot accept that brand of anti-intellectualism which dogmatically asserts that problems raised by intellectuals are of concern only to intellectuals themselves. Intelligent men may simply articulate preoccupations which are of concern to the society as a whole. Even where Yen Fu's concerns are those of the small ruling elite they are of enormous significance, since the fate of Chinese society is still shaped by the decisions of a small elite—indeed an elite which continues to share many of his preoccupations to this very day.

In dealing with the mind of an intelligent individual concerned with the plight of his own society as well as with the thought of the West, we are not simply dealing with two hypostatized entities, "Western culture" and "Chinese culture." Yen Fu is, of course, deeply immersed not only in Chinese culture but also in particularities of China's social, political, and intellectual situation at the end of the nineteenth century. His preoccupations are the very particular preoccupations of his own generation. Chinese culture is deeply involved as a pervasive presence in this situation and in his own responses to it. However, precisely when viewed through the eyes of a man like Yen Fu who still has roots in the traditional culture—who sees it, as it were, from the inside—"Chinese culture" is by no means the integrated whole envisioned by certain simple-minded schools of cultural anthropology. It is, rather, a complex of many contending and even contradictory tendencies. On the other hand, he does not respond to the "West" as an integral entity but to certain definite strands within the complex of eighteenth and nineteenth century thought. He thus forces our attention into that which is problematic in both cultures. We are dealing not only with the encounter of cultures but with problems which to some extent transcend the category of culture.

This study is not intended to be a definitive biography of Yen Fu. Attention will be focused primarily on his general concerns and ideas. One cannot, of course, erect an iron wall between an individual's public concerns and private life, or between his intellectual life (in the broadest sense) and other aspects of his existence. I would nevertheless submit that, from the point of view of the intellectual historian, it is quite legitimate to begin with the concerns of his subject as a primary datum—as the focus of attention—without attempting to reduce them to psychological or sociological origins. The concerns do not simply reflect their psychological and sociological antecedents. They are directed outward and forward in an intentional fashion to the situation within which the human being finds himself. Where a psychological trait or factor of social background seems obviously and immediately relevant I shall mention it, but the main effort here is not biographical in the psychological sense or sociological in the "case study" sense.

At the outset an effort must be made to reconstruct certain features of the Chinese environment in which Yen Fu's concerns arise. I shall not attempt to present here an account of China's total political, social, and economic situation during the latter decades of the nineteenth century. In its general features it has been described elsewhere, although much remains to be done. I shall rather focus on certain aspects of the intellectual situation among the articulate elements of the literati during the nineteenth century.

It must first of all be noted that much of what is called the "response to the West" before the end of the century takes place within a framework of concepts and categories furnished by the Chinese intellectual tradition. It could hardly be otherwise. This was still the spiritual and intellectual world within which the literati lived and breathed. Until the very end of the century some of the most active minds were still deeply preoccupied with what seemed to be familiar, recurring problems of Chinese society, and they were responding to these problems in terms of intellectual tendencies which had arisen organically out of the past. The "response to the West" was itself carried on within the setting of the intellectual currents of the Chinese world.

Even before the Opium War, corruption, rebellion, and the other telltale signs of dynastic decline had led to a growing ferment among the more sensitive elements of the literati. The eighteenth century had been dominated by the so-called "school of empirical research" (k'ao-cheng p'ai). This current, which we can only describe briefly, had itself arisen at the end of the Ming dynasty in reaction to what its protagonists regarded as the sterile metaphysical scholasticism of the Sung and Ming dynasties. The epigoni of Chu Hsi and Wang Yang-ming had, it was alleged, simply concerned themselves with abstractions spun out of their own heads which they had then read back into the Confucian classics. This irresponsible infatuation with "empty words" had turned their attention from the tasks of self-cultivation and practical statesmanship to a concern with inconsequential metaphysical disputations, thus helping to precipitate the fall of the Ming dynasty.[2]

The "school of empirical research," as represented in the first instance by Ku Yen-wu and others, raised that appeal to "reality" which so often marks new intellectual movements everywhere. Truth, it was proclaimed, is to be sought in the facts (shih-shih ch'iu shih). The facts in question, however, were not those which interested Francis Bacon but those which concerned the Chinese cultural heritage. Just as Western empiricists have usually implicitly assumed that their investigation of facts would reveal the rational system imbedded in nature, so was Ku serenely confident that the eternal normative values as well as the immutable principles of statecraft were embedded in the facts of the Confucian classical canon and in the data of Chinese history. These truths could not be recovered by armchair philosophizing. What was required was a rigorous inductive study of the contents of the classical books, based on such sciences as semantics, etymology, phonology, epigraphy, textual collation, and the authentication of texts. Nothing less than a comprehensive knowledge of the whole history of Chinese culture and institutions was required. Here was the laboratory of human experience within which the norms of the "Way" had been tested. The result of all these labors would be "statesmanship for practical use" (*ching-shih wei yung*).

It was, of course, a search for facts wholly within the limits of Confucian assumptions. Within the next century and a half this ambitious program did in fact lead to an immense scholarly achievement marked by both rigor of inductive scholarship and comprehensiveness of knowledge. The original pragmatic aim, however, tended to fade into the background. Whether this was due to the peculiar oppressive nature of the Manchu dynasty, as some Chinese historians assert, or whether a tendency to "scholarship for scholarship's sake" was latent in the original program is a question I shall not consider here. Scholarship as a way of life is a possibility that has emerged in many cultures. There can be no doubt, however, that by the end of the eighteenth century a reaction had set in among some against what was regarded as the sterility and nihilistic nature of the school. The pressing problems of the times, the demoralization of Chinese society, demanded a return to what might be called the higher concerns of Confucianism. The reaction came from diverse quarters. Some took up again a defense of the philosophic concerns of the Sung thinkers.

Others revived the mystico-historic concerns of the so-called "New Text" school of the early Han.[3] Certain common assertions recur in the writings of all these groups, however. "The ancients carried on their studies in order to regulate their own persons and to adjust the affairs of the realm (*t'ien-hsia kuo-chia*) . . . They did not separate knowledge from action," states Ch'eng Chin-fang[4] in a typical remark directed against the scholiasts. One aspect of the reaction seems to have involved a reassertion of the emotions as against the bland apatheia of the scholars. Another aspect (represented, in particular, by the so-called T'ung-ch'eng school)[5] involved a concern with beauty of style—closely associated in the minds of the school with significance of content—as against the austere indifference of the empirical research scholars to such matters.

One of the most important aspects of the reaction was the new concern with problems of state and society (*ching shih*)—with the current problems of the empire. This new concern finds expression in such works as the "Compilation of Essays on Statecraft" (*Huang-ch'ao ching-shih wen-pien*) compiled in 1820 by the noted official Ho Ch'ang-ling. This work is a collection of essays by famous officials and scholars who all share a common concern with practical problems as these are envisioned within the Chinese framework. Most of the problems dealt with are what might be called the perennial problems of the Chinese state—the administration of the six boards, taxation, the salt gabelle, grain transport, military systems, the inner Asian barbarians, sea defense, and so forth. It is under the last rubric, incidentally, that the problem of the Western barbarian is treated. It is interesting to note that the famous statesman Wei Yüan, one of the pioneers in the study of the Western barbarians, was associated with this compilation and was also an ardent advocate of the "New Text" school.

If the problems themselves are the perennial problems of the Chinese society as envisioned by the literati, most of the solutions suggested are also well within the orthodox tradition. An orientation to a concern with current problems of society by no means implied an orientation to startling new solutions.

Mary Wright, in her study[6] of the reforms undertaken by the remarkable groups of reformers who came to power during the sixties after the crushing disasters of the second Anglo-Chinese War and the Taiping Rebellion, has pointed out that men such as Tseng Kuo-fan, Wen-hsiang, Tso Tsung-t'ang, and Prince Kung were essentially engrossed in their effort to effect internal recovery within terms of the traditional framework. Their "response to the West" was still carried on within the tradition of statecraft represented in Ho Chang-ling's compilation. The second Anglo-Chinese War and the Taiping Rebellion had, to be sure, convinced them that a modernization of military technology was absolutely essential. A concern with military defense had, after all, always been a legitimate concern of the Confucian statesman. Confucius himself, despite his inherently pacifist tendencies, had conceded the need for military support of the state, given the abyss between the ideal and the actual.

If a concern with military affairs was legitimate, a concern with the improvement of military technology could also be brought within the confines of respectable Confucian statesmanship, even though ultraconservatives such as Wo Jen[7] considered the investment of energy required to master Western military technology an unseemly diversion from proper Confucian interests. Again, "barbarian" diplomacy had long been a sanctioned concern of the Confucian officialdom, so that the mastery of the techniques of handling the Western barbarians could be considered a legitimate extension of a legitimate traditional concern. While the policy of "self-strengthening" did nevertheless introduce certain novel features, on the margins as it were, the prescriptions of the T'ung-chih statesmen for internal re-

form represented the most orthodox school of political-
economic philosophy.[8] Having rescued Confucian truth
from the Taiping assault, these men were not inclined to
preside over its extinction.

Speaking broadly and crudely, traditional Chinese
thought as it had developed before the nineteenth century
offered two basic alternatives in the realm of what might
be called political-economic philosophy. One of these represented the main line of Confucian orthodoxy, while the
other was often identified as Legalist in point of origin,
even though it was supported in modified form by many
who considered themselves staunch Confucianists.

The orthodox line of Confucianism considered the main
purpose of the state to be the support and maintenance of
the moral, social, and cultural order of social peace and
harmony. This was to be achieved, in the first instance,
by the moral qualities of the ruling class itself. On the one
hand, its moral and ritual behavior would have an enormous exemplary effect on the society as a whole. On the
other hand, by the practice of a relative frugality, by curb-
ing expansionist ambitions in foreign policy, and by generally refraining from leaning heavily on the backs of the
people, the ruling class would make it possible for the people
to take care of its own basic economic needs in an atmosphere
of peace and harmony. Thus the people could be led to follow, if not to understand, the basic principles of proper
behavior.[9] The "managerial" role of the state in such activities as calendar-making, water control, and other useful
subsidiary public works is acknowledged. Since society in
actuality never completely conforms to the "Kingly Way,"
the coercive role of the state in terms of its internal police
function and in terms of military defense is also regret-
fully conceded. But both the managerial and coercive functions are regarded as marginal to the essentially moral role
of the state, or rather of the ruling class as the source of
peace and harmony. In a good state, the coercive and mana-

gerial activities of the state are reduced to modest proportions.

As already indicated, this line of thought is by no means
indifferent to the economic facts of life. On the contrary,
it is made amply clear in the *Analects*, and particularly in
Mencius, that the moral behavior of the masses is dependent on their economic welfare.[10] The ignorant masses
are economic men. Economic welfare, however, is conceived of not in terms of "economic growth" but in terms
of subsistence, of satisfaction of the basic minimum needs
of the masses. The ideal is a comfortable subsistence economy.[11] Indeed, the growth of luxury among the masses is
deplored, both for its tendency to divert them from the
basic tasks of agriculture and for its deleterious effect on
moral standards.[12] Barring natural disasters, the main
threat to the people's livelihood lies in the state's interference with its productive activities. Heavy taxes, unreasonable demands for *corvée* labor, and diversion of man-
power to military undertakings are the main sources of the
people's economic distress. The main pressures leading to
such forms of exploitation are large military undertakings,
ambitious public works, and the excessive luxuries of the
ruling class itself. It is interesting to note that within the
Confucian context no sharp line is drawn between the immorality of the individual member of the ruling class and
what might be called the immorality of state policy. In
committing itself to the pursuit of wealth and power the
state—in particular the emperor as the embodiment of the
state—is providing the same deplorable example as a collective entity as the official who pursues his own selfish
interests.

At its outer limits this philosophy even included a strain
of utopianism which was often consciously juxtaposed to
the grim actualities of the bureaucratic, centralized state
as it had existed since the Ch'in dynasty. There was the
dream of a bucolic decentralized state in which the peas-

ants would carry on their agricultural activities within the collectivity of the "well-field system" under the benevolent eyes of the local lord. This involved an idealized evocation of the "feudal utopia" of the Three Dynasties (Hsia, Shang, and Chou) to which Confucius himself and certainly Mencius looked back with deep nostalgia.

The opposing line of political-economic philosophy emerged, as it were, in conscious opposition to the original Confucian view. It emerges in the period of the so-called Warring States, when the large principalities of the ancient Chinese world were contending with one another in an all-out struggle for supremacy. The proponents of the new philosophy were "political experts" who presented themselves to the rulers of the time as practitioners of a kind of autonomous science of power. To the Confucianists who depicted the state as an agency of spiritual transformation and who practically negated the coercive bases of state power, the Legalists opposed, almost in dialectic antithesis, an image of the state (or the prince) as an engine of power. From a candid observation of the realities of the time, these "realists" conclude that the immanent goal of the state is precisely the increase of its own power both within the state and in the "international" arena. Furthermore, the authors of works such as the *Book of Lord Shang, Han-fei-tzu,* and *Kuan-tzu* were acutely aware of the relevance of economic power to military power. "Enrich the state and strengthen its military power" became the overriding motto. Within this formula, the first aim is obviously instrumental to the achievement of the second aim. The sinews of power are the revenues of the state: "The enlightened ruler must master (*t'ung*) the arts of wealth and power," asserts Han-fei-tzu (Chapter 47). The state must concern itself with methods of increasing its sources of revenue.

While all this reminds us of what has been called "mercantilism" in the West, it is important to note that some of the Legalists were staunchly "physiocratic" in their conviction that agriculture alone was the source of real wealth.[13] Others, however, were by no means unaware of the possibilities of handicraft industry and commerce as sources of wealth. Thus the Legalist ministers of the Emperor Han Wu-ti in the famous *Discourses on Iron and Salt,* which is almost a classic statement of the two opposing philosophies, expressly advocate both internal and foreign trade, praise the growth of trading towns, and advocate technical development. "The reason why the people do not have enough to eat even though our fields are fertile is because our implements are inadequate *(pu pei).* The reason why our people have no wealth even though the resources of mountains and seas are abundant is because our commerce and industry (artisan industry) are inadequate."[14] We note here that while the immediate aims of the Legalists may be narrowly fiscal, the germ of a notion of economic development is latent within this mode of thought which was to become the operating state philosophy of the hated Ch'in despotism. It is thus interesting to observe that within the orthodox line of Confucian thought the concern with the people's welfare came to be linked with the desirability of a subsistence economy—with an anti-economic stance— while the possibility of an incipient orientation to what we now call economic development was associated with the brutal and callous "wealth and power" philosophy of the Legalists.[15]

We know that during the centuries which followed the adoption of Confucianism as a state philosophy there were numerous emperors, ministers, and literati—men such as Chu Ko-liang, Chu Yuan-chang, the founder of the Ming dynasty, and Chang Chü-cheng, the famous prime minister of the Ming—who were essentially committed to the Legalist political-economic philosophy whatever their professed commitment to Confucianism. Vigorous emperors and ministers with a bent toward *Realpolitik* are, as it were, Legalist by instinct. On the other hand, it need hardly be pointed out that the Confucian dream of a state based purely on moral force, peace, and harmony was never actualized. It is simplistic to suppose, however, that an ideology or vision of reality can effect reality only by being fully realized. At the very minimum it may effect reality by precluding the application of energies to opposing goals and values— by its powers of inhibition. The orthodox Confucian political-economic philosophy may not have prevented ruthless exploitation or the pursuit of wealth by the literati[16] as individuals. Yet it may have played a considerable role in inhibiting the "rational" and systematic pursuit of "wealth and power" as state goals.

By and large, the advocates of "practical statesmanship" at the turn of the nineteenth century were firmly committed to the orthodox Confucian political-economic philosophy, as had been the advocates of practical statesmanship of the middle of the seventeenth century (men such as Ku Yen-wu and Huang Tsung-hsi). Like the latter they looked back nostalgically to the "feudal utopia" of the Three Dynasties period and shared the view that the state had become altogether too bureaucratic and centralized—that it allowed little room for the initiative of virtuous officials. As already indicated, the statesmen of the T'ung-chih restoration during the sixties essentially adhered to the same school. They did not link their "self-strengthening" motto to the old slogan, "enrich the state—increase military power." The orthodox political-economic philosophy was still part of the "Way" which they were defending. In the apt words of Mary Wright, their aims were "domestic and international peace; economic security through frugality rather than through expanding material welfare; cultural pride and devotion not to the Chinese nation but to the unique way of life of the Chinese people."[17] The only qualification that might be made to this statement is that they were professedly committed to material welfare, but in terms of a subsistence agrarian economy. Their domestic program stressed the search for "good men" in government, the revival of Confucian learning, and the rehabilitation of the agricultural economy by a policy of reduced taxation, land reclamation, and such public works as were absolutely necessary to agricultural recovery (for example, flood control). Frugality as an ideal was preached to all classes, and the anticommercial bias of Confucianism remained as powerful as ever.[18] The construction of the Kiangnan Arsenal and Foochow Shipyards, the establishment of the T'ung-wen kuan (School of Western studies), the establishment of the Tsungli Yamen, and the reluctant "entry" into diplomatic relations were still incorporated into this largely orthodox framework.

The seventies and eighties of the nineteenth century are often regarded as a period in which even this modest "response to the West" bogged down in an atmosphere of complacency, corruption, and low morale. Actually one notes during this period the influence of a much more vehemently conservative school of opinion among the leading literati at court. The current of thought represented by the so-called "Pure View" (ch'ing i) group, which exercised great influence at court and among the literati, can be defined as ultraconservative in its social-political stance. In terms of its ideology, it shared the orthodox political-economic philosophy outlined above, and even vehemently attacked the concern with barbarian technology displayed by the T'ung-chih reformers. On the other hand, it displayed an extraordinary belligerency in its attitude toward the Western scourge, evoking a certain strain of the Confucian tradition which has been little studied so far in the West—the strain of what might be called a muscular Confucianism. At the end of the Southern Sung dynasty there had been a militant party which had advocated an aggressive crusade against the northern barbarians in terms of Confucian values. The hero general Yüeh Fei, who died a martyr's death, was supposed to have fused within his person the highest Confucian virtues with all the virtues of a martial ethos. It was this tradition which was now summoned up. The barbarian could be expelled not by the use of cunning Western gadgets but by the militant and aroused spirit of the Chinese people: "what the barbarian has always feared is the consolidation of the hearts of the Chinese people," states Yüan Pao-heng.[19] "The superiority of China over foreign lands lies not in reliance on equipment but in the steadfastness of the minds of the people,"[20] states Wang Chia-pi, while Teng Cheng-hsia asserts, "When their arrogance is confronted with the zeal of our soldiers, it is bound to be defeated."[21] It is from such a point of view that one could attack the concern with Western military technology even while advocating an "expel the barbarian" policy.

However, even while this attitude, aggravated and abetted by simple complacency and low morale, was weakening the limited dynamism engendered in the sixties, subtle yet profound changes were taking place in the outlook of a small group of leading statesmen, such as Li Hung-chang and Chang Chih-tung, and of certain literati and "barbarian experts" such as Hsüeh Fu-ch'eng, Cheng Kuan-ying, Ma Chien-chung, and others. It is in these circles that we find a groping toward the realization that military technology cannot be divorced from the whole complex of Western techniques for "increasing wealth"—from the whole syndrome of what we now call industrialism. However feeble and unorganized the industrialization efforts launched by these men may seem to contemporary eyes,[22] their very commitment to commerce and industry nevertheless marks a qualitative break with the orthodox political economy. "Self-strengthening," it was now realized, could not be achieved without a major systematic application of energies to the goal of "enriching the state." It is no accident that many tracts and memorials of the seventies and eighties begin to emphasize the old suspect motto, "wealth

and power." What was being emphasized was not, of
course, a frank commitment to Legalism, but that quasi-
Legalist vein of Confucian thought which had stressed the
compatibility of wealth and power with Confucian values.
Ultimate Confucian values, it was argued, did not require
the maintenance of the orthodox political economic philosophy. "The Yellow Emperor and the Duke of Chou," states
Li Hung-chang's associate, Hsüeh Fu-ch'eng, "were certainly not merely concerned with wealth and power. Yet
placed as they were among surrounding enemies, they could
hardly turn away from a concern with the techniques
(*shu*) of wealth and power."[23] When Li Hung-chang is
attacked by a conservative memorialist for squandering the
people's wealth on industrial and commercial ventures, he
defends himself in terms of the requirements of "self-
strengthening" (a goal to which his opponents are also
presumably committed): "The fact that the military forces
of the Western states are adequately provisioned, the fact
that their machines are so cleverly devised, is due wholly
to a [policy] of wealth and power."[24]

All these men are presumably committed to the "preservation of the faith" (*pao chiao*), or to what Chang Chih-
tung[25] referred to as the "essential substance" (*t'i*) of the
Chinese "Way." They all assume, however, that the "preservation of the faith" (*pao chiao*) is inseparable from the
"preservation of the state" (*pao kuo*). Their own immediate
interests as bureaucrats or vicarious bureaucrats, and the
close identification which had always existed between the
Confucian "Way" and the existence of what we now call
the state, made such a link inevitable. As Yen Fu was later
to state in his "Ten Thousand Word Memorial" of 1898,[26]
"There can be no Way without a state and a people to sustain it." One can find, to be sure, ultraconservatives such as
the Manchu Hsü T'ung, who cries out in exasperated hostility to the reforms of 1898," "It were better that the state
perish than that we change our laws,"[27] or the eccentric

Ku Hung-ming, who was later to argue in elegant English prose that the essentials of Chinese culture could survive the demise of an independent Chinese state and even convert the conquerors in the end. Such views, however, were definitely marginal. For the bulk of the literati the preservation of the faith and the preservation of the state were indivisible. The essential core of the faith had now shrunk to certain basic features of Confucian individual and family morality, as well as to what might be called the basic monarchic constitution of the state, although in the latter point, as one may well surmise, there was a growing area of vagueness. Both Li Hung-chang and Chang Chih-tung were later shocked by what they regarded as K'ang Yu-wei's tamperings with the sacred constitution of the state. However, the orthodox political-economic philosophy was no longer an organic part of the "Way." The "preservation of the faith" involved the "preservation of the state." The preservation of the state was now inconceivable without military "self-strengthening." Self-strengthening, it was now obvious, was no longer possible without some movement in the direction of industrialization and away from the ideal agrarian-subsistence economy.

In the atmosphere of acute crisis which followed the defeat in the Sino-Japanese War, the slogan of "wealth and power" with all its associations was to win tacit acceptance among most of the articulate elements of the ruling class, and discussion shifted to new ground. What were the prerequisites for the achievement of wealth and power. The power of the West and of the new Japan was obviously not simply a matter of military technology. Perhaps it was even more than a matter of direct concern with the machinery of industry and commerce linked to military considerations. Was not the industrial and military might of the West deeply involved with the whole political, legal, and social structure of Western society? Beyond this, did not the sociopolitical organization of the West reflect the superior efficacy of Western ideas and values. Were these institutions, ideas, and values compatible with even the essential core of the Confucian faith? One could conceive of wealth and power as an outer rampart for the inner sanctum of essential Confucian values and institutions only so long as the requirements of one were not incompatible with the demands of the other. What if the construction of the fort required the destruction of the sanctum? The question now posed itself in a much more fateful form. It was no longer, How can we achieve wealth and power and preserve the state in order to "preserve the faith"? but, How can we achieve wealth and power and yet preserve the faith? If, in the last analysis, one must choose between the preservation of the state and the preservation of basic Confucian values, which shall give way?

Once the question has been posed in this form one finds oneself on the watershed which divides what we now call nationalism from any authentic, inner commitment to the traditional values. Where the commitment to the preservation and advancement of the societal entity known as the nation takes priority over commitment to all other values and beliefs, where other values and beliefs are judged in terms of their relevance to this end rather than vice versa, nationalism in a precise sense is already on the scene. It is, of course, true that every nationalist fervently desires to believe that the national community has created superior values in the past. "Pride in the national past"—in what is "ours"—is an important fuel of national sentiment. The "national past," however, particularly when one deals with a vast culture such as China, contains many things often mutually contradictory or subject to extensive reinterpretation. A commitment to the "national past" as a storehouse of good things from which one can pick and choose at will from outside the tradition, as it were, is a vastly different thing from the commitment to specific values[28] conceived of as universally true. Furthermore, particularly where the nation-state is weak and in peril, the nationalist is hardly likely to find value in those strains of the national past which run counter to the needs of national wealth and power. Occasionally, indeed, one will find in modern times the radical type of nationalist who openly proclaims that the whole national past is an obstacle to the achievement of national independence and power. The young Yen Fu— we will find—almost fits this category. The important point, however, is not whether the nationalist "takes pride" or consciously rejects the past, or even whether he cherishes universalistic messianic goals for his nation in the distant future. His immediate basic commitment is to the preservation and advancement of the national community as a societal organism. His own sense of worth and self-realization, as well as his own sense of self-interest, has come to be identified in varying degrees with the power and prestige of the societal entity.

One cannot simply analyze the responses to these issues by referring to the "interests of the ruling class." One can accept as axiomatic the proposition that the Chinese ruling class as a class was concerned with the preservation of its power and privileges. Yet this banal truth explains very little. Hume's observation, that while men act in accordance with their interests the nature of their interests is largely a matter of opinion, is most appropriate here. The literati as a stratum had every reason to believe that their interests were bound up with the survival of Confucianism. On the other hand, they had every reason to believe that their interests were bound up with the survival of the state. To pose the question in terms of the interest calculus by no means resolves the dilemma. Within the bounds of common interest (there were also, of course, innumerable divisive interests) one could arrive at the most starkly contradictory conclusions.

It is within a setting dominated by questions of this order

that the young Yen Fu achieved intellectual maturity, and it is against this background that we must view his effort to transvaluate traditional values—his effort to find the true secret of Western wealth and power.

CHAPTER II

The Early Years

T H E biographical tradition of China does not dwell on the psychological subtleties of childhood. There is in fact a fixed convention for dealing with the childhood of famous men. Having furnished some examples of their astounding precocity, one then passes on to the serious business of their formal education. Unfortunately most of what we have on Yen Fu's childhood is written in this traditional mode.

Yen Fu[1] was born in 1853 in the village of Yang-ch'i-hsiang in the Hou Kuan prefecture of Fukien. The Yen family was a respectable scholar-gentry family which had originated in Honan during the T'ang dynasty. The province of Fukien itself, while geographically isolated, had long been known as an uncommonly active center of intellectual and scholarly activity, precisely because of the presence of gentry families of this type.

The physical environment of Yen Fu's native village was

quite different from that of the northern Chinese plain. We read of deeply wooded ravines, swift-flowing streams, and high tree-clad mountains, effectively isolating one valley from another. Without attempting to speculate on the effects of early physical surroundings, one may at least safely assume that Yen Fu's first years were spent in an environment entirely untouched, in any direct way, by the "Impact of the West."

One finds the usual anecdotes concerning Yen Fu's childish precocity, and one need not doubt that he was an extraordinarily bright child. His father, Yen Chen-hsien, engaged in the practice of medicine and evidently enjoyed a certain reputation throughout the district. His mother's family were evidently commoners,[2] since the biographies provide us with no imposing genealogies. Yen Fu speaks of her, with great tenderness, in one of his reminiscent poems of old age. He describes her bitter struggles to support the family[3] by needlework after the father's death. He recalls over the years her heartrending sobs during the early hours of the morning when she thought the children were asleep.

Before his death in 1866, Yen Chen-hsien supervised the education of his young prodigy with painstaking care. The prospects of the attainment of an official career via the well-worn examination path loomed brightly ahead, and at the age of ten Yen Fu was provided with the best tutor his father could find.

The tutor, Huang Shao-yen, remained with the youngster for two years before their relationship was terminated by his death. The pupil is said to have "grieved no end" for his master,[4] indicating that their relationship had been a happy one. One may indeed surmise that the tutor exercised a considerable influence over his young charge who was at a most impressionable age. The terse remark that "he placed equal weight on Han and Sung learning" would indicate that Huang Shao-yen was not an uninspired hack but a thinker deeply involved in the intellectual trends of the time. In the broadest sense, the "Han learning" refers, of course, to the "School of Empirical Research" (briefly described in the preceding chapter), while "Sung learning" refers to the broad philosophic concerns of the thinkers of the Sung, Yuan, and Ming dynasties. Now, one of the schools which was coming to the fore during the first half of the nineteenth century (its most illustrious representative was Tseng Kuo-fan) insisted that the essential values of the "Han" school—the respect for factual truth, rigorous method, and comprehensive knowledge of the cultural heritage—were entirely compatible with the more vital philosophic, moral, and social concerns of the Sung philosophers. Thus we find Huang Shao-yen setting his twelve-year-old pupil the task of studying the lives and thought of the illustrious thinkers of the Sung, Yuan, and Ming dynasties. One is tempted to speculate that Yen Fu's later combination of enthusiasm for the metaphysical sweep of the Spencerian cosmology and equal enthusiasm for Mill's inductionist logic and empirical method reflects to some extent the efforts of his teacher to combine the values of "Han and Sung."

In general, one has the impression that in spite of the abrupt termination of Yen Fu's formal traditional education at the age of fourteen, his eager mind, encouraged by the efforts of his tutor, had absorbed a substantial amount of knowledge. His training, though brief, had been thorough and intense, and undoubtedly it was richly supplemented in later years by his own efforts. All his subsequent writings give evidence of a thorough grounding in the classical and historical literature. His much admired "ancient style" and his equally admired poetry with its rich burden of classical allusion presuppose a considerable immersion in the traditional culture. In spite of the abortive nature of his traditional education, Yen Fu is certainly not one of the semideracinated young men of the next generation. From all one is able to glean, the stamp of tradition on what might be called his personal culture remained indelible. Whatever his opinion of this or that aspect of the traditional culture, he does not view it from the outside. In his own individual existence, as a matter of fact, he remains a traditional gentleman no matter how far his ideas on general political and social issues may stray. The transvaluation of values does not penetrate the marrow of his own being. His personal and domestic life, as far as we know, do not stray far from the accepted patterns of Confucian behavior.

As in the case of so many Chinese literati, we can learn very little about Yen Fu's domestic life. We know that he was married at fourteen to a girl of the surname Wang, who bore him a son (Yen Po-yü) and subsequently died in 1892. Ch'en Pao-chen's biographic epitaph informs us that she was a virtuous and upright woman. He married a second wife in the same year, who bore him four daughters. From private sources we are informed that he was a kindly father. We know that he firmly applied his convictions concerning the education of women to his own daughters, but in other respects the family life was probably in the patriarchal mode. There is, of course, no evidence whatsoever of revolt against any of the traditional ways in matters of emotional life, and we shall find that the demand for sexual freedom or romantic love is irrelevant to the transformation of values which Yen Fu later advocates.

With the death of his father in 1866, the prospects of further education leading to an official career were abruptly cut off. Such sudden steep reverses in the fortunes of Chinese gentry families, due to the death of a father or some sudden reversal in the fortunes of an influential family member, were by no means uncommon in Chinese society. It was only in the latter half of the nineteenth century, however, that the pursuit of "Western studies" emerged as one more bleak alternative for those whose path to an official career had been blocked. Yen Fu's fellow provincial, Lu Hsün, born some twenty-seven years later, furnishes an account of his youth amazingly similar to that of Yen Fu. His father's death had left the family in dire straits, and his widowed mother, with tears of frustration in her eyes, was forced to send him off to a school of "Western affairs" (*yang wu*). The early "self-strengtheners" who had endorsed Western military technology in the abstract had not really changed even their own basic attitudes toward technologists in the flesh. Their own personal ideal of manhood was still so deeply biased by tradition and class prejudice that it was difficult for them to thrust themselves wholeheartedly into efforts to change the "patterns of incentive." Some of the earliest "self-strengtheners," such as Lin Tse-hsü and Wei Yüan, had even hoped that Western military technology might be mastered by skilled artisans and craftsmen. The T'ung-chih statesmen were, to be sure, already aware of the "theoretical component" in Western science. Hence their willingness to recruit young men like Yen Fu for the Foochow Shipyard School.[5] Yet neither they nor their successors (such as Li Hung-chang) gave much sustained thought to the question of career incentives for experts in Western affairs.

Yen Fu gained his admission to the naval school of the Foochow Shipyard School only through the patronage of Shen Pao-chen,[6] at the time superintendent of the shipyard. He happened to be from the same county, and he was also a friend of the family. It is interesting to note that the composition subject set for the entrance examination to the school was hardly in the spirit of "vocational aptitude" tests. The topic was "Life-long filial devotion to One's Parents." One of Yen Fu's biographers[7] surmises that his essay on this seemingly stereotyped theme may have revealed genuine depths of emotion, given the recent death of his father and the struggles and sorrows of his widowed mother. There certainly is no evidence in Yen Fu's life of any revolt against parental authority or even of any particular intellectual animus against the value of filial piety, even though he did come to question other aspects of Confucian family morality. At no point, we shall find, was he inclined to seek precisely here the root of China's weakness.

Yen Fu's essay won him first place among the entrants and he was allowed to choose between the School of Naval Architecture, where the French language and French instruction prevailed, and the School of Navigation, where the language of instruction was English. His choice of the School of Navigation was to determine the whole course of his life. His medium of access to Western ideas was to be the English language. Great Britain was to become his ideal model, and English ideas were to dominate his intellectual development. At the school he studied the English language, arithmetic, geometry, algebra, analytic geometry, trigonometry, physics, mechanics, chemistry, geology, astronomy, and navigation. In addition, Chinese studies were not entirely neglected. It should be noted at this point that Yen Fu's later enthusiasm for Western science was based on a first-hand, albeit rudimentary, contact with the actual methods and data of the natural sciences, rather than on vague associations with the slogan, "science." The precision and discipline of Western science were here added to the sense of the precise and rigorous which he may have derived from his early training in the methods of the "Han" scholarship. Up to a point he can be said to have come to his enthusiasms for science from within science itself.

After five years of study Yen Fu graduated with high honors in 1871 and then actually went to sea. He sailed the training ship *Chien-wei* south as far as Singapore and Penang and north as far as the Gulf of Chih-li and the Gulf of Liaotung. In 1872 he cruised the Yellow Sea on the *Yang-wu* and even visited Japan. His performance aboard the *Yang-wu* won the high praise of the English commander, Tracey, who later helped make possible the further pursuit of Yen Fu's studies in England. In 1874 he was even sent on an actual naval mission when Shen Pao-chen used the *Yang-wu* to take soundings of various ports in eastern Taiwan in connection with the Sino-Japanese crisis of that year.

When Yen Fu was finally sent to pursue his studies in England in 1877, he had already been exposed to a life experience which sharply set him off from the overwhelming bulk of his fellow countrymen. One may assume that, even before his departure, the credit he had won in his Western studies, his interest in these studies, and his pleasant associations with his "barbarian" instructors had already dissolved in him those notions of Western moral, intellectual, and spiritual inferiority which were still shared by most of the contemporary literati ranging from the "pure stream" partisans to the most open-minded specialists in "Western affairs." This may not be entirely true of many of his classmates who did not deviate from their professional aims and who later achieved some status as naval officers. Yen Fu, one may assume, responded to his experience with an intellectual sensitivity quite unique in kind.

In Yen Fu we note, in fact, the beginnings of a phenomenon which was to occur again and again among "overseas students" in subsequent generations. Sent abroad to study some specific field of "practical" knowledge, the most gifted seldom found themselves in a proper state of mind for unrelieved attention to their chosen field of professional study. The enormously unsatisfactory general condition of China, contrasted with the wealth and power of the host country, inevitably turned their attention to general problems. Their preoccupation with the general plight of China was often heightened, particularly in the next generation, by an enormous sense of personal insecurity concerning their own future prospects. In the case of Yen Fu, there is no reason to suppose that he anticipated all his future career frustrations, but the orientation to general problems is unmistakable. His performance in naval science at Portsmouth and then at Greenwich was evidently quite creditable, but he was not the first in his group, as has often been claimed.[8]

He seems to have arrived in England already obsessed with the question which was to underlie all his subsequent investigations. It was not a question he himself had formulated, but one which was, as we have seen, already dominant in the milieu of "Western affairs" experts with which he had become involved. What was the secret of Western wealth and power? Above all, what was the secret of Great Britain's wealth and power, for in 1877 Great Britain was by all odds the pristine exemplar of wealth and power. It was this burning preoccupation and not idle curiosity which led to Yen Fu's eager study of British political, economic, and social institutions, and finally even to his entirely unprecedented concern with contemporary British thought.

It was probably Yen Fu's eager search for understanding which attracted the attention of China's first ambassador, Kuo Sung-t'ao. We are told that, in spite of the enormous difference in status and age between them, "they often spent whole days and nights discussing differences and similarities in Chinese and Western thought and political institutions."[9] Yen Fu himself recollects many years later in a commentary in his translation of the *Spirit of the Laws* that after spending fascinating days visiting the British law courts he remarked to Kuo "that the reason why England and the other countries of Europe are wealthy and strong is that impartial justice (*kung li*) is daily extended. Here is the ultimate source."[10] The ambassador, he relates, heartily agreed.

Kuo Sung-t'ao was one of those who had already gone beyond the "self-strengthening" formula of the T'ung-chih statesmen to the realization that nothing less than a full devotion to the goals of wealth and power would suffice.

What is more, his stay in England was leading his thought in the same direction as that of his young fellow country-man, and well beyond that of Li Hung-chang. Political insti-tutions, legal institutions, social arrangements, and even values and ideas all were involved in the wealth and power of the West. His premature boldness in enunciating such views was to have a most decisively adverse effect on the future course of the ambassador's official career.

Upon his return to China in 1879, Yen Fu began to experience that series of frustrations which was to lend a sharp edge of personal resentment to his general exas-peration with the plight of China. His first position as teacher at the Foochow Arsenal School was soon abandoned when he was summoned by Li Hung-chang to be a sort of dean (*tsung chiao-hsi*) at the newly established Peiyang Naval Academy in Tientsin. One biographer suggests at this point[11] that the death of his patron and sponsor, Shen Pao-chen, in 1879 seriously jeopardized his career in spite of his apparent rise on the career ladder. In spite of Li Hung-chang's respect for his attainments, Yen Fu was not really a member of Li's personal organization. Nevertheless, he was finally promoted to the position of superintendent of the academy in 1890.

All of this seems to suggest a steady rise in status. In actuality, however, Yen Fu remained an "outsider" unable to influence policy decisions, and here lay the source of his frustration. The insights he had gained during his stay in Great Britain had made him acutely aware of the inade-quacy of Li Hung-chang's self-strengthening program. He seems to have realized that an enterprise such as the crea-tion of a modern navy could not be successful in a society which had not undergone profound social and psychological changes. In a reminiscence written some years later,[12] he recollects a conversation with Sir Robert Hart, in which the latter had compared a navy to a tree which requires a fa-vorable environment in which to grow and bear fruit. Yen

Fu relates that he was deeply impressed with this analogy. His depression over the fact that his talents were not being used was aggravated by the state of corruption, unthinking conservatism, complacency, and indolence which he now observed for the first time among the high officialdom in Peking and Tientsin. His own patron Li Hungchang was, of course, deeply inured to this environment in spite of his commitment to self-strengthening, and was himself tainted by its corruption. The biographical epitaph written by Ch'en Pao-ch'en tells of Yen Fu's profound distress over the loss of the Liu-ch'iu Islands to Japan. The Japanese who had been his fellow students in England were all able to apply their energies directly to the creation of Japanese wealth and power, but he remained on the outside. "In another thirty years," he is quoted as saying, "all our dependencies will be swallowed up and then they will pull us around by the nose like an old cow."[13] Such remarks did not endear him to the ever bland and discreet Li.

It was during this period that Yen Fu first succumbed to the opium habit. Whether this addiction reflected his depression over China's plight and his own career frustrations, or whether it reflected other aspects of his personal life or psychological make-up we shall never know. His capacity for bitterness and resentment apparently was profound, but he does not seem to have pushed as hard as he might have against the obstacles which stood in his way; one may indeed wonder whether he would have become a decisive man of action even if Li Hung-chang had given him *carte blanche* at the Academy and even if he had risen high in the state bureaucracy. In a sense, opium symbolizes that quietist mystical strain in Yen Fu's outlook which was to remain, as we shall see, the obverse side of his religion of wealth and power. It is entirely conceivable that his true vocation was the intellectual vocation into which his energies were finally channeled.

During the next few years, however, he did make some

effort to escape from his position as Li Hung-chang's administrative underling. At one point, he invested some money in a coal mine enterprise launched by Wang Shou-yün in Honan.[14] This interest in private enterprise reflected both his desire to achieve financial independence and the new values he had brought home from England. He could not be deflected very long, however, from an effort to penetrate the traditional bureaucracy. Deeply engrained habit and the plain realization that respectability and influence could only be won by treading the examination path finally led him in 1885 to prepare for the triennial examination for the *chü-jen* degree. He did not pass, nor was he to succeed in his three subsequent attempts to cross the examination barrier.

As we know from the careers of others, such a failure can hardly be taken as a reflection on Yen Fu's intellectual capacity or even as evidence of neglect of his Chinese studies. It may simply indicate an inability to conform completely to the fantastically formalistic rules and conventions of the systems as it existed at this time. Undoubtedly, Yen Fu's humiliating experiences in these years added an edge of personal bitterness to his extraordinarily vehement attack on the system after 1895. In spite of these failures, however, Li Hung-chang again made a half-hearted gesture toward his Western expert in 1890 by promoting him from the position of dean to the position of superintendent (*tsung-pan*) of the Academy. However, as one of Yen Fu's biographers states, "This was simply an empty appointment. He was not taken into Li Hung-chang's confidence."[15]

Such was the bleak tale of Yen Fu's career until the fateful Sino-Japanese War of 1894–95. It was after the war that he finally found his voice and became one of the leading intellectual publicists of China. It was only then that all his pent-up thoughts finally found public expression. It would be idle to speculate on the relative weight to be assigned to private resentments and public concerns in explaining his ideas. Both were prompted by the same situation, and both moved in the same direction. The same complacent and arrogant officialdom which was denying him a rightful place in the councils of the state was responsible for the miserable failure to make China wealthy and strong.

There are available certain clues to Yen Fu's intellectual development before the explosion of 1894–95, when in his own words he felt "things choked up in my breast, which I had to vomit forth."[16] The revolutionary notion that the secrets of Western wealth and power are to be found in the writings of Western thinkers was already his at the time of his return from England, and during all the subsequent years he continued to read writings in "the horizontal script." As early as 1881 he had read Spencer's *A Study of Sociology*,[17] which proved to be a major intellectual event in his life. In his preface to the translation of this work written many years later, he tells us something about his first reactions to it. Since the thought of Herbert Spencer was to dominate Yen Fu's whole subsequent development, it may be worth while to consider his initial response to Spencer's work.

A Study of Sociology was written in 1872 at the request of Spencer's ardent American disciple, Professor Youmans. It does not itself give an account of Spencer's system of sociology, which must be sought in its later version in the mammoth *Principles of Sociology*. It is, rather, a sort of prolegomenon to the study of sociology, which outlines all the emotional, ethical, and intellectual predispositions necessary to the creation of that queen of sciences, sociology. In many chapters richly interlaced with his own innumerable biases, Spencer depicts all the subjective biases and objective difficulties which impede the emergence of a truly objective, scientific sociology.

While the *Study* does, of course, reflect Spencer's whole evolutionary outlook, one need not suppose that this accounts for Yen Fu's particular enthusiasm for it; he had become familiar with Darwinism in England and was also reading Spencer's other books at this time. He himself relates that he found in the book a remarkable confirmation of one of the basic insights of Chinese thought expounded in such ancient classics as the *Great Learning* and the *Doctrine of the Mean*. Just as the *Great Learning* and the *Doctrine of the Mean* establish a profound link between sincerity of purpose and rectitude of mind and the pursuit of true knowledge, so does Spencer find that the pursuit of knowledge is organically linked with the overcoming of emotional and moral distortions—with a certain high detachment which is essentially a moral attainment. "Wishing to rectify their hearts," states the famous passage in the *Great Learning*,[18] "they first sought to be sincere in their thoughts, they first extended to the utmost their knowledge. Such extension of knowledge lay in the investigation of things." In this passage, to be sure, moral perfection seems to be a "fruit of knowledge," while Yen Fu stresses the reverse relationship of sincerity (lack of bias—intellectual honesty in this context) to the achievement of knowledge. The basic point, however, is that the moral qualities and the scientific attainment "go together."

I shall not linger at this point over Yen Fu's motives for his effort to find identities between Western and Chinese thought—an effort which marks the whole development of his thought—for the problem of his relation to the cultural tradition will be given more detailed consideration below. One obvious motive would seem to be to raise the credit of barbarian studies in the eyes of the overwhelmingly hostile literati by pointing to the highly ethical basis of Western science. Was this, however, merely a strategic device, or can we believe Yen Fu's assertion that he himself was profoundly stirred by what seemed to him to be the common principles of Spencer and the Four Books? He himself says that until he read Spencer he had "always stated that life tends to lop-sided extremes (or to biases)."[19]

Spencer had, as it were, revived his faith in the possibility of the kind of high moral detachment and unclouded intellectual vision which the ancient books describe.

However, Spencer's tract was *not* exciting merely because he, a Western thinker, had reconfirmed the insight of the ancient sages, but because of his clear demonstration that the true "knowledge"—the knowledge which both reflected and led to "sincerity" (*ch'eng i*)—was precisely the knowledge to be found in the methods of Western science. The sciences which Yen Fu had studied at Foochow and at Portsmouth and Greenwich were not merely significant for their specific practical applications. The methods involved in them contained the key to truth itself. It was precisely cultivation of the sciences which led to that purgation of all the beclouding by the passions dreamed of by the ancient sages, or, alternately, it was precisely Western science which presupposed the moral qualities, the adherence to the "mean" (Ezra Pound's "Unwobbling Pivot") described in the *Doctrine of the Mean*.

Beyond this, however, Spencer's book was most exciting because it demonstrated the relevance of the method of Western science to the problem of ordering human society (*chih kuo p'ing t'ien-hsia*): "Science, sincerity, and rectitude are made the foundations for ordering society." Yen Fu expresses a particular enthusiasm for those chapters of the book (Chapters XIII–XVI) labelled "Discipline," in which Spencer gives an account of the contributions made by all the separate sciences to the master science of sociology: "For sociology is a science in which all other sciences are included." Each of the sciences contributes "a certain habit of thought" absolutely essential to the mastery of this most complex of all sciences. In order to demonstrate this thesis, Spencer proceeds to describe the essential principles which lie behind all the separate sciences, and to fit each of the sciences into its proper niche. Thus mathematics and logic "furnish an unshakable belief in necessities of relation."

Physical and chemical science add "strength to the consciousness of cause, use, and effect," biology teaches "continuity, complexity, and a contingency of causation," and so forth.

This discussion arouses Yen Fu's enthusiasm on two counts. The scientific disciplines are suddenly explained in terms of large philosophic principles and placed within an over-all grandiose scheme in which each is assigned its proper place. "These three chapters furnish the correct method for studying Western science. They are indispensable for intellectual training." Secondly, a direct link is here established between the principles of the various sciences and Yen Fu's own immediate burning preoccupation with the ordering of state and society, for was not sociology essentially the science of ordering the state and society (*chih-p'ing*)? As he later states in his essay "On Strength,"[20] "Spencer applies the methods of evolution to explain human relations and the ordering of society. He also uses the most recent principles of science to illumine [the principles] of self-cultivation, to regulate the family, to govern the state, and set the world at peace."

It will immediately be noted that all these traditional Chinese phrases give a somewhat odd twist to Spencer's prosy tract. This terminology, in fact, imposes a prescriptive, programatic interpretation which would have scandalized the master. Spencer is not providing prescriptions for social action by an intellectual elite. He regards himself as an Olympian, detached observer describing the process of social evolution. In his view, one of the basic lessons which social science should convey, at least to the Englishman and American, is precisely that one should not tinker from the "outside" with the majestic, impersonal processes of social evolution. As applied to Western industrialized societies, it may indeed be said to be a prescription for nonaction as far as vicarious statesmen and would-be social reformers are concerned.[21] As for the inhabitants of pre-industrial societies, the book was certainly not written for them. The science of sociology was not designed as a tool for consciously reshaping society as in "applied science," but as a tool for understanding an on-going impersonal process which was obviously moving in the right direction.

To Yen Fu, however, the principles do not merely describe society. They presumably provide prescriptions for transforming society—prescriptions for achieving those goals of wealth and power which had obviously been achieved in Spencer's England and to which Spencer's own ideas provided a necessary clue. Yen Fu's overwhelming preoccupation is to apply the scientific principles of society to the achievement of these all-absorbing goals. The difference in the direction of thought which we already note here will run through all his subsequent interpretations of Western thought. It is quite clear from this brief indication, however, that Yen Fu had already found the clue to the secret of Western "success" in the Spencerian synthesis, years before the crisis of 1894–95.

It was also during these years that Yen Fu incidentally became a pioneer in the strategy of using Western thought itself as a weapon against the missionary. Yen Fu had never been attracted by the religious message of the missionary. Neither the traditional nor the antitraditional components of his thought predisposed him to any sympathy toward theistic religion. He was, in fact, one of the first Chinese to become aware of the conflict between the Christian tradition and the infidel thought of eighteenth- and ninteenth-century Europe. He had been preceded in this only by the "Western affairs" expert, Wang T'ao,[22] who had vaguely heard of something called positivism (*pu-ssu-tieh-ni-chiao*), which could be used as a weapon against the missionary. Yen Fu had already begun to note that affinity between the monistic, pantheistic tendency in Chinese thought and the monism of his favorite Western thinkers (which will be discussed below).

We will, to be sure, find that in his capacity as a vicarious statesman he will occasionally speak in high praise of the social-ethical effects of Christianity—particularly its effect on the masses. In his essay "On Strength" he contrasts the widespread and profoundly effective religio-ethical education of the masses in the West with the criminal neglect of the moral training of the masses in China. However, his fundamental antipathy to the theology of Christianity is quite clear. Rejecting as he did the basic message of the missionaries, he no doubt fully shared the animus of his fellow literati against their activities.

It was his good fortune to make the acquaintance of Alexander Michie, an intelligent Scotsman—obviously not orthodox in his religious views—who wrote a tract in 1891, called *Missionaries in China*, which presented a penetrating yet judicious attack on the methods of the missionaries in China. It was probably the following year that Yen Fu translated this tract into Chinese, hoping, no doubt, to provide his fellow literati with a formidable new arsenal of anti-missionary arguments from the mouth of the foreigner himself,[23] at a time when incidents involving missionaries were rife throughout the country. There seems to have been little response to this effort, however.

Our main attention at this point is drawn to Yen Fu's preface to his translation, since it raises an interesting question concerning his relation to tradition during this early phase of his intellectual development—a phase which is described by one biographer as the phase of "all-out Westernization." In answering the frequent missionary allegations that China simply had no religion, Yen Fu bases his reply on Michie's own notion "that the heart of Chinese religion is the idea of filial piety." The view that filial piety was the heart of Confucianism was not, of course, a new notion in China, but Yen Fu finds in it a possible Chinese equivalent to the role played by Christianity in Western society—a sort of all-embracing inner social discipline for the masses in particular. "All action [presumably moral action] derives its origin here [in filial piety]. Extending it to the service of the lord it becomes the virtue of loyalty. When applied to an elder brother it is fraternal piety. In its farthest extension it even determines the Chinese attitude of reverence toward heaven,"[24] and to this extent coincides with religion in the Western sense.

The striking fact is that here, and even in later writings, Yen Fu often evinces a relatively positive attitude toward this most traditional of values. As we have noted, in his adolescence he had probably felt the subjective hold of this value on himself. Now, however, he was examining it from the outside, with the cool eye of the statesman, as a possible Chinese equivalent of that Christian piety in the West which made it possible for even the common man "to face death without regard for self-interest." We will, to be sure, find Yen Fu attacking various facets of the family system in China, particularly the subjugation of women. We will also find him attacking the notion of the family as the supreme focus of loyalty. Yet the possibility that the virtue of filial piety with its in-built spirit of self-sacrifice and self-abnegation might provide the moral fuel for a spirit of nationalist self-sacrifice among the masses, as was presumably the case with Christianity (of the English puritanic variety), was a possibility which he continued to entertain from time to time. His main indictment against Chinese society was precisely the fact that it had grossly failed to educate the masses, even in terms of this traditional moral value.

How this relatively favorable attitude toward the value of self-sacrifice as embodied in filial piety can be reconciled with Yen Fu's commitment to modernization in general and to an ethic of individualistic utilitarianism is a question which might well be raised at this point.

It might simply be stated in passing that Yen Fu's conception of the possible synthesis of modern and traditional elements obviously does not rest on certain assumptions now prevalent among some Western social scientists. In terms of certain Weberian categories—universalism, impersonality, achievement versus status, and so forth—filial piety as a value is a supreme obstacle to "modernization." Yen Fu, like some contemporary statesmen of Japan[25] who had just promulgated the famous "Educational Rescript," regards the whole matter from a somewhat different perspective. The value of filial piety fosters a habit of disciplined subordination and acceptance of authority—notions of self-abnegation which can perhaps be transferred from the family to the factory and nation. There is no reason why the particularistic aspects of the value cannot be confined to the family itself. Subsequent Chinese history has not tended to support Yen Fu's hopes concerning the compatibility of filial piety and modernization on a Japanese model within a Chinese context. Whether historic contingency or important differences in the Chinese and Japanese conception of filial piety have played the leading role here is something we shall not venture to consider at this point. It was not, however, entirely absurd for Yen Fu to believe, in the early nineties, that filial piety as a moral force among the masses might be harnessed to advance the course of wealth and power. The question of the compatibility of filial piety with Yen Fu's commitment to "liberalism" raises the question of the nature of his liberalism and of the connection between modernization and liberalism, which will be one of our main problems. Furthermore, it must be noted that the positive attitude toward filial piety by no means implies that Yen Fu was attempting to construct a "national Confucian religion" in the manner of K'ang Yu-wei. The "preservation of the faith" had at this time receded far from the center of his concerns.

These few glimpses of Yen Fu's thought before he bursts forth in print after 1895 would indicate that some of his basic preoccupations were already present and that some of his basic ideas had already taken shape long before they found expression. Spencer, the chief deity in his pantheon, had already won his profound devotion. The Sino-Japanese War simply overcame his final inhibitions against the public expression of his burning convictions.

CHAPTER III

Declaration of Principles

THE Chinese defeat of 1895 produced an almost traumatic change in the climate of literati opinion. The defeat was not expected even by those who were acutely aware of China's deficiencies in the realm of wealth and power. Between the general awareness of Chinese weakness and the concrete demonstration of weakness there still lay a palpable hiatus. The defeat of China by France had not been unexpected. The discrepancy between the military might of the Western powers and of China was by now generally realized. However, the discrepancy between the self-strengthening efforts of the Chinese and those of the "eastern dwarfs" had not been generally realized. The traumatic effect of these events, the sudden sense of urgency, the acute fear that China might now finally be "cut up like a melon" by the great world powers were certainly felt by all those literati who were as much concerned with "preserving the state" as with "preserving the faith." By now this included all but a small fringe. In this new climate, tongues were loosed which had previously kept silent, and it was in this atmosphere that Yen Fu, who does not seem to have been endowed with an extraordinary measure of civic courage, finally burst forth in print.

During the years 1895–1898 we have from his pen a whole series of essays with such titles as "On the Speed of World Change,"[1] "On Strength,"[2] "On Our Salvation,"[3] and "In Refutation of Han Yü."[4] These essays, written in the space of one year (1895), shed an extraordinary light on Yen Fu's entire image of the world at this time. They articulate all the basic assumptions which are to underlie his translation efforts of the next few years. The numerous commentaries which interlace his subsequent translations of Huxley, Smith, Montesquieu, and Mill somehow take on an unexpected degree of mutual consistency when viewed in the light of the essays. These constitute in effect a sort of prolegomenon to the whole translation enterprise; further, they are diffused with the high passion of a man who has much to say and has long held back.

THE REALM OF IDEAS

The fundamental thesis is stridently proclaimed. The ultimate source of Western power—of the difference between East and West—lies not merely in weapons and technology, not simply in economic or even political organization, or in any institutional arrangement. The ultimate source is an entirely different vision of reality. It is to be sought in the realm of ideas and values.

One finds here an extraordinary stress on the role of "ideas" in human history. We have already noted before the voluntaristic twist which Yen Fu gave to Spencer's highly deterministic scheme. He found in it a program for "changing the world" rather than simply a theory for describing it. He is not entirely unconscious of the problem of the relation of "destiny" (*yün-hui*) to consciously directed human action. As a matter of fact, in his essay "On the Speed of World Change" he even seems to lean for a moment toward the deterministic side. The ultimate cause of historic change, he states, is, after all, "destiny." "Once the [process of] destiny had been fulfilled, the sages could not force it from its course, for after all, the sages were themselves a factor (*i wu*) within the course of destiny. It is unreasonable to assert that they could change the course of destiny. The sages were men who knew the direction of the process and were able to anticipate its ultimate course . . . They were then able to regulate it, complete it, to cooperate with it, and thus lead the world (*t'ien hsia*) to a state of peace. Later men, observing their success, came to believe that the sages were actually able to change the course of destiny."5

This passage actually seems to imply a commitment to a kind of historical determinism. Where Yen Fu uses the old expression *yün-hui* one may already read "process of evolution." Simultaneously, however, we find him making vast claims for Western thought as the primary factor accounting for the difference between China and the modern West. "The greatest difference in the principles of West and East, that which is most irreconcilable, is the fact that, while the Chinese love the ancient and ignore the modern, Westerners stress the new in order to overcome the old. The Chinese think of the process of nature (*t'ien hsing*) and of human affairs (*jen shih*) in terms of a cycle of order and disorder, prosperity and decay. The Westerners make their ultimate principle of learning and political action the idea that the possibilities of daily progress are inexhaustible, that prosperity once achieved will not decline, and that order will not fall back to disorder."6 One might, of course, maintain that this Western outlook is itself a fruit of the evolutionary process, just as the ability of the ancient sages to perceive the "direction of the course of destiny" was a result of destiny itself. Here, however, Yen Fu immediately confronts a conundrum which was to be with him constantly. The impersonal forces of evolution described by Darwin and Spencer are universal. Why then have they bogged down in China and achieved realization only in the modern West? Obviously, it is because the sages of the modern West have clearly understood the processes of evolution. It is their grasp of the "course of destiny" which has made possible the unrestricted operation of the forces of evolution as determinants of modern social development, just as China's ancient sages based their static view of society on their grasp of the static and cyclical aspects of nature. By the same token, the sages—and Chinese culture in general—never attained a grasp of the mechanisms of evolution. One might say that if the sages were unable "to change the course of destiny" they somehow seem to have had the power to thwart the evolutionary process, by inihibition as it were. Ideas are enzymes which can either release or hold back the forces of evolution.

It is not modern Western thought as a whole which has comprehended the evolutionary course of destiny. It is specifically that strain of thought which finds its ultimate embodiment in the writings of Darwin and Spencer. "Since the publication of this book [*The Origin of Species*]," Yen Fu states, "vast changes have occurred in Western learning, government, and philosophy.[7] Those who assert that the teachings of Mr. Darwin have done more to renew the eyes and ears and to change men's thoughts than Newton's discovery of physical laws are perhaps not indulging in empty words."[8] Darwin's theories do not merely describe reality. They prescribe values and a course of action. They are, in truth, "a source of strength." In the brief preliminary exposition which Yen Fu presents of the main tenets of Darwinism, the language is already that of social Darwinism: "Living things struggle among themselves in order to survive. Nature (lit., 'heaven') selects [among them] and preserves the superior species. It is his view that humans and living things are born within a given space and together feed on the environment (heaven and earth) and on the benefits of nature. They come into conflict with each other. Peoples and living things struggle for survival. At first, species struggle with species; then as [men] gradually progress, there is a struggle between one social group and another. The weak invariably become the prey of the strong (ch'iang-jou), the stupid invariably become subservient to the clever."[9] What interests Yen Fu here is not so much the Darwinian account of biological evolution qua science, even though science is a cherished value. It is precisely the stress on the values of struggle—assertive energy, the emphasis on the actualization of potentialities within a competitive situation. The image of "nature red in tooth and claw" does not depress him. It exhilarates him.

It is no accident, of course, that, having made his reverential bow to Darwin, Yen Fu immediately passes on to the more pertinent Herbert Spencer, for it was Spencer who (in his view) made the all-important application of these truths to human affairs. "Spencer is also a native of England, and a contemporary of Darwin. His books actually appeared before the *Origin of Species*. He based himself on the theory of evolution to explain the origins of human relations and of civilization. I call this science the science of social groups[10] [sociology], for, as Hsün-tzu states, man's superiority over the beast lies in his ability to form social groups."[11] Through Spencer the catch-phrases of Darwinism become immediately linked to Yen Fu's fundamental preoccupation. Is our goal the wealth and power of our state? We must know the laws of society which explain why some states are strong and others weak. It is Spencer who has laid bare the laws which govern the evolution of individuals within given societies, as well as the evolution of whole societies on the intra-societal plane.

It is true that lesser heroes are also invoked in these essays. The whole technical base of modern Western industry stems from the truths revealed by Newton. The power of Western ships and vehicles is based on the discoveries of Watt. Adam Smith is already referred to as the man who ultimately deserves credit for "all their methods of regulating livelihood and ordering wealth." We shall, however, find that Yen Fu is able without difficulty to fit the partial insights of all these prior or lesser deities into the grand synthesis created by Spencer.

Herbert Spencer's reputation has sunk low in the twentieth century. Yet I suspect that it is not simply the obsolescence and mediocrity of his thought which explains the fact that we no longer read his books. His synthesis may be a compendium of commonplace and typical nineteenth-century views, but many of these views still form part of the unstated creed of our age.[12] In part, it is because so many of his notions are so widely accepted that they seem commonplace. To Yen Fu, of course, these notions are by no means commonplace. They are the fresh and creative ideas, encompassed within a vast and satisfying synthesis, which divide the modern West from the stagnant East.

Before probing further the essential difference between West and East as perceived by Yen Fu, we might pause to raise the question whether this fervent commitment to Spencer marks a rupture with the totality of Chinese tradition. Has he become, in the words of his biographer Chou Chen-fu, "an all-out Westernizer"—an "antitraditionalist" in the manner of the young people of the May Fourth generation? The enthusiastic embrace of Western thinkers whose ideas and values run directly counter to cherished Chinese values represents an assault on Chinese pride at its most vulnerable point. The notion of China's superiority in this sphere was the last bastion of resistance of the "Western affairs" school and even of the reformers of the 1898 period.

Liang Ch'i-ch'ao, the young protegé of K'ang Yu-wei, was

during this period profoundly influenced by the essays and translations of Yen Fu. Yet, like his master K'ang, he continued to cling to the "preservation of the faith" although the nature of his faith had itself become highly problematic. K'ang's "new text" conception of Confucianism with its vision of Confucius as the uncrowned Messiah king— the whole blending of the cryptic doctrine of the Kung-yang commentary on the *Spring and Autumn Annals* with Western ideas of progress—represented a strain of "faith" which was entirely exotic to the overwhelming majority of the respectable community of Confucian literati. It was, as a matter of fact, a form of Confucianism so emptied of specific doctrinal content that it could accommodate within its empty spaces the whole of modern nationalism and the very transformation of values contemplated by Yen Fu himself. Yet in a significant exchange of letters between Yen Fu and Liang Ch'i-ch'ao in 1897[13] we find the former asserting in categorical terms that "the faith cannot be preserved, and if one asserts that we should advance even while preserving the faith, it is not the original faith which is being preserved."[14] Liang Ch'i-ch'ao's reply to this extremely bold assertion would indicate that he himself was tending in the direction of Yen Fu and away from his master K'ang. His defense of the faith is couched in highly pragmatic terms. If the strength of the state depends on the people, then the powers of the people must be consolidated. In their present state the Chinese people can only be united by an authoritarian government. "While democracy offers the best method of 'saving the times,' the spirit of the people today is still unenlightened and we must first rely on the power of the sovereign to change it. This is what he [K'ang] means by the faith."[15] In other words, the "faith" is conceived of here as the quasi-religious source of legitimation of the monarchy—it is again the statesman's "religion for the people." (Whether K'ang himself thought of his brand of Confucianism at this time in these coldly calculating political terms is highly doubtful.)

Yen Fu, however, refuses at this point to make any commitment to Confucianism even in its most attenuated form. As a statesman, he certainly accepted Liang's provisional justification of the monarchy. As a matter of fact, the chain of reasoning in Liang's letter might well have derived from Yen Fu's own writings. He refuses, however, at this point to concern himself with the very real question of the traditional bases of legitimation of the monarchy. He is much more concerned with the tasks of renovation which the monarchy must now undertake. Nor does he feel any need to persuade himself that K'ang Yu-wei's brand of Confucianism is indeed the original faith.

His fundamental point of view is expressed most succinctly in his "Letter to the Editor of the *Wai-chiao-pao* on Education"[16] (written five years later). "What are China's principal troubles? Are they not ignorance, poverty, and weakness? In a nutshell, any method which can overcome this ignorance, cure this poverty, lift us out of this weakness, is desirable. The most urgent of all is the overcoming of ignorance, for our failure to cure poverty and weakness stems from our ignorance. In overcoming ignorance we must exert our utmost efforts to seek out knowledge. We have no time to ask whether this knowledge is Chinese or Western, whether it is new or old. If one course leads to ignorance and thus to poverty and weakness, even if it originates with our ancestors or is based on the authority of our rulers and teachers, not to speak of persons of a lower order, we must cast it aside. If another course is effective in overcoming ignorance and thus leads to the cure of our poverty and weakness, we must imitate it, even if it proceeds from barbarians and wild beasts, not to speak of persons of a higher order." He then points to the Meiji Japanese, to Frederick the Second, and to Peter the Great, who "in their ardent exertions to strengthen themselves abandoned century-old institutions and national customs like so much chaff." The basic shift here is unmistakable. Values, institutions, ideas—the whole content of culture—must be judged in terms of one criterion: will it preserve and strengthen the nation-state? Nothing in the tradition which impedes the achievement of this goal is sacred. Furthermore, at this point Yen Fu's disposition is to regard almost the whole Confucian stream of thought referred to in the phrase "preservation of the faith" as incompatible with this goal.

Why, then, must one hesitate to define Yen Fu as an "all-out westernizer" or as an "antitraditionalist"? In the first place, the whole concept of "traditionalism" is not available to him. It is only later that the nineteenth-century Western term "traditionalism" is translated into Chinese. "Chinese Tradition" as an all-inclusive abstract category does not become a target of his attack, because it is doubtful whether the tradition presents itself to him as an integrated synthetic whole. Where he can find support for his views in Lao-tzu, Buddhism, the *Book of Changes,* or the words of Hsün-tzu he will do so. We are, of course, tempted to link him at this point with a whole vein of apologetics which had developed during the seventies and eighties, designed to prove that all the innovations of Western civilization had ultimately come "from the East" (*tung-lai*), that is, from China. This device obviously represents an effort to salvage cultural pride (or later nationalist pride). At times, this line of argument was used by ultraconservatives to discredit Western innovations: Chinese culture had been quite capable of producing Western technology and institutions but had not deigned to turn its energies in that direction. More commonly, it was used as a device to legitimate innovation. Actually, however, Yen Fu explicitly rejects the crude notion that the West had borrowed its civilization from China.[17] One will, to be sure, find in his preface to the

Evolution and Ethics the claim that one can see in ancient thought some of the basic categories of logic and physics which underlie the spectacular scientific development of the West. The notion expressed by Ssu-ma Ch'ien that "the *Book of Changes* is based on the hidden, which is then made manifest, while the *Spring and Autumn Annals* pushes back from that which is seen to that which is hidden"[18] contains in essence a reference to something like the notions of deduction and induction, while the basic categories of "number, logic, mass, and motion" are all contained within the *Book of Changes*. However, the crucial point here is that "while the ancients discovered the beginnings of these principles, later men were unable to follow through."[19]

It is not our concern here to consider the validity of such assertions. Actually, these particular assertions concerning logic and science seem far less plausible than other later assertions of resemblance between given strains of philosophic thought in the West and in China. Our interest is in Yen Fu's motivation. Was it timidity which drove him to present new ideas in familiar trappings in order to avoid persecution? The environment, it is true, still called for some degree of prudence. Yet we have already noted the bold assertion that the "faith cannot be preserved," and we will further note that his specific attacks on specific Chinese traditions are proclaimed without the slightest reservation. Again, he may simply be using the pedagogical device of explaining the unfamiliar in terms of the familiar, and the suspiciously novel in terms of the respectably ancient. Finally, if the term "nationalist" can already be used to describe Yen Fu, then must we not assume the presence of that pride in national accomplishments which seems to be an indispensable ingredient of all nationalism?

All of these elements are undoubtedly present. I would suggest, however, that we must also be open to another possibility—that Yen Fu genuinely senses similar elements in both cultures. He is, after all, neither a cultural relativist who thinks of cultures as closed, isolated monads, nor a historicist in the sense that he would deny a priori the possibility of comparing ideas across the gulf of time. He lives enough within the tradition to know that it is not all of a piece, and within it he finds that which attracts him and that which repels him. He accepts without undue wonderment the notion that Chinese thought and Western thought may have dealt with similar problem areas; he may genuinely feel that he discerns, rightly or wrongly, affinities between elements of Chinese thought and elements of Western thought. In sum, Yen Fu is no longer committed to anything in the tradition which lies in the way of the search for wealth and power, yet he is no doctrinaire "antitraditionalist." The question of his relation to the totality of thought currents which constitute Chinese tradition remains open and indeterminate.

Thus Yen Fu's rapturous embrace of Spencer by no means marks a total rupture with Chinese traditional thought on all levels. Strangely enough, it is precisely at the "deep" metaphysical cosmological level that Spencer's image of the universe seems most congenial to certain inveterate Chinese modes of thought. The vaguely pantheistic-naturalistic, immanentist monism of Spencer, in which the manifold phenomena of reality "evolve" out of the womb of the "Unknowable" and are mediated through the abstract categories of space, matter, time, motion, and force, is readily translated by Yen Fu into language derived from the appendix to the *Book of Changes,* from Lao-tzu, or from Sung philosophy. Spencer's world of the "heterogeneous and organized" evolving out of "the homogeneous and simple" is easily transposed into elegant classical Chinese prose. "There is contraction (*hsi*), and matter is drawn together. There is dispersion (*p'i*), and force is released (*ch'u li*). In the beginning there is the Simple. It changes and turns into the variegated and mixed (*tsa niu*)."[20]

Here we have the "ten thousand things" emerging in all their variety out of the womb of non-being. It is, of course, true that this particular mode of metaphysics is often associated in China with a kind of cosmical cyclical theory in which the "ten thousand things" achieve full differentiation only to be reabsorbed into the void, and with a characteristic emphasis on the cyclical great return rather than on irreversible progress "from the homogeneous to the heterogeneous." It is also true that all this does not necessarily involve any theory of evolution in the precise nineteenth-century connotation of that term.[21] Yet, the common features are obvious. We shall have to consider whether Yen Fu's emotional attitude toward the "Unknowable" is the same as that of Spencer. Whatever may be the case, the bare ontological structure of Spencer's metaphysics is not alien to him. The same Spencerian "monistic superstition" and "block universe" which infuriated the defiantly pluralistic and individualistic William James and which ran counter to certain central tendencies of the whole Judeo-Christian tradition offer no stumbling block to that which is most traditional in Yen Fu. Needham is probably quite right in asserting that certain brands of monistic metaphysics which have come to the fore since the seventeenth century in the West are closer (at least on the strictly metaphysical level) to what might be called the *philosophia perennis* of China than to certain dominant tendencies of ancient and medieval Western thought. Whether this type of thought should be called "organismic philosophy" in Whitehead's sense, as Needham asserts, may well be doubted. Herbert Spencer's seamless monism would seem to have far greater affinity to this deep stream of Chinese perennial philosophy than Whitehead's system with its enormous pluralistic emphasis on the reality and value of particular "actual entities."

If Spencer's ultimate metaphysical notions offer no offense to that which is most familiar, it is certainly not this affinity which has excited Yen Fu's burning enthusiasm. It is rather the fact that embedded in this familiar metaphysical framework he finds a vision of natural and human reality which divides Spencer off from China by a bottomless abyss. It is, after all, not the identity but the difference which commands Yen Fu's overwhelming attention.[22] "Our Chinese sages," he states in one of the most pregnant passages in all his writings, "were not unaware that the universe is an inexhaustible storehouse [of infinite possibilities] and that if the subtle powers of the human mind are given free vent, human ingenuity and intellectual capacity can attain unfathomable results. However, we simply turned aside [from the pursuit] and did not concern ourselves with it. In our philosophy (tao) of sustaining the people we aimed only at harmony and mutual sustenance."[23] This turning away from a fearless application of human intellectual energies to the exploitation of the infinite resources of the universe was motivated in part by the kind of quasi-Malthusian consideration which can already be found in the writings of Hsün-tzu. "The products of heaven and earth are limited but the lustful desires of men are limitless. The procreation of children increases constantly, the cultivation of the soil is ever more extended. In the end there is an insufficiency of food. The insufficiency leads to struggle but struggle is [in their view] man's greatest calamity. Hence they preferred to preach contentment with one's lot (chih-tsu, lit., 'knowing what suffices'). They saw to it that everyone was content with a rustic simplicity and a dull confined existence, that they cultivated the soil in the service of their superiors."[24]

The sages—those symbols of Chinese culture—had, as it were, made a deliberate choice. They were not unconscious of the infinite resources of the universe or the infinite capacity of human constructive energies to wrest wealth and power from the universe. (Later we will find that Yen Fu stresses not only intellectual power, but Spencer's famous triad of physical, intellectual, and moral energies.) Some of them were even aware of the role of overpopulation in the economy of the universe. Within the Darwinian scheme, however, overpopulation plays a positive, dynamic role. It is the teeming of creatures which leads to the struggle for existence. It is the struggle for existence which leads to natural selection and the survival of the fittest—and hence within the human realm to the greatest realization of human capacities. To the sages, however, the energetic pursuit of survival and mastery as ends, the prospect of strife and conflict, represented the demonic—the ultimate evil. They thus shrank back from the actualization of men's potentialities, settling for peace, harmony, and order on a low level of human achievement.

In the last analysis, the fact that the Chinese "loves the ancient and despises the new," the fact that the West envisions limitless progress while China accepts a cyclical view of human history, rests on this more fundamental difference. The sages had succeeded in their attempt to freeze the process of evolution at a given stage of social equilibrium. The Taoist philosophers had even longed to reverse the process by taking refuge in the womb of non-being. One loves the old because the old embodies the values of peace, harmony, simplicity, and tranquil social order. "Alas, such was the consummate skill of the sages in constraining the world, in preventing struggles and putting an end to disorder, they were unable to foresee that people's knowledge would decline steadily and their energy would steadily deteriorate!"[25] So long as China remained isolated, it did not suffer the consequences of its failure to accept the tasks imposed by the evolutionary process. Now, however, China was reaping the sinister harvest of this failure.

Here we find, then, the very crux of the difference between East and West. On the one hand, we have a vision of reality which stresses the primacy of force in the universe at large and the thrust of energy in the biological and human world. The key terms are energy, dynamism, struggle, self-assertion, and the fearless realization of all human potentialities on ever higher levels of achievement. The same Spencer who proclaims the category of force as "the ultimate of ultimates"[26] on the cosmic plane makes the "energy of faculty" the key term on the human plane. On the other hand, we have a vision which exalts passivity and quietude, which shrinks from struggle and strife, and positively fears the assertion of human vital energies. Paradoxical as it may seem, these differences of vision probably go "deeper" in Yen Fu's view than the formal affinities of metaphysical structure which he finds in Spencer and the mainstream of Chinese philosophy. We can, of course, easily perceive how directly this vision relates itself to Yen Fu's immediate preoccupation with wealth and power. It is the uninhibited flow of the evolutionary process in the West which has accounted for Western wealth and power. It is the inhibition of the evolutionary process which is the ultimate source of China's poverty and debility.

Spencer not only provides a new dynamic vision of the cosmos as a whole—he also provides the enormously exciting and illuminating image of the "social organism." He not only indicates the paths to salvation; he also defines precisely what it is that is to be saved. To Yen Fu, groping toward the notion of China as a society-nation rather than a culture, the concept of the social organism as almost the exact analogue of the biological organism (a concept worked out in incredibly exhaustive detail in the *Principles of Sociology*) provides the most vivid possible image of the nation. It is an organism among other organisms within a Darwinian environment struggling to survive, to grow, and to prevail. "When a social group is formed, in terms of its structure and functions, in terms of its capacities, it does not differ from a biological entity. While differing in magnitude, there is a similar correspondence of organs and functions [Spencer's "mutually dependent parts"]. Knowing the principles of sustaining the life of my own person,

I also know the principles of the survival of the social group. Knowing what makes for long life in the individual, I know what maintains the strong pulse of the nation. In the individual, body and spirit depend on each other. Within the society, physical strength and virtue are mutually dependent. In the individual, liberty is esteemed. In the nation, independence."[27] Another notion closely linked by Spencer with the physiological conception of social organism is the notion that the quality of the social "aggregate" depends on the quality of the "units" or individual cells. The logical relationship between the "social organism" notion and the emphasis on the quality of individuals is actually quite feeble,[28] as has often been pointed out, in spite of its surface plausibility. Yen Fu, however, is not inclined to question this linkage, since both notions are immediately and directly relevant to his most overwhelming concerns.

What Yen Fu finds essentially in Spencer is the most graphic possible image of the nation-society, as conceived of in the purest nationalism. As a cell of the organism known as China, the duty of the Chinese individual is not to any set of fixed, universal values or fixed beliefs. It is above all a commitment to the survival and growth of the social organism of which he is a part.

The analogy between the social and biological organism seems fresh and new to Yen Fu. To those inclined to stress the "social organic" emphasis of Chinese culture this may seem somewhat strange. In the "individualistic" West we know that the analogy goes back as far as the Greeks and was certainly a commonplace by the time of Hobbes. Spencer, to be sure, adds a dynamic "evolutionary" element, but the basic image itself is extremely ancient. One cannot assert that traces of the analogy cannot be found in the immense corpus of Chinese literature. There is, for example, an occasional comparison of the relationship of emperor and ministers to the relationship of head and limbs.[29] What is more common, however, within "magical"

Taoism and Chinese medicine is the reverse analogy according to which the human body itself is conceived of as a kind of organized state with its various departments and bureaus. The focus in all works of this type is not on the state or society but on the magico-hygienic regimen of the human body.[30]

It is, of course, true that in the Confucian tradition the individual is subordinate to the "social." The "social" here, however, is the web of social relationships within which the individual is involved. It refers to social structure rather than to society as a whole conceived of as an organism in some sense. The entire ecumene of the Chinese world (t'ien hsia) was certainly not regarded as a closed organism, and the biological analogy was not immediately obvious. Hence Spencer's biological metaphor, particularly within its Darwinian framework, strikes Yen Fu with all the force of a blinding revelation.

There has been no reference thus far to liberalism. Most Chinese textbook accounts of Yen Fu's thought at this time label him quite unproblematically an advocate of "Western liberalism."[31] Spencer, of course, is universally known as an almost classical representative of nineteenth-century British liberalism. Richard Hofstadter[32] is able to discuss Spencer's impact on the United States almost wholly in terms of his role as the philosopher of "rugged individualism" and classical economic orthodoxy. Spencer himself had undoubtedly come to his nonconformist brand of individualism long before he had elaborated the synthetic philosophy.[33]

Yet in discussing the impact of Spencer on Yen Fu, I do not think that I have upset the proper ordering of topics in leaving the strictly "liberal" aspects to the end. The cult of energy, of struggle, of the maximum assertion of all vital powers, and the biological image of the social organism must here be given first priority. It is within the setting of these ideas that we must now locate the strictly "liberal" aspects of Spencer's outlook as viewed by Yen Fu.

As already pointed out, the quality of the social aggregate in Spencer is based on the quality of the individuals who compose it. The individuals themselves are conceived of as units of latent energy—the famous triad of physical, intellectual, and moral energies. The dynamic principle which sets these energies in motion is the search for individual happiness. Spencer, however, draws a sharp distinction between his own conception of human happiness—his own happiness ethic—and what he regards as the passive hedonism of the Benthamite utilitarians. The conditions under which happiness is achieved are conditions in which all healthy vital capacities reach their full realization. Happiness is vouchsafed only to him in "whom the functions are duly fulfilled . . . Pains are correlative to actions injurious to the organism, while pleasures are the correlative of actions conclusive to its welfare."[34] (with the proviso that "special and proximate pleasures and pains must be disregarded out of consideration to remote and diffuse pleasures and pains").[35] Happiness is concomitant to the full realization of the "energy of faculty." The "egoism" advocated by Spencer is thus entirely different, in Yen Fu's view, from the passive, consumer "egoism" with which he was so painfully familiar in the Chinese society of his time. The "individualism" of Spencer must be sharply differentiated, on the one hand, from the "romantic" individualism preoccupied with the limitless strivings of the passions and imagination, and also from a passive hedonism of immediate pleasures. It is a sober pursuit of self-interest which results in the positive propulsion of the "constructive" human energies—physical and intellectual. The assertion of these energies results in a Darwinian struggle for existence within which acting individuals "grind and polish each other . . ."[36] "Beginning in mutual antagonism they end by completing each other."[37]

Freedom within this context means the free exercise of all human capacities and functions—the creation of conditions which release and encourage constructive human energies and actualize the capacities of men. While the sages did everything to confine and inhibit the energies latent in the individual, the West has in modern times created institutions and fostered ideas designed to release these energies. The motive power of these energies is the enlightened sense of self-interest in the individual. Here we find the nexus of libertarianism, classical economic ideas, and Darwinist imagery which constitutes the liberalism of Spencer. Yen Fu derives from him the profound conviction that the energies which ultimately account for the wealth and power of the social organisms of the West are energies latent in the individual; that these energies are powered, as it were, by the drive of enlightened self-interest; and that liberty, equality, and democracy provide the environment within which this enlightened self-interest manifests itself —within which human physical, intellectual, and moral potentialities are realized.

Freedom of the individual is thus inevitably linked to a repudiation of a cardinal tenet of the orthodox Confucian ethic—the principle that the pursuit of self-interest, of *li*, is the ultimate source of evil. At this point, Yen Fu must place himself in blatant opposition to tradition. It is in his translation of Adam Smith's *Wealth of Nations* that we shall find him squarely facing this irreconcilable conflict of values.

It should be added, however, that Spencer with his facile reasoning also spares Yen Fu the necessity of facing the unmitigated confrontation of issues. The fact is that a legitimization of self-assertiveness on the part of the individual, a justification of the limitless pursuit of self-interest within a Darwinian environment, is probably as inherently irreconcilable with the notion of universal liberty for all men as it is with Confucianism. Ernest Barker has pointed out that among Spencer's many incongruities is the notion that a Darwinian conception of individuality, which simply posits a blind self-assertiveness on the individual's part, can be reconciled with the notion of an innate moral sense which will hold back the individual from ignoring the liberty of others. The recognition that the liberty of others must be respected is, of course, an assertion of a "natural rights" doctrine. This is a residue of Spencer's earlier liberalism which actually has no place in a Darwinian universe in which the biological entity possesses only those "rights" which it can assert.[38] In Barker's words, "Man must not claim (but Spencer gives no reason why he must not claim) any rights of action which interfere with his fellows."[39] If human society is, in fact, a field of action in which the behavior of individuals is completely determined by Darwinian mechanisms, the notion of respect for the liberty of others is entirely unwarranted, at least during the stages of evolution preceding the final utopian equilibrium.

Yen Fu, however, is not inclined at this point to raise questions concerning the relations of "natural rights" theory to Darwinism. He welcomes both Spencer's "egoism" and his "altruism." There is a realm in which the individual asserts his powers to the full and without inner restraint and another realm in which he restrains himself in the interests of others, and in both realms (in the West) his actions redound to the supreme benefit of the social organism. Spencer's effort to leave a place for the other-regarding virtues actually helps to mitigate the stark contrast between the Confucian ethic with its absolute rejection of "egoism" and Spencer with his affirmation of aggressive self-interest. It even makes it possible for Yen Fu to find common features in the Western concept of freedom and the Confucian value of reciprocity (shu). "To kill, injure, or steal another man's property are all extreme violations of human freedom."[40] My freedom can be preserved only as long as I do not invade yours.

Having made this bow in the direction of lending a certain respectability to the value of freedom, however, Yen Fu immediately proceeds to emphasize the essential difference, for it is precisely the new and the different which attract him. "The two [reciprocity and liberty] cannot be said to be the same, for while the Chinese virtues of reciprocity and good standards of behavior (*chieh-chü*) focus exclusively on the treatment of others, the freedom of the Westerners while involving the treatment of others is focused in the first instance on the preservation of self."[41] The Chinese ethic achieves its purpose only by diminishing the energies of all—by a subtraction on all sides. Freedom (as understood by Spencer) achieves its goal by advancing the interests of all and hence by heightening the energies of the society as a whole.

Hence we see the close connection between the absence of freedom and the negation of man's Promethean energies. The energies made manifest in the spectacular dynamism of modern Western society are energies stored up, as it were, in the individual atoms of society and set free only by the conditions created by freedom.

The key term is freedom.[42] The principles of equality and democracy, which are also extolled, are, as it were, corollaries of the principle of freedom. At one point Yen Fu uses the old Chinese substance-function (*t'i-yung*) dichotomy to describe the relations of freedom and democracy. "Freedom is the substance, democracy the function."[43] "From the difference [between China and the West] on the matter of freedom there arises a whole host of other differences. To mention but a few—while China honors the three-fold network (*san-kang*) of proper social relations above all else, the Westerners place equality first; while China favors relatives, Westerners esteem the capable; while China bases the whole social order on filial piety, Westerners base it on impartiality (*kung*); while China reveres the ruler, the West exalts the people."[44]

The principle of equality simply involves the recognition of the equal freedom of all. The equality in question is primarily the "equality of opportunity," for it is only where equality of opportunity exists that true human capacities and potentialities can be freely exercised. The struggle for existence in human society should be carried on wholly in terms of real capacities and not distorted by "artificial" inequalities. An interesting indication of the extent to which Yen Fu's "liberalism" is permeated by Darwinian assumptions is furnished by his observations on the question of economic inequality in the West. The fact is that he is fully aware of the existence of such inequalities and is even familiar with socialist trends in Western thought ("the party of those who would equalize the rich and the poor").[45] The economic inequality of the West far exceeds that of China. While the rich are extraordinarily rich, the poor are just as prone to crime, vagrancy, and sundry misfortunes as the destitute in poor countries.[46]

Yet this observation by no means diminishes his enthusiasm for the West or inclines him, as in the case of Sun Yatsen, towards an assertion of the superiority of Chinese traditional concern for "people's livelihood" over the brutalities of modern Western capitalism. "Western economists and sociologists are aware of the existence of this evil . . . The source of the evil must be sought, however, in men's minds, customs and habits. If one wishes to equalize the noble and the mean, the rich and the poor, the people must all be rendered worthy and the number of the unworthy reduced; the people must all be rendered intelligent and the numbers of those without capacity reduced. It is only when all have knowledge and ignorance has been reduced that such equality is feasible. Even if a country's wealth were now completely equalized, tomorrow we would again have inequality because those who incline to indolence would not be made industrious and those who love luxury would not be made frugal."[47] It is precisely in the West, however, that the conditions have been created for increasing the intellectual, moral, and physical capacities of the people.

In the end those who survive will enjoy both freedom and equality. When this equality is achieved, however, it will not be an equality of weakness and austerity achieved by a diminution of human energies, such as is envisioned in the Chinese ideal of the "Great Peace" (*Taiping*). It will be an equality which arises out of assertion of energy and bitter struggle—an equality of those who deserve to survive.

Democracy is, of course, that system of government which provides ideal conditions for the exercise of individual freedom. It is also, we shall find, that type of polity which most effectively calls forth the patriotic loyalty of the people—and channels their energies in the service of the collective wealth and power of the state.

The most radical statement of Yen Fu's ultimate commitment to democracy is to be found in his essay entitled "In Refutation of Han Yü."[48] In his essay "On the Way" (*"Yuan-tao"*) the famous T'ang literatus had furnished an account of the origins of human culture. Such accounts are quite common in Chinese literature and Han Yü's does not differ in its basic essentials from others, although it may be somewhat more extreme than many in its formulations. "In ancient times," we learn, "men suffered acutely, but when the sages appeared they taught them how to live together and sustain themselves. They became their rulers and teachers. They drove away noxious insects, serpents, and wild beasts, and settled the people in the Middle Land. They clothed them when they were cold and fed them when they were hungry. At first, when they lived in trees they would fall and when they lived in earth dwellings they became sick. They therefore built them dwellings and trained artisans to supply them with tools, merchants to exchange their goods, doctors to prevent their early death. They established the rites of mourning, burial, and sacrifice to nurture their feelings of love, and ceremonies to teach them the proper precedence of social relations . . ."[49] Had it not been for the sages, the human race would long since have perished. Why? "Because men had no wings, no fur, scales, nor fins to protect them against the heat and cold and no claws and fangs with which to procure their food."[50]

Now this account of the origins of human culture infuriates Yen Fu. Not only does it inflate the image of the sages to superhuman proportions.[51] What is worse, it portrays the mass of mankind as a totally inert, mindless clay incapable of initiative in any realm of human activity. It must again be stressed that the image of the mass of mankind as the passive object of the civilizing activities of the sages is by no means unique to Han Yü. It runs throughout Chinese political thought. It is by no means incompatible with the notion that the rulers' main task is to provide for the welfare of the people. Nor is it incompatible with the notion that superior man may rise out of the mass of the people. But it is incompatible with any notion of cultural creativity of the "ignorant people" as such.

We have seen elsewhere Yen Fu's attack on the sages for failing to develop the capacities of the people and settling for social harmony at a low level. Here the accusation is somewhat different. Having done everything to inhibit the vital energies and capacities of the people, the ruling class simply came to believe that the people had no creative capacities. Looking down from their high pavilions on the stolid peasantry toiling in the fields, they found it difficult to attribute to them any creativity whatsoever. Yen Fu attacks the obvious fallacies of this account. Did the sages come equipped with fur or claws and fangs? Did they not suffer from cold and illness and all the vicissitudes of other mortals? If they were human like all the others, where did they acquire their peculiar wisdom? If mankind had had to wait for the sages to teach them the barest rudiments of culture, would they not have perished long before the sages arrived?[52]

Actually the emergence of government itself presupposes a long cultural and economic development. Governments were established in order to perform a specific coercive function—to suppress internal violence within society and to defend the society against enemies from without. The people "set aside a tithe of their product in order to establish rulers to administer punishment and carry out military defense."[53] This, of course, clearly reflects Spencer's conception of government as the police weapon of society and drastically reduces the role of the rulers from the status of creators of culture to the role of policemen of society.[54] Furthermore, in China the rulers have on the whole performed their function badly, at least since the establishment of the Ch'in dynasty. At this point Yen Fu takes up a theme very common among his more radical young contemporaries, such as Liang Ch'i-ch'ao, T'an Ssu-t'ung, and others—namely, that the truly tyrannical period of Chinese government had begun with Ch'in Shih Huang-ti.[55] H'an Yü's grotesque exaggeration of the role of the sage-ruler reflects the centuries of arrogant authoritarianism which had intervened between the rise of the Ch'in empire in the third century B.C. and his own lifetime. If the sages themselves had done little to foster the energies and capacities of the people, the post-Ch'in rulers had done their best to suppress them. In the modern West, on the other hand, the state is regarded as the common property (*kung-ch'an*) of the people, and the rulers are regarded as servants of the people.

Here we find Yen Fu's most vehement statement of democratic protest against the authoritarian repressions of the past. Yet before drawing too sharp a contrast between the "radicalism" of this essay and the "conservatism" of some of his later writings, we must scrutinize this essay more closely. In the first place, we immediately note that Yen Fu has by no means forgotten his overriding concern with the wealth and power of the state. The gross underestimation of the physical, mental, and moral capacities of the people which is reflected in Han Yü's essay had itself been one of the major causes of China's lamentable weakness.

Having failed to do anything to encourage the creative energies of the people, the ruling classes did not believe they existed. As a matter of fact, since nothing was done to foster the capacities of the people, these capacities did indeed atrophy and are now merely potential rather than actual. At present the masses are, in fact, "incapable of ruling themselves."[56] Their abilities have not been developed, their physical powers have not been enhanced, their moral powers have not been consolidated."[57] If, as Spencer insists, the quality of society as an aggregate (and hence, in Yen Fu's view, the quality of the state) arises out of the quality of its units, the reasons for China's debility are obvious. Were a new sage-ruler now to arise in China he would say, "I must exert myself night and day to seek means of advancing my people's intellectual, physical, and moral capacities, to eliminate that which obstructs their intellectual, physical, and moral capacities . . . To see to it that they do not deceive each other, rob each other, and harm each other, I shall completely respect their freedom, for the freedom of the people is endowed by heaven. How dare we obstruct it? If by good fortune the people arrives at the point of being able to rule itself, I shall be happy to grant it self-rule. If the state advances daily in wealth and power, I and my posterity will derive advantage therefrom. Why should I attempt to maintain the realm as my private property? If I truly pursue this course and if the people does not attain harmony and good order within thirty years and if within sixty years China is not able to vie with Europe in wealth and power—may I then be accused of misrule."[58] Freedom is thus conceived of as the release of the "energy of faculty," while the wealth and power of the state remains the ulterior goal toward which this energy must be applied.

In stressing Yen Fu's persistent preoccupation with the wealth and power of the state, I by no means intend to imply that his commitment to values such as science, freedom, equality, and democracy is not authentic. One need not even assume that in the end these are not conceived of as values in themselves, or that he does not have ultimate visions of human welfare. Nevertheless, the foreground of his concern remains very much occupied by an overwhelming anxiety concerning the survival of the state. It would be a grave mistake to assume that the universal ultimate hopes are more important in determining the shape of his thought than this proximate goal. On the contrary, it is within the setting created by this preoccupation that all his commitments must be viewed. If science, freedom, equality, and democracy had not, in his view, been immediately relevant to this concern, one may well doubt whether his commitment to "liberalism" would have been so passionate. These principles might possess an abstract, intrinsic value of their own, but it is their immediate value as *means* to wealth and power which arouses his most fervent response.

What is even more relevant in judging the "radicalism" of this essay is the fact that Yen Fu's commitment to democracy is even here not immediate but ultimate. Spencer with his nineteenth-century gradualistic evolutionism has inoculated him quite effectively against any eighteenth-century notion that the ideal polity can immediately be realized within any given socio-historic situation. Democracy can come into being only when the historic conditions for its existence have matured. The condition of the Chinese people is due to the repressive authoritarianism of the past, but the condition itself cannot be wished away. Ignorance, physical debility, and lack of "public spirit"[59] are incompatible with self-government, and these defects can only be overcome under the guidance of an enlightened elite which assumes the initiative in coping with them. "Can we now abandon the lord-subject nexus [the principle of authoritarian government]? Decidedly not! Why not? The time has not yet come. The 'mores' [of the people] have not been perfected, and they are not prepared to govern themselves."[60] Unlike the sage-rulers of old, however, the enlightened rulers of the present will say yes to the potential energies of the masses. They will educate the people, and render them capable of moving toward self-government. What is needed in the immediate future is an enlightened elite which will prepare the ground for democracy. Thus, the very essay which contains Yen Fu's most radically "democratic" statement also contains the premises of his "conservatism."

So far we have found that all the views of Yen Fu can be connected with some strand of the Spencerian synthesis. The monistic quasi-pantheistic naturalism; the vision of the universe as an "inexhaustible storehouse" of force and energy constantly embodied in ever more heterogenous, complex, and differentiated structures; the Darwinian mechanisms of evolution as interpreted by Spencer; the biological analogy of the social organism; and the particular interpretation of the values of liberalism all have their Spencerian inspiration. It would nevertheless be more accurate to say that Yen Fu's vision of truth is a composite vision derived both from Spencer and from the observation of Spencer's England. He sees Spencer in terms of England and England in terms of Spencer. If Spencer is to him the philosopher of Victorian England, it is also true that he reads Spencer in terms of what he has seen in England. If he is at all aware that Spencer heartily disapproved of many developments in Great Britain during the latter decades of the nineteenth century—that he regarded the increasing intervention of the state in the internal affairs of society and growing imperialism abroad as a "retrogression"[61]—this awareness does not penetrate the deeper levels of his consciousness. As refracted through his own preoccupation with wealth and power, Spencer and Victorian England somehow blend into one harmonious whole.

One theme running through all Yen Fu's writings which cannot be clearly traced to any element of Spencerianism and which probably rests squarely on his own observations of English life is the praise of Western "public spirit" (*kung-hsin*). He had been profoundly impressed not only with liberty, with the growing equality of opportunity, and with self-government, but also with a value which encompassed and amalgamated all these others—the value of public spirit. It is to this value, above all, that he refers when he speaks of "people's morality" (*min-te*). The miracle of the West (particularly Great Britain) lies in its ability to promote the constructive self-interest of the individual, to release individual energies *and yet* harness these energies to collective goals. As a matter of fact, the very institutions of liberty, equality, and democracy which make it possible for the individual to pursue his private interests in peace and security cause him to identify his own interests with the interests of the social organism as a whole. The wonderful paradox of the West is that self-interest and the interest of the social organism reinforce each other. By sedulously creating an environment favorable to the interests of the individual, the people are led to identify these interests with the public interest—that is, with the interest of the nation-state.

Again, to the Westerner who has been indoctrinated concerning the "social virtues" of the Chinese, it may seem surprising to see the "public spirit" of capitalist England contrasted with the narrow selfishness of Confucian China. In part, Yen Fu's indictment of China involves the charge that the traditional values are no longer operative in the society which he knows. Basically, however, there is, in his view, a qualitative difference between the public spirit of the West and China's social morality. At best China harnesses the social sense of the individual to limited "particularistic" relations—to other individuals and to very small groups. In the words of Liang Ch'i-ch'ao (who was evidently much influenced by this theme in Yen Fu), "In China there are duties of individuals to individuals. There are no duties of individuals to society."[62] When the Chinese pursues his own interest or the interest of his family, it must be at the expense of the state. Again, the kind of interest he pursues is the sort of cancerous consumer self-interest which can only weaken the social organism as a whole, and not the constructive self-interest of the Western entrepreneur. The loyalty to the sovereign which should provide the nucleus for a nationalistic "public spirit" cannot exist, because there can be no sense of identity of self-interest with national interest. In the recent Sino-Japanese War there had been absolutely no sense of the fact that the state is like a body—that "when the head is attacked all four limbs must respond; when the stomach is stabbed, the whole body must suffer." On the contrary, the whole burden of defending the realm had fallen upon "one corner of the northeast." The old virtue of "loyalty" as applied to the emperor can simply not be compared to Western public spirit.

It is not, however, merely the identity of self-interest with national interest which accounts for the quality of the "people's morality" in the West. The "altruistic" side of Western mass morality is also infinitely more alive and available to collective goals that the mass morality of China. Christianity (particularly of the British puritanic variety) itself has proved an excellent teacher of public virtue, however erroneous its theology. Here Yen Fu takes up a theme we have met before. Even the poor, who may not, after all, perceive any very concrete connection between their own material self-interests and the interests of the nation-state, can also be led to regard "the common enemy of the state as their own private foe."[63] For one thing, Christianity helps to foster a sense of quality. The fact that on the Sabbath all the people, from princes to paupers, flock to church—where they are imbued with a sense of God's majesty and hear the promise of eternal life, where they learn that from a religious point of view they are all God's children—enhances their sense of equality and of self-esteem.[64] Furthermore, their religious education imbues them with the feeling that "God is watching them even in their inner chamber," so that even the man of the people is guided by a kind of inner "moral check" on anarchic, anti-social tendencies. All this serves to channelize the energies of the individual in socially constructive directions, and makes even the masses dutiful citizens ready to die for their country.

The vicarious statesman sees here a genuine superiority of Christianity over Chinese tradition in terms of its social effects. It is not only the superiority of Christianity on the matter of equality. It is also the fact that in the West a genuine, successful effort has been made to indoctrinate the masses in their own religious ethic, while in China no conscious effort has been made to propagate Confucian values among the people. "The idea of establishing schools for the people—let alone women [an idea which had presumably been implemented in ancient China]—has long since disappeared, and even if such schools existed now as in the past we would only pick the select among the people and educate them. As for the children of the poor, they receive no kind of instruction." Even if traditional values such as filial piety and loyalty might have provided a foundation for the creation of "public spirit," these values are not available to the masses. In the end we return to the original indictment. The sages and the ruling classes in China had no inclination to develop the potentialities—physical, moral, and intellectual—of the people, and no belief in these potentialities. Hence the ingredients of a national public spirit are completely lacking.

Summarizing the salient features of Yen Fu's synthesis at this point, one might say that in Spencer he finds the concept of human freedom in terms of the release of individual "energy of faculty." The intellectual, physical, and moral capacities of the people thrive and grow in a milieu of free institutions and uninhibited struggle for survival within the economic sphere. Simultaneously all these released energies are organized and fused: "Their wills are combined"[65]—in the service of the wealth and power of the social organism (the nation-state), which must also carry on a struggle for survival on the level of social organisms. More concretely, it is Great Britain's commitment to liberal values which has made that nation the most powerful state in the world.

At this point, of course, some may begin to detect what seems to be a fundamental, grotesque distortion of the whole Spencerian outlook. Spencer himself had regarded the synthetic philosophy as a cathedral dedicated to the God of individual liberty. The nation-state and its aims form no part of his vision of the good society. The good society will be a society in which the happiness of individuals will be the paramount and exclusive goal and in which the individual will suffer not external restraints and coercions. While he occasionally evinces a kind of instinctive British chauvinism,[66] nationalism is abhorrent to Spencer, and nothing could be more foreign to his outlook than the notion that the value of individual liberty lies in its power to advance the wealth and power of the nation-state. He had, after all, divided the evolution of mankind into two neatly distinguished periods—the "militant stage" and "the industrial stage." The nation-state is a relic of the militant phase of human evolution. During this stage mankind had become aggregated for mutual defense into large nation-states which required an extreme coercive military apparatus to carry on the external struggles with other societies and to create a harsh social discipline within the social organism. Such states are authoritarian and hierarchic and tend to control every facet of human society. "This structure which adapts a society for combined action against other societies is associated with the belief that its members exist for the benefit of the whole and not the whole for the benefit of its members."[67]

As the industrial structure gradually becomes dominant,

however, coercion within society gives way to voluntary cooperation. Free contract comes to govern civil life. Representative government emerges, militarism declines. The need for "coercive" methods of discipline disappears. Society is held together by the spontaneous habits of social discipline created by industrial organization. The struggle for existence continues to flourish in the sphere of healthy economic competition among individuals, but the collective struggles of states among themselves should gradually recede into limbo. Spencer belongs to that considerable group of nineteenth-century thinkers, including Karl Marx and the orthodox economists, who managed to convince themselves before the latter decades of the century that the nation-state was a relic of the past and that nationalism was about to recede from the stage of history. By the seventies, to be sure, he was forced to confront many unaccountable "reversions to the militant stage." There were the ominous power struggles on the Continent and the Tory imperialism of Disraeli. Spencer could only explain these developments to himself in terms of willful tampering with the proper course of social evolution—as a kind of unaccountable atavism.

We know from Yen Fu's later work[68] that he was not unaware of Spencer's periodization scheme, of the distinction between the monarchic society and industrial-democratic society. Yet the sharp antithesis drawn by Spencer between the belligerency and aggressive rivalry of states in the "militant stage" and the pacific and nonaggressive nature of the "industrial stage" makes no impression upon him. He is diverted from it by his own preoccupations and by what he sees before his eyes in the contemporary West. He does not forget for a moment that Great Britain is still the world's mightiest power. If Spencer regards Great Britain's growing imperial might with dismay, Yen Fu is only too acutely conscious of what seems to be its growing wealth and power. What he sees is not an antithesis but a functional relationship. Great Britain is strong and power-ful *precisely because* it has fostered ideas and institutions which liberate the energies of the individual and has consolidated these energies in the interests of the state. It is precisely because it is now in its "industrial stage" that Great Britain can assert its paramountcy in the world of struggling powers; individual freedom and national power are mutually reinforcing, and nothing can convince Yen Fu that national power presents a "retrogression" in any sense.

There can be no doubt that Yen Fu is here distorting Spencer's most deeply felt values. There can be no doubt that Spencer's American interpreters such as Sumner and Youmans, who interpreted him as the philosopher of economic individualism and anti-statism, divined the intentions of his heart much more accurately than the Chinese vicarious statesman who could not forget the goal of state power. Yet there remains a serious question whether the basic premises of Spencer's metaphysic and sociology as such are really more favorable, from a logical point of view, to his own conclusions than they are to Yen Fu's. Does the whole thrust of the Spencerian synthesis lead more inexorably to Spencer's "anarchistic" individualism than to Yen Fu's view of the individual as an instrument to ulterior state goals?

It must first of all be pointed out that the ontological status of the individual in Spencerian metaphysics is most feeble. Individuals are simply the particles through which the abstract impersonal forces of the universe—Force, Mass, Evolution—manifest themselves. The "abstract" individual, to use Hegel's term, has no more significant role to play in Spencer's cosmos than in Hegel's. The human individual is subject to a plethora of servitudes. Over and above the physical and biological forces which shape his being at every instant, whatever residue of his being is left is completely controlled by the "superorganism" of society. Spencer, of course, never tires of preaching that the quality of the total aggregate of society is a product of the quality of the units. Yet it is entirely obvious that the individual unit is only a cell of the social organism and that the quality of the unit is itself a result of the evolution of the whole social organism. The superiority of "industrial" man over "militant" man is certainly not due to the creative efforts of individuals but to an impersonal socio-historic process "into which man enters," to use Marx's phrase.

It may, of course, be argued that while individuals play no creative role in Spencer's universe, while this universe hardly treats individuals as ends in themselves on any level, Spencer is nevertheless convinced that the individual is the ultimate beneficiary of the whole process. It is also quite obvious, however, that to Spencer it is not any individual qua individual who is to be valued but only those individuals who embody the highest intellectual, physical, and moral capacities. The sacredness of the person of the misfit and the failure forms no part of his gospel. He is willing to see any number of "inferior" individuals sacrificed to produce that generation of superior individuals, those embodiments of capacity, who will be the ultimate beneficiaries of the whole process. Freedom, political equality, self-government are fundamentally instrumental to the achievement of this goal.

Beyond all this there is, of course, an enormous *non sequitur* at the very heart of Spencer's whole social-biological analogy. After entire chapters of the *Principles of Sociology* in which analogies between the social organism and the biological organism are spelled out in fantastic detail, in which the evolution of a coordinated nervous system, the ganglia, and finally the brain itself are compared to the growing consolidation of the state, he is suddenly forced to beat a hasty retreat. In the biological world the ever greater development of the brain, its ever increased power of coordination and control, becomes almost the goal of the whole evolutionary process. The evolution of the whole organism is toward ever-increasing subordination of parts to the welfare of the whole. Obviously, this analogy points to the ever-growing role of the state and the subordination of all sub-organs of society to the goals of the state; yet it is precisely this obvious conclusion that Spencer must do everything possible to avoid. "The welfare of the aggregate," we are suddenly informed, "considered apart from that of the units is not the end to be sought . . . The society exists for the benefit of its members not its members for the benefit of society. The claims of the body politic are nothing in themselves and become something only insofar as they embody the claims of its component individuals."[69] All this is based on the assertion that there is no social "sensorium"—that is, that while the social organism seems analogous to the biological organism in every other conceivable respect it does not embody a living consciousness. Consciousness rather resides in the cells. One cannot help feeling here that Spencer's views in this instance are guided by his individualistic bias rather than by the inherent logic of his sociology. Is there any logical reason why the conscious "cell of society" should not be sacrificed in the course of evolution to serve the purposes of the social organism, even though the latter is not conscious in the individual sense? Why must one assume that evolution has any particular predilection for the fact of consciousness? Indeed, is there any reason why one should not assume the existence of a kind of higher consciousness in the social organism, in the manner of Durkheim?

In human society, presumably, the period of the dominance of the "brain" belongs to the earlier, less mature "militant stage" of society, while it gradually shrinks and becomes vestigial in the "higher" industrial stage. In Spencer's analogy, the industrial system is analogous to the self-regulatory digestive system. Thus, as Ernest Barker aptly remarks, "while the evolution of the animal is toward the triumph of the nervous system, the evolution of the social organism is toward the triumph of the alimentary system . . . The stomach is, after all, the end of the social organism."[70]

It is not at all surprising that Yen Fu, who is so deeply impressed with the original biological analogy, does not seem to be particularly sensitive to Spencer's final retraction or to the anti-statism from which it springs. Both the logic of the idea itself and the candid observation of the contemporary European scene naturally lead to the view that the body politic is pre-eminently the beneficiary of the whole course of social evolution. Again this does not preclude the possibility that the individuals may also be the beneficiaries in the long run, but Yen Fu himself is more deeply engaged with the more immediate claims of the body politic.

There is little evidence in any of Yen Fu's writings that he really accepts the whole sharp antithesis between the "compulsory," externally imposed type of organization characteristic of the militant stage and the "voluntary" co-operation based on internalized habits of social discipline characteristic of the industrial stage. He fails to appreciate the sharp distinction drawn here between the nature of the machinery designed to produce wealth and the machinery designed to produce power. In his "On Strength" he speaks of the perfection of "governmental, industrial, military, commercial, and legal institutions" in the West, using one of those Chinese cluster phrases (*kuan, ping, kung, shang, fa, chih*) which strongly suggest that we are dealing with one and the same complex. The old Chinese Legalist association between the systematic organization of the machinery of wealth and the machinery of power makes it possible for him to reach beyond Spencer to something like Max Weber's view of the rationalization of society. To Weber also the bureaucratic organization of the state, the organization of the modern military machine, the rationalization of law, and the industrial system are all aspects of an over-all process of rationalization in modern society, and belong to one complex. In all these areas, the West has applied the moral, physical, and intellectual energies of individuals to "public" goals. The professional bureaucrat, the technically competent military man, the engineer, and the industrial entrepreneur all represent the happy cooperation of science, freedom, and public spirit. Industrial corporations are as much the manifestation of the power of organization and of the moral virtue of individuals (who subordinate immediate interests to long-term interests) as are bureaus of government and military organizations.

On the other hand, the ready acceptance of discipline on the part of the individual in the government bureaucracy and in the armed forces seems to be neither more nor less "compulsory or voluntary"[71] than his acceptance of discipline in the economic sector. In all these cases Yen Fu accepts an identity between his private interests and the public interests. From the point of view of the state, "private" railways, ship lines, and the innumerable private economic activities of individuals contribute as much to the state's wealth and power as do the activities of government bureaus or the army and navy. As in the case of many of the statesmen of Meiji Japan, who were acutely aware of the need of conscious direction from above in creating even a "capitalist economy," the whole blown-up distinction between the impersonal, spontaneous nature of economic growth and the conscious, artificial nature of political and military organization simply does not come through. The "entrepreneurship" of the large private entrepreneur consists of the fact that he imposes rational organization on areas of economic life where it has not existed before. His individual energies translate themselves into the extension of rational organization and of social discipline. In all these areas—military, political, economic, and educational—the West has achieved a happy, mutually reinforcing mixture of individual initiative and social organization, self-interest and social interest. China has not achieved this mixture in any sphere of its social organism.

Yen Fu can perceive nothing retrogressive or atavistic in the growing "struggle for existence" among the great powers of Europe at the end of the nineteenth century. This struggle is not an incomprehensible throwback to a presumably obsolete militant phase of history. It is rather the logical culmination of the release of human energies and their consolidation within national societies. The two levels of social Darwinism described by Spencer—the struggle of whole societies for existence, and the struggle of individuals among themselves within society—do not necessarily belong to different periods of human development. A candid glance at Europe, America, and Japan shows that the two levels are contemporaneous and mutually reinforcing. Indeed, it is because the fruitful struggle among individuals has been given free rein within British society that Great Britain has achieved a position of ascendancy on the plane of international struggle. Can one really say at this point that the mid-Victorian oracle living in the heart of the West has a stronger grasp of current realities than the Chinese literatus looking in from the outside?

In sum, Yen Fu has derived most of the elements of his thought from Herbert Spencer. The chemistry of this thought has, however, undergone a subtle transformation. The elements of the original synthesis as refracted through Yen Fu's preoccupation have come to be juxtaposed in new ways which might have shocked the British oracle. Can one, however, speak here of a simple distortion, or is it possible that Yen Fu's unexpected perspective actually illumines some of the anomalous features of the Master's teachings not obvious to his Western disciples?

THE REALM OF ACTION

One can hardly deny the essentially "radical" nature of the basic ideas expressed in the essays of 1895. They strike at the root. They transvalue values which had lain at the very heart of Confucian culture and present a new vision of

both cosmic and human reality. Furthermore, these ideas
are boldly presented as Western ideas. Yen Fu's prominent
contemporary, K'ang Yu-wei, had also, to be sure, embraced
the notion of inevitable progress in human affairs but had
attempted to derive this notion from a suppressed strain
(the New Text School) of Confucian thought. Yen Fu
finds no need to seek a Chinese garb for that which is new
in his vision. The Western values of dynamism, self-assertion, realization of capacities—of freedom, democracy, and
science—starkly confront the Chinese exaltation of inertia,
sterile social harmony, and the negative authoritarianism
which had dammed up the physical and intellectual energies
of the race. The biographer Chou Chen-fu is not entirely
mistaken when he treats Yen Fu as the main representative
of "all-out Westernization" at this time, although, as indicated, the reservation must immediately be added that this
Westernization does not preclude a sense of affinity between certain aspects of Chinese philosophy and certain
aspects of modern Western thought. It is a Westernization
which does not require any dogmatic "all-out antitraditionalism."

When we turn to the realm of action, however, we find,
on the whole, that in his practical recommendations Yen Fu
does not go beyond the positions of the 1898 reformers and
that the events of the great year of the Reform find him on
the sidelines of political action. One should perhaps draw
a distinction between the factors which account for his
relative personal inactivity in the Reform movement and
the factors which account for his relative caution in the
area of policy recommendation. In surveying this man's
life as a whole, one can only feel that he is not an "organization man"—that he even confronts the prospect of actual
political responsibility with a certain terror. The old Chinese assumption that the man of thought should also be the
man of action is still very much part of his ethos, and he
complains bitterly throughout his life that he is not "being

used." Yet one cannot help feeling that his lack of success in the realm of politics is due, in part, to his failure to seek out opportunities and his essential unwillingness to play the game.

During the entire period from 1895 to 1898 Yen Fu continued to occupy his frustrating post as superintendent of the Tientsin Naval Academy. In 1896 he helped to organize a Russian language school in Tientsin in conjunction with the new secret Sino-Russian Treaty negotiated by Li Hung-chang.[72] He also lectured at a new school of Western studies (T'ung-i hsüeh-t'ang, lit., 'School of all the Arts') founded by Chang Yüan-chi[73] in Peking. In 1897 he founded with others a new Chinese daily in Tientsin, the famous *Kuo-wen-pao*, and a weekly journal, the *Kuo-wen hui-pien*. It was also during these years, of course, that he began his translation enterprise and completed his most famous translation-commentary, on Huxley's *Evolution and Ethics*. These are, thus, years of considerable and fruitful activity on the part of Yen Fu the educator and publicist. One might indeed say that his activities in this sphere most logically reflected his own conception of the priority of tasks in China. Before the intellectual elite could begin the Gargantuan task of enlightening the masses it would have to enlighten itself, and Yen Fu was here assuming the role of educator of the elite.

The fact is, however, that in many ways Yen Fu remained the outsider. To the extreme conservatives he was, of course, anathema. To the cautious reformers, such as Chang Chih-tung, who were still profoundly concerned with "preserving the faith," his professed indifference to this goal was most offensive. We know that Chang was deeply offended by his "In Refutation of Han-yü" and actually instructed Tu Jen-shou to write a rebuttal.[74] In many ways Yen Fu was an outsider even to K'ang Yu-wei and his group. The younger members of this group, such as Liang Ch'i-ch'ao and T'an Ssu-t'ung, were, to be sure, profoundly stirred by his writings. It is, indeed, quite clear that Yen Fu's influence on Liang Ch'i-ch'ao's subsequent development was to be far more profound than that of his own master K'ang. Yet K'ang and his disciples had, after all, come up through the examination system and were still profoundly concerned to set their ideas within a traditional frame of reference. They constituted a learned clique in the full Chinese sense of the term, and Yen Fu was outside of their circle. He was still the man who had not passed the official examinations.

When one adds to these factors the diffidence and strain of timidity noted above, one can understand why Yen Fu observes the stirring events of the summer of 1898 from the sidelines. Some gestures were indeed made in his direction. Yen Hsiu, a member of the reformist party in Kweichow, had suggested that a special examination on political and economic sciences be created for capable people such as Yen Fu who had not come up through the examination route. This suggestion was approved by the emperor. However, before the examination could be administered, the coup d'état which terminated the famous hundred days had already taken place.[75] While the Kuo-wen-pao in general supported the whole reform effort of 1898, Yen Fu's only direct participation in the summer events took the form of his "Ten Thousand Word Memorial" and of an audience with the emperor. His memorial was never submitted for imperial perusal, since the coup d'état of August took place one week after his imperial audience.[76] The contrast between the boldness of Yen Fu the thinker and his passivity in the realm of action did not pass unnoticed, and he was accused in certain quarters of being a man "who can sit and talk but not act."[77]

Whatever may have been the causes, temperamental and circumstantial, for his failure to plunge into the maelstrom of reform politics, the logical consistency of his views on current policy matters is unimpeachable. We must at this point draw a sharp distinction between two dichotomies which are frequently confused—the dichotomy of traditionalism versus Westernization and the dichotomy of conservatism versus radicalism. If Yen Fu's relative conservatism and caution may have temperamental roots, they also derive with a most rigorous logic from the particular Western ideas which he espoused, and not simply from the Chinese "love of the old." Evolution as presented by Spencer is a painfully slow, cumulative process which proceeds by minute steps and without leaps. China was simply not ready. It had not yet progressed very far on the road from monarchy to democracy. As we have seen, even in his most radical outbursts against Han Yü's contempt for the powers of the people, Yen Fu admits that in the immediate future the people can not lift itself by its own bootstraps. Spencer has rendered him forever immune to the mystique of revolution, and nothing that he will find in Montesquieu, Smith, Huxley, or Mill will contradict this disbelief in the miracle of sudden transformation. The ignorant are not rendered wise in a day.[78] The weak do not become strong in a day, nor are the demoralized and selfish imbued with "public spirit" in a day.

Yen Fu's concrete suggestions for reform can be found scattered throughout his writings of these years, and they are particularly concentrated in his "Ten Thousand Word Memorial." The latter was published in installments in the Kuo-wen-pao in the early months of 1898. It was, as indicated, never submitted to the throne.

While most of Yen Fu's concrete suggestions are hardly unique, he does confront the Reform group with a certain air of superiority. His views on reform are, as it were, "scientific"—based on a clear sense of priority of tasks derived from Spencer's description of the "laws" of social history. In a letter written to Liang Ch'i-ch'ao in 1897, we find him cautioning the latter that "in thinking of reform B one must first carry out reform A."[79] In his own writings on reform the young Liang Ch'i-ch'ao had, in Yen Fu's view, simply piled up pell-mell a list of all possible desiderata without any conception of their proper priority in time or relationship to China's actual socio-historic situation. It was in this manner, indeed, that Liang Ch'i-ch'ao and his master K'ang Yu-wei were to proceed in the famous hundred days. China's situation was urgent, and what was required in their view was an attack from all four quadrants—a "revolutionary," across-the-board reform, as it were. It is ironic to note incidentally that this is the same letter in which Yen Fu denies that "the faith can be preserved." While K'ang Yu-wei and Liang Ch'i-ch'ao derive from their peculiar form of Confucian "faith" the simple belief that "institutions can be changed," Yen Fu derives from his new Spencerian gospel a profound sense of the difficulties of change—a sense that institutional change must be based on a cautious analysis of the possibilities provided by the objective situation.

In his memorial Yen Fu refers to two orders of reform— the "fundamental" (pen) and the "external." The external involves matters such as military modernization, financial reform, and proper diplomacy. The fundamental involves matters such as the nurture of men of ability and changes in customs and of "men's minds" (jen hsin). The fundamental thus involves a change in the famous triad of the people's physical, intellectual, and moral powers[80]—of the basic human material on which a nation's power rests. Yen Fu reminds us here of those conservatives who were urging that "changes in laws" (pien fa) are not as important as "change of heart." The resemblance is, however, superficial. What Yen Fu desires is a "change of heart" in an entirely new direction—a thorough transvaluation of values. Furthermore, he by no means negates the urgency of external reforms.[81] "When the circumstances are urgent we must give priority to the external reforms." However, such external reforms will have no sustained effect unless some progress is made in that which is fundamental.

While there is no reason to suppose that Yen Fu opposed any of the external reforms of the summer of 1898, his own concerns tend to revolve about those particular external reforms which were in his view most relevant to the fundamental. He never tires of warning that unless the old is transformed the new cannot be implemented and wealth and power can never be achieved. Consistently, most of his suggestions tend to fall under the heading of "that which will advance the physical, intellectual, and moral power of the people." Under the heading of physical, he dwells on the need to rid China of the curse of opium and the practice of foot-binding,[82] and on the need to transform the attitudes of the Chinese people toward the value of physical fitness,[83] which is closely associated in his mind with the psychological values of physical courage and the power of physical endurance. In some ways, the affirmation of man's physical powers and what might be called the physical virtues would provide the most dramatic manifestation of the new transformation of values.[84] What is more striking, he even pleads for the physical education of women, particularly on the grounds that healthy mothers produce strong children.

It is, however, the category of the "intellectual" which arouses by far his most animated response. This is, after all, the keystone of the arch. Until the elite's vision of the world was changed, one could hardly hope to change much else. Nor was there much doubt about what required first attention in this area. The primary incubus which had to be removed was the content of the examination system. Yen Fu's most ferocious essay of 1895, "On Our Salvation," is directed primarily against the "System." "Unless China reforms it must die. Where must such reform begin? Nothing is more urgent than the abolition of the eight-legged essay."[85] The examination system as it existed had deformed the minds of the entire elite and perverted its morals. All the arguments of Spencer and Huxley against a purely literary and bookish education are hurled with devastating effect against the examination education and, beyond that, against the whole content and method of the education of the literati—in effect, against every school of traditional thought. There were many traditionally minded literati in China who opposed the empty formalism of the examination system and who raised the banner of this or that school of Confucian thought—the Sung philosophy, the "empirical research" school, the New Text school of K'ang Yu-wei, the Wang Yang-ming school, and so forth. Yen Fu passes them all in review as a possible basis for education and finds them all wanting. "Summing it all up in a word—they are all not useful."[86] They cannot contribute to China's wealth and power. "They will not save us from destruction." Whatever truths they may contain, these truths are not immediately relevant to the tasks at hand. "For the time being they should all be put away on a high shelf."[87] What is needed is quite clear—it is Western scientific education which forces men to face facts directly and to derive from the facts by rigorous induction those unshakable truths which are most immediately relevant to wealth and power. It should, of course, immediately be added that the basic tenets of social Darwinism as interpreted by Spencer in his psychology and sociology, the basic truths of classical economics, and so forth, are all among the truths of Western science, derived inductively from a direct observation of the facts. At this particular point in time, Yen Fu does not concern himself at all with the role of traditional studies in the new educational curriculum. In the area of education, he is ready for revolution.

A negative corollary of his views on the effects of Chinese education is his firm conviction that the "monopoly" of government position by those who have been thoroughly molded by the old system must be broken. Here too, one can detect the note of personal involvement. One of the main recommendations in his "Ten Thousand Word Memorial" is that—to use Huxley's phrase—some provision be made for the "descent of incapacity." This he urges as one of those measures which must precede a general reform. The conservative party in the state, even though it contains many "gentlemen," is the major obstacle to reform (and here Yen Fu points to the example of Wang An-shih, whose reforms had all been obstructed by a conservative stranglehold on government).

Under the category of "reforming the people's morality," we find recommendations of measures designed to create a sense of national identity—a sense of "public spirit." Oddly enough, it is under this rubric that Yen Fu recommends in 1895 the inauguration of a deliberative assembly. "How can we induce our people to think of China as their private possession? Let us establish a national assembly at the capital and have all the provinces and prefectures nominate representatives. In this way one will instill in the people loyalty and love [for China]."[88] This conception of the parliamentary institution as a means of creating national loyalty by leading the individual to identify his own interests with those of the state is, of course, entirely in keeping with Yen Fu's conception of democracy and reminds us of a type of argument very common among the Japanese "liberals" in the early Meiji period. Actually, within the next few years he was to retreat even from this recommendation on the grounds of its prematurity in terms of China's stage of development. In his memorial he also puts forth an interesting, albeit more cautious, suggestion—namely, that the emperor turn himself into a beloved symbol of the nation by carrying out a tour of the realm and establishing close contacts with the people. In this way the dormant loyalties of the people would be aroused, thus creating an entirely new atmosphere in which other reforms could proceed.

Another curious but interesting suggestion is that the emperor carry out a world tour with the aim of convincing

the World Powers that their own interests will be best
served by a common agreement to guarantee Chinese security. The weakness of China, Yen Fu reasons, is one of the
factors making for world insecurity. Great Britain, France,
Russia, and Japan are in constant dread of the possibility
that their protagonists will win a position of predominance
within a collapsing Chinese empire. This leads him to the
hopeful premise that "all these countries deeply desire to
see China strengthen itself." A world tour by the emperor
might go far in convincing the chancellories of Europe to
provide China with a breathing spell within which to
carry out necessary reforms.

However fanciful this proposal may be, it does indicate
how far Yen Fu is from any inclination to attribute to
"imperialism" the main responsibility for China's ills. He
states quite explicitly that 70 per cent of China's difficulties
derive from "inner ills." His social Darwinism makes it impossible for him to stand in moral judgment on the imperialist powers of the West. China's weakness in the struggle for
existence stems from its own unfitness. It is entirely inevitable that those states which are fit should struggle among
themselves for predominance. China must itself bear the
heavy onus of its failure to adapt.

On balance, Yen Fu's basic concern throughout these
years (1895–1898) is with education in the broadest
sense and, in the first instance, with the education of the
elite. It is only when the elite is imbued with the new vision
and the new knowledge that it can proceed to unlock the
potentialities of the people. China's whole experience since
the sixties had amply demonstrated that without this new
vision, "external" reforms would have no staying power.
The gospel of education itself does not derive from Spencer.
Spencer had not assigned to education or to ideas any particular role as a dynamic principle pushing forward the
evolutionary process. It is, rather, "evolution" as a total
process which pushes forward all the separate aspects of

human culture. Yen Fu, however, living in a society where the process had stalled, cannot help hoping that the idea of evolution will itself inspire those effects which the process of evolution has unaccountably failed to bring about.

CHAPTER IV

Western Wisdom at Its Source:
Evolution and Ethics

IF EDUCATION is the first order of business, it is the liberating ideas of the western sages which must provide the first content of education, and there can be no more effective way of presenting these ideas than in their original form. The Chinese literati must be made to confront the wisdom of the West at its sources. As early as 1891, Yen Fu had, as we have seen, attempted without undue success to seek support in Michie for an exposure of the missionary movement, and it was as early as 1895 (or perhaps even 1894)[1] that he began to work on his great chef d'oeuvre, the translation of Huxley's *Evolution and Ethics*.

Yen Fu's fame rests primarily on his role as a translator and commentator. The latter role must, incidentally, be stressed, for most of the translations are interlaced with Yen Fu's commentaries, and it is certain that the commentaries aroused quite as much attention as the texts themselves. If in the preceding chapter I have dwelt at some length on Yen Fu the early essayist, it is because the essays and letters of the 1895–1898 period provide, it seems to me, the matrix in terms of which the whole translation effort must be understood. In a sense, the corpus of translations simply provides an elaborate and imposing commentary on the basic notions elaborated in the essays. One need not assume that the choice of works to be translated followed any blueprint, or that Yen Fu's ideas did not change in any respect during the years of the great translation enterprise. Yet the assumptions which first emerge in the essays continue to permeate, to illumine, and to provide a framework for the whole subsequent effort.

THE MEDIUM

One of the most fascinating aspects of Yen Fu's translations is, of course, their language. The effort to incorporate into classical "ancient style" (*ku wen*) Chinese the concepts and categories of eighteenth- and nineteenth-century Western thought is an effort which probably merits a separate monograph in itself. There are, indeed, schools of cultural anthropology which might be inclined to deny the feasibility of the enterprise a priori (for example, Marcel Granet, Benjamin Whorf). Since it is my own conviction that Yen Fu does succeed on the whole in transmitting the essential thought of his Western sages, I shall not linger at great length on the linguistic problem, fascinating as it may be.

One need not wonder why Yen Fu did not attempt to translate into "vernacular" Chinese (*pai-hua*). The whole *pai-hua* movement still lay in the future, and if it had existed he might have rejected its basic premises (as he did in his latter years). The audience to which he appeals is the elite, and he is determined to use a language which will appeal to this elite. He has no illusions that the masses will immediately read his translations.

Even within the gamut of styles available in what is crudely called in the West "classical Chinese," his style is extraordinarily abstruse, elegant, and highly allusive—to such an extent that the young Liang Ch'i-ch'ao while praising the translation of Smith's *Wealth of Nations* feels forced to complain that, in spite of Yen Fu's absolute pre-eminence in China as an interpreter of Western thought, "in his style he is too much concerned with profundity and elegance. He is firmly bent on copying the style of the pre-Ch'in period, and those who have not read many ancient books found his translations most difficult to comprehend."[2]

The reference to the pre-Ch'in period reminds us that Yen Fu was actually affiliated with a very definite stylistic school—the so-called T'ung-ch'eng school referred to above.[3] His mentor on matters of style was the well-known Wu Ju-lun,[4] who was himself a protégé of the famous Tseng Kuo-fan. As already indicated, the founders of the school in their own eyes represented a revulsion against the colorless and formless notational style of the Ch'ing Empirical Research school, as well as against the florid and exuberant rhetoric of the "double-harness style" (*p'ien t'i*) of the Six Dynasties. They were seeking a style which would be adequate to matters of serious philosophic concern and simultaneously provide an aesthetically satisfying vehicle for this concern. Thus, in line with the "Old Style" movements of the T'ang and Sung dynasty they looked back to the philosophers of the Chou dynasty for stylistic models. Here one could find a happy combination of precision and richness, terseness and profundity, clarity and elegance. While most members of the school were hardly noted for the originality of their thought, Yen Fu himself was entirely convinced that this style would meet his three criteria of good translation—faithfulness (*hsin*), comprehensibility (*ta*), and elegance (*ya*).[5]

One may ask with Liang Ch'i-ch'ao why elegance is a

primary requirement in conveying the thought of Herbert Spencer or Adam Smith. Yen Fu's reply is that "where language has no refinement, the effects will not extend very far." Furthermore, "in using the style and syntax of the pre-Han period one actually facilitates the comprehension of the subtle principles and abstruse phrases [of the translated text]."[6] Again, of course, this would be true only for the educated literati. In reply to Liang's assertion—"The change in style of language which has taken place in Europe, America, and Japan is in direct ratio to their level of civilization . . . Unless profound and abstruse books of this type are rendered in a flowing and incisive style, how can our students profit from them? The object of translation is to spread civilized ideas among the people, not to make a useless reputation"—Yet Fu simply states that "the books with which I concern myself are profound and abstruse. They are not designed to nourish schoolboys and I have no hopes of their deriving profit from them. I have translated precisely for those Chinese who do read many ancient books."[7] Beneath the surface, Yen Fu's flair for elegance may, of course, also reflect his own aesthetic bent, as well as his pride in his own virtuosity. Yet the motive of swaying the style-conscious literati by demonstrating that Western thought lends itself to the noblest Chinese prose was certainly present. So successful was Yen Fu in this endeavor that many conservative literati were actually induced to read his translation of *Evolution and Ethics* for its beauty of style, and, contrary to his own expectations, he was also to be avidly read by schoolboys for his message.

Nevertheless the basic question remains. Can the authentic thought of eighteenth- and nineteenth-century Europe be transposed into classical Chinese—a linguistic medium soaked in the categories of a totally alien culture? If we accept the notions of Granet or Whorf that the thought world embodied in classical Chinese represents a self-contained cultural monad hermetically sealed off from the cultural world embodied in the languages of the modern West, then Yen Fu's enterprise must be considered impossible by definition.

It is my own considered opinion that this view is unjustified; that, taken in the aggregate, Yen Fu's translations do communicate the essence of the thought which he is attempting to communicate; and that his language deals with the same universe as that of Mill, Montesquieu, and Spencer. This does not mean that there are no problems. Yen Fu himself constantly groans over the magnitude of the task which confronts him. From the very outset, he makes no attempt at literal translation. Almost all his translations are paraphrastic. The translation of *Evolution and Ethics* is, in fact, not so much a translation as an abridged summation of the original. In other cases, he adheres more closely to the original text. What he tries to do, he informs us, is to grasp the essential meaning of whole sentences or passages containing whole thoughts and then to communicate their meaning in idiomatic Chinese. In actuality, the creation of new terms required infinite pains. In his own words, he sometimes "pondered for a month over one term." On the whole, he does not employ many of the neologisms which had been created by the Japanese during the previous decades. (Here the pride of the Chinese literatus, thoroughly convinced that he understands the resources of his own language infinitely better than the upstarts of the "eastern country," coalesces with the resentment of the modern nationalist.[8] Furthermore, his philosophy of style called for the maximum use of the allusive categories of ancient Chinese philosophic thought in rendering Western concepts. Ironically enough, however, most of his own neologisms were to perish in the struggle for existence with the Japanese creations. With the abandonment of classical Chinese as an instrument of translation, with the flocking of Chinese students to Japan and the flood of translations of Japanese translations, the line of least resistance was toward the wholesale adoption of the new Japanese vocabulary. Does the use of ancient Chinese terms produce distortion of meaning? Does the use of *t'ien* (heaven) to render the word "nature" introduce some shift of meaning? Does *t'ien* contain the connotation of a directive, purposive power? Yen Fu himself is not unaware of the problem; in a note in *A Study of Sociology* he points out that the word *t'ien* had accumulated a whole series of levels of meanings. It meant the "Great Empyrean," the Supreme Deity (*shang ti*), as well as "an uncreated formative substance (*hsing-ch'i*) governed by cause and effect." If the word *t'ien* is ambiguous, however, what about the word "nature," or even "evolution," when used as the subject of an active verb? Yen Fu, on the whole, seems justified in assuming that the word *t'ien* covers a range of ambiguity not far removed from that of the word "nature." With other terms the range of congruity of meaning may be somewhat smaller, but generally the area of overlap is considerable. Furthermore, the consistent use of the same term in highly diverse contexts tends to reduce the area of incongruity.

One cannot, to be sure, measure the unanalyzable change of "feel" which may take place when such concepts as "the struggle for existence" and "the survival of the fittest" are rendered by phrases such as "Things struggle"—"superior victorious, inferior defeated," but can one deny that the basic idea has been communicated? It does not seem to me that the difference in cultural tone is more significant than the identity of the idea.

The method of paraphrastic translation does, to be sure, facilitate occasional serious distortions of meaning. On the whole, those distortions arise not so much out of the nature of Yen Fu's linguistic medium as from the pervasive distorting perspective of the preoccupations through which all his translations are refracted. Turning again to *A Study of Sociology*, we find in one passage one of Spencer's typical diatribes against legislative meddling with the evolutionary process. "The ordinary political schemer is convinced that out of a legislative apparatus properly devised and worked with due dexterity may be had beneficial State action without any detrimental reaction. He expects to get out of a stupid people the effects of intelligence and to evolve from inferior citizens superior conduct."[9] In Yen Fu's paraphrase this emerges somewhat as follows: "They say that the rise or fall of the society depends wholly on the legislative system (*fa chih*), on our system of laws, and that weak people can be used to create a strong state, a poor people can be made to create a rich state, a stupid people can be made to make a wise state. This is like dreaming of food and hoping to be satisfied!"[10]

Here we see Yen Fu's central preoccupation with the power of the state creeping into his paraphrase of passages which say nothing on the subject. The fact is that Spencer nowhere introduces the wealth and power of the state into his argument. Neither he nor those whom he attacks are concerned with the power of the state. Presumably all are concerned with the people's welfare. It is not the state as an end but the state as instrument which is under discussion. The whole passage is concerned with the benefits which individuals and groups hope to derive from *state action* ("Why does not Government, out of its inexhaustible resources, yield us this benefit?").[11] The argument is between those who believe that benefits can be achieved by state action and those, like Spencer, who are convinced that only the unimpeded march of the forces of evolution, unobstructed by state meddling, can achieve the greatest good of the greatest number. With Yen Fu the language of general welfare almost imperceptibly translates itself into the language of the wealth and power of the state. We shall note these same transpositions elsewhere. We are not dealing here, however, with a distortion created by the language medium as such. We are dealing with the pervasive presence of Yen Fu's own preoccupations. Where these preoccupations do not intrude, the general meaning of the original comes through essentially unharmed.

EVOLUTION AND ETHICS

The most relevant and revolutionary strain of Western thought is that embodied in the Darwinian theory of evolution as interpreted in Spencer's system. We can, thus, well understand Yen Fu's ardent desire to present a brief and succinct account of its main tenets directly out of some Western source. Fully conscious as he is of the formidable problems of translation, he could hardly hope to translate the *Origin of Species,* which would, in any case, not have related itself directly to his immediate concerns. He is not fundamentally interested in Darwin's contributions to biology or in his painstaking disquisitions on variation among pigeons. He is overwhelmingly concerned with the implications of Darwinian principles for the sphere of human action.

It was naturally his highest ambition to translate the work of his true master, Herbert Spencer. However, as he informs us in one of his commentaries on *Evolution and Ethics,* "Spencer's writings are abundant, profound, and vast. They cannot hastily be translated."[12] In 1897 he did begin to translate two chapters of *A Study of Sociology* for the *Kuo-wen-pao,* but he never was to feel himself capable of translating *First Principles* or any of Spencer's other works. What was needed immediately was some manageable tract which would summarize in attractive form some of the main principles of Darwinism.

We do not know how Yen Fu came upon Huxley's recently published (1893) Romanes Lectures on "Evolution and Ethics," but his decision to translate them was reached either in 1894 or 1895. According to one account he had already finished a first draft in 1895.[13] Here one may note, if one will, the direct impact of the Sino-Japanese War. Most accounts place the completion of the translation in

1896 and publication in 1898. It is, however, quite possible that he was already deeply involved in this enterprise even while writing his essays of 1895.

T'ien-yen lun (*On Evolution*) was to be Yen Fu's most resounding success.[14] Not only did it cause a stir among Yen Fu's contemporaries in the ranks of the literati, but a whole literature of memoirs and reminiscences testifies to its resounding impact on the youth of the dawning twentieth century. As the first serious attempt since the Jesuits to present contemporary Western thought to the literati, and to demonstrate the high seriousness of this thought, it was bound to create a sensation.

In his introduction Yen Fu again takes up the theme we have alreay met—namely, the notion of an affinity between certain elements of Chinese traditional thought and elements of modern Western thought. John Stuart Mill had pointed out, he states, that in order to understand the language and literature of one country one should study the languages and literatures of many countries. The study of modern Western thought actually throws light on ancient Chinese thought. Not only are some of the ideas of the modern West compatible with ancient Chinese thought; they actually enhance our understanding of that thought. Thus the Western logical categories of induction and deduction throw a blinding light on certain obscure passages in the appendices to the *Book of Changes* and in Ssu-ma Ch'ien's *Historical Records*.

Again one may point to the obvious motive of wrapping barbarian ideas in a mantle of respectability. Again, however, it is entirely conceivable from everything we know that Yen Fu himself sincerely believes in the affinities between certain ancient Chinese ideas and modern Western ideas. Yet even while pointing out that the ancients may have had intimations of modern Western truths, he insists that more weight must be placed on the fact "that later generations were unable to amplify and apply them . . . [we cannot use the fact that] our ancients anticipated them in order to praise ourselves."[15] He explicitly disassociates himself from the notion that the ideas of the Westerners "came from the East." The decisive fact in the end, however, is not that Huxley's book discusses much "that is in harmony with our ancients" but that it constantly deliberates on matters which are directly relevant to "self-strengthening and the preservation of the race."[16] It is the latter fact which has impelled Yen Fu to translate the book. It is the latter fact which arouses the enormous excitement of the young men who read it. It is not the affinities with the sages, but the strident slogans of social Darwinism which occupy the center of the stage.

Yet here we confront the enormous paradox. Huxley's lectures are decidedly not an exposition of social Darwinism. They actually represent an attack on social Darwinism! They must be understood in terms of that widespread revulsion against Spencerian orthodoxy which set in at the end of the century in both Great Britain and the United States. While Huxley had won himself a reputation as the indefatigable defender and expounder of Darwinism against attacks from all quarters, these lectures are by no means intended as yet another résumé of Darwinian principles. On the contrary, Huxley's overwhelming preoccupation is that of protecting human ethical values against the efforts to create an "evolutionary ethic." It is most significant, incidentally, that while the original title is *Evolution and Ethics*, Yen Fu simply calls his translation *On Evolution*. The whole tract is expressly directed against Spencer and other advocates of an evolutionary ethic. After spending a lifetime preaching what seemed to be an integral naturalism, Huxley announces that "ethical nature while born of cosmic nature is necessarily at enmity with its parent."[17] He cannot stomach Spencer's crass and brutal cosmic optimism. The whole mood of the lectures is subdued and melancholy. While Huxley rejects the extreme pessimism of the Buddhist "world deniers" and stoic ataraxy, there is a distinct withdrawal from the exultant belief in the cult of energy and in a cosmically sustained, unlimited progress. We are reminded again that the theory of evolution is not the same as a theory of irreversible progress. Evolution, we are told, includes "the phenomena of retrogressive metamorphosis that is of progress from a condition of relative complexity to one of relative uniformity,"[18] as well as the reverse. The central thesis of the whole work is that "social progress means a checking of the cosmic process at every step and the substitution for it of another, which may be called the ethical process . . . The ethical progress of society depends not on imitating the cosmic process, still less in running away from it, but in combatting it."[19] Nothing could have been further from Huxley's pathos at this point than Yen Fu's ardent desire to find in the Darwinian cosmos prescriptions for human behavior. Nothing—it need hardly be added—was more remote from Huxley's concerns than Yen Fu's preoccupation with the wealth and power of the state.

Why then does Yen Fu choose to translate a work so little in tune with his basic message? We can, of course, only speculate. First of all, imbedded in Huxley's lectures we do find a brief, vivid, and almost poetic account of the main tenets of Darwinism. While Huxley's aims are not expository, in contrasting the cultivated garden of human society with the rank growths of unsubdued nature he does provide a vivid description of the natural process. His illustrations based on the metamorphosis of the bean and on the natural history of "the countryside visible from the windows of the room in which I write" have a trenchant power which no amount of purely scientific discourse could convey. There is enough material here to provide Yen Fu with a point of departure for his own disquisitions on topics such as the Malthusian theory of population. Again, since Huxley is more interested, in these lectures, in the plight of man than in the evolution of the cosmos, we find him ranging widely over the whole history of human thought. We find here a disquisition on the history of the idea of evolution since the pre-Socratics, and a discussion of the attitudes toward human life in both the Orient (Buddhism in particular) and in ancient Greece. One of the grand themes is the attitude of different cultures toward the problem of evil and suffering, which has always been a concomitant of the whole evolutionary process. The pre-Socratics had realized that suffering was endemic to the process, as had the ancient Indians. The Greeks had at first found "fierce joys" in life, but the later Stoics had sought release in apatheia, while the Indians in their realization that high culture and suffering are indissolubly linked had turned their backs on the whole evolutionary process. The discussion of Brahmanism leads to a discussion of Buddhism and the conviction that all reality is "a mere flow of sensations, emotions, volitions, and thoughts devoid of" any substratum. This in turn leads to a discussion of Berkeley and idealistic philosophy in the West.

Diffuse and rambling as all this may be, it provides Yen Fu with an extremely broad canvas of human intellectual history and creates a wonderful sense of the essential transcultural unity of mankind. Buddhism, with which Yen Fu's audience is not unfamiliar, is here brought into one framework with various schools of ancient Greece, with ancient Judea, and the Modern West. While Huxley's references to Berkeley provide Yen Fu with an excellent opportunity to discuss the whole epistemological trend in Western philosophy since Descartes, Huxley's lectures provide an opportunity for Yen Fu to communicate to his reader a sense of the underlying unity of mankind vis-à-vis the grand problems of the race. Nothing could be more effective than this essay in corroding the literatus' sense of a qualitative abyss dividing barbarian from Chinese.

Above all, the very anti-Spencerian animus of Huxley

provides Yen Fu with an excellent opportunity for defending the views of Spencer. From the very outset he is, of
course, fully aware of the basic tendency of the book and
explicitly states in his introduction that Huxley wrote this
book in order to refute Spencer's view, which "bases the
human order in nature" (*jen t'ien wei chih*). His commentaries abound in panegyrics of Spencer and defenses of
his positions on various matters. It would, indeed, be no
exaggeration to say that *T'ien-yen lun* consists of two works
—a paraphrase of Huxley's lectures, and an exposition of
Spencer's essential views as against Huxley.

What then are the basic issues? Huxley rejects all the
"multitudinous attempts" of Spencer and others "to apply
the principles of cosmic evolution or what are supposed to
be such to social and political problems." Huxley's humani-
tarian ethic is deeply repelled by the "ethic of evolution" in
the two forms in which it has appeared. On the one hand,
there are those who envision a kind of despotic society run
by social engineers "endowed with a preternatural intelligence."[20] This elite "would systematically and ruthlessly
apply the principle of improvement through selection to
human society."[21] It would assume nature's task (which
nature has unaccountably failed to assume) in human society. On the other hand, there are the Spencerians who
would allow the supposedly beneficent, impersonal forces of
evolution to run their course without any human "meddling." In fact, whatever decency exists in the human world
has actually come from man's "horticultural" interference
with the general tendencies of the cosmic process both outside himself and within himself. Huxley is profoundly repelled by that "fanatical individualism"[22] which uses the
notion of an "ethic of evolution" to bolster men's "natural"
callous indifference to the sufferings of others. "Social progress means a checking of the cosmic process at every step
and the substitution for it of another which may be called
the ethical process. Just as human art runs athwart the

cosmic process in horticulture so does human morality run athwart the cosmic process. If the conclusion that the two are antagonistic is logically absurd, I am sorry for logic . . . The history of civilization details the steps by which men have succeeded in building up an artificial world within the cosmos."[23] It is only within his own human sphere that man is able to restrain the amoral anarchic energies of the cosmos, even though these energies exist within man himself.

Yen Fu finds himself profoundly opposed to this vision on every level—religious, metaphysical, ethical, and sociopolitical. Both that part of him which is still organically linked with the Chinese past and that part of him which is most antitraditional place him squarely on the side of Spencer against Huxley.

First of all, Huxley's enmity to the cosmos offends Yen Fu's deepest religious proclivities. It may seem somewhat strange at this point to speak of Yen Fu's religious propensities. His hostility to Judeo-Christian theism[24] is quite explicit, and none of his western idols are particularly noted for their religious attitudes. Yet in many of his remarks scattered throughout this work we note a clear affinity for the mystical core of Lao-tzu and Chuang-tzu, as well as for Buddhism, and even Advaita Vedanta of India. Unlike Joseph Needham[25] he does not see an unbridgeable abyss dividing the mystical core of Taoism from the mystical core of Indian religion, for unlike Needham he is not inclined to talk down the mystical element in Taoism. The mystical elements in Taoism, in Buddhism, and even in Sung Confucianism imperceptibly coalesce in his mind with Spencer's "Unknowable," which becomes in his translation the "Inconceivable" (*pu k'o ssu-i*). Just as the world of the "ten thousand things" in Lao-tzu or the appendices to the *Book of Changes* emerge out of the womb of non-being or the "Inconceivable," so does Spencer's world of the complex, heterogeneous, and organized emerge out of the "Unknowable."[26] Spencer's insistence on the unknowability of ultimate reality and on the absolute inability of human reason or human language to cope with it does not diminish Yen Fu's profoundly religious orientation toward the ultimate. Had not Lao-tzu, Gautama, Chuang-tzu, and others expressed themselves exhaustively on the ineffability of the Ultimate, and does not the *Classic of the Way and its Power* open with the sentence, "That the way of which one can speak is not the true way"? As a matter of fact, the insistence on the ineffability and unknowability of the Ultimate is a common feature of mystical literature everywhere.

However, the aura of feeling which surrounds Yen Fu's use of the word "inconceivable" is infinitely removed from Spencer's supercilious nod in the direction of the "Unknowable." Having paid his cool respects to the Unknowable, Spencer resolutely turns his attention back to that realm of the Knowable in which he regards himself as master of all he surveys. To Yen Fu, however, Spencer's Unknowable is Gautama's Nirvana, the Brahma of the Advaita Vedanta, and even the "Principle" (*li*) of the Chu Hsi school of Confucianism ("The Supreme One Principle into which all the separate principles of things are absorbed"), and, as such, a realm toward which he entertains sentiments which can only be called profoundly religious. "The vulgar think in their ignorance that Buddhism and Taoism, in the last analysis, preach extinction and nothingness. Hence, why should they long for this? The enlightened know, however, that one passes from the transient into the Everlasting and from pain and suffering to supreme ineffable joy."[27] The "Inconceivable" remains for Yen Fu the source of ultimate comfort and consolation, even in this, his most aggressively Westernizing mood. It is perhaps not easy to explain this Janus-like attitude. Yet it is there. One face is oriented toward wealth and power, toward the cult of dynamism, energy, self-assertion, struggle, and the reali-

zation of all human capacity, while the other face still
seeks solace for life's sufferings in a mysticism which radically denies the significance of the whole phenomenal
world and all its works. For Yen Fu the same "Unknowable"
which lies behind the whole process of evolution is also
the ultimate refuge from life's storms.

It might be pointed out, incidentally, that Yen Fu's
attraction to Buddhism is not an individual vagary. It is
interesting to note that many of his contemporaries in the
late nineteenth and early twentieth century—men such as
K'ang Yu-wei, T'an Ssu-t'ung, Liang Ch'i-ch'ao, Chang
T'ai-yen, and Wang Kuo-wei—were also concerning themselves with Buddhism at this time, and, while the motives
involved in all these cases undoubtedly differ, there seems
to have been a strong urge in all of them to find some
support beyond the "rationalism" of Confucianism, which
seemed to absolutize the current social and ethical order.

Yen Fu does not accept Huxley's hostility to the cosmos.
He is a yea-sayer to the universe on two levels. On his
mystical side, he feels a strong piety toward the Ultimate
(Spinoza's Natura Naturans), and on his activist side he
enthusiastically accepts "Natura Naturata" as made manifest in the process of evolution. Like Spencer he finds "no
radical vice in the constitution of things"[28] at either level.

Huxley's own ultimate grievance against the universe is
ethical. The universe displays an absolutely callous indifference to the myriads of individual creatures which it
spawns. Paradoxically, one might say that Huxley's bitter
rejection of the Judeo-Christian religious tradition springs
from his deep commitment to the Judeo-Christian ethic
with its stress on the infinite worth of the individual. (He
himself acknowledges elsewhere his commitment to "Bib-
lical ethic." His commitment to persons as such (both "fit"
and "unfit") is infinitely more genuine than the much
touted "individualism" of Spencer, and it is precisely this

concern which he finds it impossible to reconcile with his Darwinian image of the universe.

Yen Fu, however, is doubly steeled against Huxley's Job-like dilemmas by his own brand of mystical pantheism, as well as by his hearty acceptance of social Darwinism within the human realm. When he reads Huxley's passionate assault on "the moral indifference of nature" this reminds him of the famous passage in Lao-tzu: "Heaven and earth are not benevolent, they treat the ten thousand things as straw dogs."[29] Unlike many Western interpreters of Lao-tzu, however, Yen Fu does not see in this statement a kind of nineteenth-century Western "humanistic" outcry against the universe. "The non-benevolence (*pu jen*) of which Lao-tzu speaks is not really non-benevolence. It is something which transcends the dichotomy of benevolence and non-benevolence."[30] The pathos of Lao-tzu is not one of tragedy but a kind of boisterous glee,[31] for the Taoist sage is able to identify himself not with the evanescent ten thousand things but with the inexhaustible Tao— with the larger cosmic process which produces them. If the existence of individuals has no intrinsic worth in itself, Huxley's grievance against the "Unknowable" loses its raison d'être and falls to the ground. Hence Yen Fu cannot share Huxley's view that the "microcosmic atom should have found the illimitable macrocosm guilty."[32] Spencer's "Unknowable," on the other hand, is the ultimate source of both religion and science, and in its scientific aspect it wholeheartedly accepts the applicability of the Darwinian "ethic of evolution" to the explanation of human society.

Yen Fu argues most trenchantly against Huxley's juxtaposition of the cosmic and human process. "His attempt to derive social ethics (*ch'ün tao*) from the feeling of sympathy inverts cause and effect. What causes men to enter society and leave their state of dispersion is the interest in security. In the beginning, man does not differ on this from birds, beasts, and other lower forms. It is not his fellow-feeling which leads to the formation of society, but his interest in security. The process of evolution determines that those who can form social groups survive and those who cannot shall perish. Those who form effective social groups survive, those who do not, disappear. What makes them effective? The ability to develop a sense of mutual sympathy. This ability to feel sympathy is, however, an effect of the process of natural selection and not something which was there from the outset. Those groups which do not effectively develop this fellow-feeling are eliminated in the struggle for existence . . . Huxley seizes here upon the secondary (*mo*) to explain that which is fundamental (*pen*). His grasp of the principles of sociology is by no means as thorough as that of Spencer."[33]

Not only is the element of sympathy in human society adequately explained by Spencer in terms of the cosmic process itself, but the other "egoistic," "self-assertive" component of human nature which Huxley so profoundly mistrusts is also part of the cosmic strategy spurring on human progress. Huxley does not, of course, completely reject the self-assertive instincts, and he concedes them a certain role in man's economic life.[34] Basically, however, he regards them as a survival of the beast in man, and, as against the "fanatical individualism" of Spencer, he heartily approves of all ethical and social efforts to curb them. Spencer has, however, taught Yen Fu a profound respect for these self-assertive instincts as the spur of progress. Both the social virtues which unite men and the competitive pursuit of self-interest which leads to the release of men's highest capacities are manifestations of nature, and, like Spencer, Yen Fu takes a sunny view of the whole process. He has not accepted the entire metaphysic of evolution in order to reject its social implications. On the contrary, it is the social message which first attracted him to the metaphysic.

It must be noted that the fundamental philosophic issue as between Huxley and Spencer—the whole question of the relation of the cosmic process and the human process— gives rise to many familiar resonances in the mind of Yen Fu. It reminds him of centuries of controversy within the streams of Chinese thought. Had not Hsün-tzu and Mencius already been concerned with these issues? Huxley's position is that all efforts to find a ground for man's higher ethical tendencies in the non-human cosmos are futile. In this he strongly resembles Hsün-tzu and Liu Tsung-yüan of the T'ang dynasty. To Hsün-tzu also "cosmic nature is no school of virtue."[35] The latter even uses the expression *wei*—"artificial" or "man-made"—to describe human culture, just as Huxley uses the word "art." At one point Yen Fu states, "According to the previous passage, the dominance of force is an aspect of the natural process (*t'ien hsing*); the dominance of virtue is a result of order established by men (*jen chih*); where there is strife and disorder nature is dominant and where there is peace and order man is dominant. This view is in harmony with the ideas of Heaven of Liu Tsung-yüan and Liu Yü-hsi [as expanded in their essays on Heaven] and in direct contradiction to the views of the Neo-Confucianists since Sung who attribute the rational principle (*li*) to heaven [nature] and lusts to men. In general, among philosophers both ancient and modern, Eastern and Western, there have been two schools: the religious school which attributes the principles of morality to heaven (the cosmos) and selfish passions to men; the scientific outlook which attributes the dominance of force to heaven and the dominance of ethics to men."[36] Huxley's position in all this is that while he attributes rational organization to nature he will attribute ethical values only to man.

In all this we see a concrete illustration of Yen Fu's tendencies to find universal issues of human thought which transcend the dichotomy of Western and Chinese culture. The whole discussion is highly matter-of-fact and does not suggest, at least to this reader, the motive of seeking a source of pride in the fact that Chinese thinkers were involved in areas of the problematic which also involved thinkers in the modern West. In part the purpose may be pedagogic. Yen Fu is explaining the unfamiliar in terms of the familiar. The pedagogic motive is, in fact, imbedded in his very language, since most of his Chinese terminology bears within itself an association with the various schools of Chou and Sung thought. Again, beyond this natural pedagogic device it is entirely conceivable that Yen Fu sincerely believes that the question under discussion does cut across differences of time, place, and culture and that there is no reason, a priori, why Huxley should not be aligned on certain issues with Hsün-tzu and Liu Tsung-yüan as against Spencer, Lao-tzu, and Chu Hsi.

The question of whether human values are rooted in the cosmos or whether they cut athwart the cosmic process may have arisen in both cultures. Yet Yen Fu remains acutely aware of the novel setting within which the whole Western discussion takes place. Like Lao-tzu and Chu Hsi, Spencer finds the root of his ethic in the cosmos. His ethic, however, is entirely new. He affirms the role of force, of "self-assertion," in the cosmos at large and approves its manifestation in the human sphere! The neo-Confucianists approved of the universe because (like the Stoics in the West) they believed that the universe lent support to their negative, inhibitory ethic. Hsün-tzu and Huxley do not approve of the universe as a school of ethics because the universe as they see it does not seem to support a restraining inhibitory morality. Spencer approves of the universe precisely because it affirms the ethic of self-assertion and enlightened self-interest even while creating mechanisms for keeping these energies within reasonable bounds. It is Spencer and not Huxley who has provided the cosmic sanction for social Darwinism.

If Yen Fu is Spencer's partisan on the religious, ethical, and socio-political level, he also finds that it is Spencer, not Huxley, who fills his most deeply felt intellectual needs. The system as an integrated whole is overwhelmingly attractive. Again and again he mentions the fact that Spencer has created a system which explains all the phenomena of reality. "He has explained all transformations in terms of evolution. He has written books and composed treatises which embrace heaven, earth, and man under one principle."[37] He shows how the principles can be applied to illumine the laws of agriculture, commerce, military affairs, language, and literature. Spencer's law that all things "develop from the simple to the complex" applies to all things, from the formation of the stars to the ordering of the state. After giving a short account of the whole synthetic philosophy, Yen Fu exclaims in rapture: "What a joy to be able to grasp all this; to be able to comprehend it after deep thought!"[38] Spencer's architectonic monistic "block universe" is deeply satisfying to him, for, like many in his generation, he is seeking not only a cure for China's immediate ills but a clear and all-embracing vision of reality. Huxley's wanton introduction of a breach into this closed system, his effort to create a discontinuity within the whole, runs counter to all Yen Fu's predispositions.

In sum then, *Evolution and Ethics* provides Yen Fu with a point of departure for presenting his own interpretation of Spencer's evolutionary philosophy. Huxley provides, as it were, a foil for the master. In the course of the discussion Yen Fu's own religious, metaphysical, and ethical commitments are made clear. Above all, it is in the *On Evolution* that he makes clear his profound commitment to social Darwinism and to the ethic implicit in social Darwinism. He is acutely aware that this ethic implies nothing less than a revolution of values in China, and it is to this revolution that he now turns his attention. To many of his younger readers, it was precisely the slogans of social Darwinism which were to constitute the central significance of the book.

CHAPTER V

The Wealth of Nations

Y E N F U had been aware from the very outset of the crucial importance of economics. The concern with wealth and power which he had carried with him to England naturally drew his attention most forcefully to England's machinery for creating wealth. Implicit in the phrase itself is the assumption that wealth is the fuel of power. Economics is also central, of course, to the whole Spencerian synthesis. The emergence of the "industrial stage" of human development marks the highest stage of human evolution, and Spencer's views of the evolution of the industrial stage manage to incorporate all the assumptions of the classical economists. The "egoistic" energies which are celebrated in Spencer's writings are, above all, the energies of the industrial entrepreneur. This was the constructive egoism which Yen Fu was now prepared to defend against the highest values of Confucianism. Here again, it is not merely the doctrine of Spencer but the concrete fact of Great Britain's unprecedented economic power which leads him back to the man who was widely acclaimed as the intellectual fountainhead of this phenomenal development—Adam Smith. His first reference to Smith, as already noted, can be found in his "On Strength." "When we of the East contemplate the enormous wealth of the West, its countless techniques for increasing livelihood and regulating finances, we find it difficult to account for this state of affairs."[1] In the West itself, Yen Fu informs us, it is commonly held among those in a position to know that the credit for this is to be ascribed to the "book of Adam Smith." Again, in a commentary on a passage of the *Evolution and Ethics* in which Huxley makes a somewhat lukewarm concession to the positive role of self-interest in men's lives,[2] Yen Fu ardently defends the positive role of self-interest. He states: "The wealth and power of modern Europe are attributed by experts to the science of economics. Economics began with Adam Smith, who developed the great principle . . . that in serving the greater interest (*ta li*) the interests of both sides must be served."[3]

Here again, we note what may be considered an excessive weight placed on the role of ideas or of "sages" in shaping the course of human events. This attribution of England's economic process to the doctrine of one man seems to be in conflict with Yen Fu's own new-found faith in the vast impersonal forces of evolution. Here again, however, we may refer back to discussion of the relationship between "destiny" and "the sages" in Chapter III. The fact that England produced a sage who was able to articulate the dynamic principles of economic growth while China produced no such sage is a fact which Yen Fu cannot overlook. The sages may be only "a factor in destiny," but they seem to be an indispensable factor nevertheless.

The motives for undertaking a translation of the *Wealth*

of Nations thus emerge quite clearly. Yen Fu began this enormous undertaking in 1897 and had completed half the book by the end of 1898. The entire translation was completed by the end of 1900 and was again favored with a foreword (as in the case of *T'ien-yen lun—Evolution and Ethics*) by his stylistic mentor, Wu Ju-lun. The translation is somewhat more literal, less paraphrastic, than the *Evolution and Ethics* translation and is copiously interlaced with commentaries.

It must further be noted that while Yen Fu regards Adam Smith as the source of economic wisdom, he is by no means unconscious of all that has happened in economics since Smith. The evolutionary-historic sense which he derives from Spencer has not deserted him. In his translator's introduction, he mentions Jevons and Marshall, in particular, as economists who had developed economics into a deductive science, while Smith, in his view, had derived most of his views inductively. This, of course, is entirely in keeping with Mill's views on the natural evolution of the sciences. "Economics has made great advances in the last two hundred years. If one wished to have a total picture of economic science in addition to Smith's *Wealth of Nations* one would have to translate Mill, Walker, and Marshall."[4] He has chosen Smith's work because it is the fountainhead rather than the last word. Throughout his many commentaries he points to the vast economic changes which have occurred since Smith, some of which have rendered certain views of the master obsolete. While he is on the whole convinced that most of these changes have simply confirmed Smith's perspicacity, occasionally he points to revisions and improvements introduced by later economists such as Ricardo, Mill, and Rogers. At one point he presents a long and difficult exposition of Ricardo's theory of rent,[5] and elsewhere he takes some issue with the labor theory of value.[6] The translation, together with the commentaries, provides a good elementary course in the tenets of classical economics in its whole development, at least through Marshall.

Throughout the book we remain constantly aware of the familiar preoccupation with the wealth and power of the state. How, then, is this concern reconciled with Smith's economic individualism? Is not Smith known in the textbooks as the deadly enemy of mercantilism, and is not economic growth for state power almost the heart of mercantilism? Eli Heckscher in his classical work on mercantilism defines mercantilism at one point as that system which "would have had all economic activity subservient to the state's interest in power,"[7] and he also says that "mercantilism as a system of power was thus primarily a system for forcing economic policy into the service of power as an end in itself."[8] Here we have a definition of the fundamental nature of mercantilism which draws it very close to Yen Fu's own preoccupation with wealth and power. How can Smith be used for mercantilist purposes?

First of all, we must note that Adam Smith, like the utilitarians in general, is no Max Stirner. He does not pit the Ego in irreconcilable conflict against society and the universe. To him the complement of the enlightened self-interest of the individual is the general interest of the community. Like Bentham, he is ultimately concerned with the greatest good of the greatest number. The whole notion of the "invisible hand" is that of a pre-established harmony between the enlightened self-interest of individuals and the interests of society as a whole. He constantly uses terms such as "the general interest" or "public happiness,"[9] or simply the word "society" itself (as in the statement that "the study of his own [the individual's] advantage naturally, or rather necessarily, leads him to prefer that employment which is most advantageous to society")[10] to designate the ultimate beneficiary of all economic activity.

Of course, the word "society" is to be understood in

Smith (with an extremely important reservation which we shall note below) as designating the sum total of individuals who compose a society. In this sense the ultimate beneficiaries are individuals. On the other hand, when he refers to "a society" he generally refers to the nation-state societies with which he is most familiar, so that the words "society," "nation," and "country" are interchangeable, as is clearly indicated by the title of the whole work, *An Inquiry into the Nature and Causes of the Wealth of Nations,* or when he entitles one of his chapters, "How the Commerce of the Towns Contributed to the Improvement of the Country." We can thus immediately see how all language in Smith which refers to the "general interest" or "the nation" or "society" easily becomes transmuted in Yen Fu's translation into language which refers to the state interest.

Again, one need not assume that Yen Fu is completely uninterested in the greatest happiness of the greatest number as an ultimate goal, but words such as *ch'ün* (the "social organism") and *kuo* ("nation-state") are already heavily freighted with the connotation of state power as an end in itself. If to Smith the "wealth of nations" refers in the first instance to the wealth of the sum total of individuals who compose the nation-society, to Yen Fu the wealth of the *kuo* refers in the first instance to the wealth and hence to the power of the nation-state as a collective entity struggling for existence in a world of similar collective entities. We thus emerge from the study of Yen Fu's *Wealth of Nations* with one overriding conclusion—that the system of economic liberalism developed in the book of Smith and demonstrated in the living example of Victorian England is a system admirably designed to achieve the wealth and power of the state. Here again we come back to the theme we have met before—that the wealth and power of the state can only be achieved by a release of energies and capacities (in this case specifically economic) of the individual.

Again and again in his commentaries Yen Fu takes up

this theme. Thus in the very last chapter of *The Wealth of Nations*—"Of Public Debts"—we come across a passage in which Smith deplores the practice of increasing the national debt by funding. He points out that this kind of large-scale borrowing from subjects and mortgaging of revenues is possible only in a state of society where commerce and manufacture have achieved a high state of development. He also points out that war has, on the whole, been the main cause of large-scale fundings of this type. However, while he regards "perpetual funding" as a "ruinous expedient,"[11] he concedes that Great Britain has so far not suffered from "the weakness and desolation" which the practice of funding has caused in other states. In England "the frugality and good conduct of individuals seem to have been able, by saving and accumulation, to repair all the breaches which the waste and extravagance of government has made in the general capital of the society. At the conclusion of the late war, the most expensive that Great Britain ever waged, her agriculture was as flourishing, her manufactures as numerous as they had ever been before. Great Britain seems capable of supporting a burden which half a century ago nobody believed her capable of supporting."[12] In spite of this admission, however, the whole tenor of Smith's discussion is negative. In the end, excessive funding must ruin even England.

Yen Fu, however, is profoundly struck by one fact above all else—the fact that Great Britain has been able to maintain and increase its wealth even while increasing its national debt. What perspicacity and what a depth of patriotism are revealed in Smith's explanation of this paradox! "Even though the [national] debt of England is heavy, the state continues to gain in wealth and power! . . . There is always a reason for things . . . The policies which account for England's growth in wealth and power since Smith are innumerable . . . The growth of scientific knowledge, the effectiveness of her steam and electric powered engines, the enlightenment and knowledge of her sovereign and ministers and the daily innovations which are introduced by them. However, the most relevant factor was the adoption of the principles advocated in this book . . . They have eliminated the fetters of mercantilism (*hu shang*) and have adopted a policy of free unrestricted commerce." In Great Britain, where everything has been done to encourage and release the economic energies of the people, the state has been able to tap this inexhaustible source of wealth for its own purposes. If this was true in Smith's own day when mercantilism (in the narrower sense of "protecting commerce") prevailed, how much more has this been the case since Smith's death, when his principles have been applied and the fetters on economic acitivity which still existed in his day have been eliminated!

What a contrast with China! Ever since the Sino-Japanese war and the Boxer Rebellion, China has become more and more indebted to foreign powers. It cannot tap the economic energies of its own people, which remain woefully undeveloped and fettered, and the increase in national debt can lead only to an ever greater and more abysmal poverty. Throughout Chinese history, as a matter of fact, any increase in national debt or in taxation could result only in an abstraction from the wealth of the society as a whole, since the economy was static both in conception and in fact. Where the people are oriented toward production, the state can assume more and more burdens without fear of impoverishment.[13]

So impressed is Yen Fu with this insight that it is brought up again and again and is even mentioned in his short introductory biography of Adam Smith, where he states, "The English have not been free of national debt for a day. Although their financial burdens are heavy, their treasure is abundant. Is not the fact that instead of growing poor and weak they have become wealthy and powerful due to the fact that they have broken the locks, opened wide

the doors, and allowed the people to exercise their freedom?"[14] When Smith soberly warns, "Let us not, however,
upon this account rashly conclude that she [Great Britain]
is capable of supporting any burden nor even be too confident that she could support without great distress a burden
a little greater than what has already been laid upon her,"[15]
and when he further advises that England "accommodate
her future views and designs to the real mediocrity of her
circumstances,"[16] Yen Fu is able to point out from his
vantage ground in time that Great Britain has not followed
Smith's advice and that its "views and designs" have expanded enormously since Smith's day. It is precisely because
Great Britain has realized Smith's principles that it has been
able to ignore his advice and increase its national debt
astronomically. Smith simply failed to realize the nuclear
potentialities, as it were, of the economic liberation which
he was proposing.

When Smith points out the necessity of opulence, given
the expense of modern (eighteenth-century) military technology,[17] Yen Fu is again able to refer to the undreamt-of
expansion of the state's burdens in this area. "Comparing
the military expenses of European states in Smith's day to
those of our own, they seem like child's play . . . As a result
of the extension of popular rights in Europe ever since the
Ch'ien-lung, Chia-ching period [the end of the eighteenth
and beginning of the nineteenth century] and of the spectacular advance of various industries, it is no exaggeration
to say that more has been accomplished in a hundred years
than in the previous millenium. As the states have become
daily richer, their defenses have become ever more formidable . . . The power or weakness of a state depends on various sources of wealth, and if one wishes to enrich the state,
one must expand the people's knowledge and improve its
economic system (lit., 'system of finances')."[18] The lesson
for China is clear. If it is ever to overcome its debility, the
Chinese state must enormously increase its financial bur-

dens, and this can only be done, as Smith has shown, by orienting the people toward economic activities and releasing their economic energies.

Here again, to the extent that Adam Smith's aims are purely economic, to the extent that his ultimate goal is the welfare of individuals, Yen Fu's argument that economic freedom is to be justified precisely because it makes possible an enlargement of the state's "designs" might appear to be a monstrous and unexpected inversion of Smith's own doctrine.

The fact is, however, that Smith is more complex than the school which claims him as a father. While much of his polemic is directed against mercantilism in the narrow sense of that term, what he rejects fundamentally is the mercantilists' conception of means. He does not totally reject their end—the enhancement of the wealth and power of the state. Living in the world of monarchic eighteenth-century states, he accepts as a matter of course this world of contending states and the considerations of *Staatsräson* so characteristic of the age. He is not, to be sure, a nineteenth-century nationalist, but neither is he a doctrinaire nineteenth-century cosmopolitan like some of his own orthodox followers (or Herbert Spencer), who believe that the nation-state is about to be dissolved by the inexorable march of free trade and a liberal economy. He certainly has no notion that the "militant stage" of human history is about to disappear. Hence, alongside his general social aims he also accepts the aims of the state qua state as a legitimate concern. In his very definition of political economy he asserts that it has two distinct objects. "It proposes to enrich both the people and the sovereign."[19] In defining the duties of the sovereign he states, "The first duty of the sovereign— that of protecting society from the violence and invasion of other independent societies—can be performed only by military force."[20] Elsewhere in his defense of the Navigation Act he goes so far as to maintain that "defense is of much more importance than opulence,"[21] and in the chapter on the "Employment of Capitals" he states that "the great object of political economy is to increase the riches and power of that country"[22]—language which translates itself without the slightest distortion into the language of Yen Fu's concerns.

Thus we find that, if Yen Fu distorts, the distortion is mainly one of emphasis. In the total context of the *Wealth of Nations* the concern with "public happiness" in terms of the economic welfare of the sum total of individuals certainly overshadows the concern with state-power goals. In Yen Fu's commentaries the concern with welfare (*min sheng*, "people's livelihood") is by no means absent, but it is overshadowed by the more immediate concern with state power. To both Smith and Yen Fu, liberal economic principles admirably serve both ends. However, while Yen Fu finds little difficulty in relating Smith's economic principles to his own "mercantilist" purposes, his real problem lies elsewhere. He must confront head-on the contradiction between the exaltation of enlightened self-interest and the Confucian detestation of material gain as a conscious object of pursuit. From the Confucian point of view, Adam Smith's economics are infinitely more subversive than Herbert Spencer's metaphysics.

There is, to be sure, a kind of *laissez faire* in the orthodox line of Confucian political economic theory. The state is constantly admonished not to engage in activities which are properly those of merchants, and a good state, as we have seen, is one which refrains from interfering overmuch with the livelihood of the people.[23] It is a *laissez faire,* however, which has nothing whatsoever to do with any exaltation of economic pursuits. There is an extremely modest conception of what merchants are to be "allowed to do" and the whole anti-economic morality is simply assumed.

As we have seen, by the nineties a considerable number of the literati had tacitly revised their Confucian views on the pursuit of wealth by the state as a collective entity. Li Hung-chang, Chang Chih-tung, and others had certainly embraced the aims of wealth and power, but the resistance to an acceptance of the morality of enlightened self-interest as applied to individuals was still profound. The prejudice against any revaluation of the merchant and his presumed ethos was still bone-deep and grounded solidly on both the class interest and the deepest convictions of the literati.

It is interesting to note that Yen Fu's friend and mentor, Wu Ju-lun, in his introduction to the translation, also finds the crux of the matter in this area. "Unless we make every effort to change our mental habit of shunning all talk of interest (*li*), unless we resolutely break our attitude of emphasizing agriculture and suppressing commerce, our wealth will remain undeveloped . . . If interest is taboo (*hui*) there can be no science of economics."[24]

Yen Fu does not shrink from confronting the issue, but, as we have already noted elsewhere, he does attempt to mitigate it. Adam Smith himself, like Herbert Spencer, comes to his aid. Yen Fu is well aware of the fact that the same Adam Smith who had written *The Wealth of Nations* had also written *The Theory of Moral Sentiments*.[25] Smith by no means reduces the whole man to the model of economic man. Here we see the advantage enjoyed by Yen Fu in knowing Smith, Spencer, and his other heroes from the source rather than from textbook simplifications. In areas other than the economic, Smith differs from the philosophers of his time who trace the origins of social morality to self-interest alone. In his *Theory of Moral Sentiments,* he claims that "morality arises out of the feeling of sympathy in the human heart."

It is interesting to note that Spencer and Huxley had both been influenced by Smith's moral theory; Huxley specifically refers to it in *Evolution and Ethics*.[26] Yen Fu himself is inclined to accept Spencer's view of egoism as the ultimate source of social solidarity and sympathy as derivative, but

from all these sources (as well as from John Stuart Mill)
Yen Fu is able to derive the view that both self-interest and
sympathy or "reciprocity" (*shu*) may subsist side by side.
Unlike the puristic Bentham, who had fanatically insisted
on explaining everything in terms of the single principle
of self-interest, Smith had not taught that righteousness (*i*)
must completely give way to self-interest (*li*) but that both
are, in some sense, complementary. "There may be those
who maintain that Smith's book is concerned purely with
utility (*kung-li*). They say that according to the economists
human morality is a matter of calculating gains and losses
and that if mortality is to be nothing more than a matter
of self-interest and the pursuit of profit, the principles of
heaven will be lost. Such is their harsh judgment! What
they do not understand is that science concerns itself with
questions of truth and falsehood and not with whether its
findings coincide with benevolence and righteousness.
What [the economists] discuss is economics. They decidedly do not discuss that which lies outside the realm of
economics. But they do not assert that human morality
is nothing but a matter of economics. If one were to con-
demn them, how would this be different from reading
books on military strategy and censuring them for dealing
with matters of violence (lit., 'subjecting other countries'),
or from reading treatises on acupuncture and moxibustion
and blaming them for advocating the infliction of pain!"[27]

The argument here is most shrewd. Military technology
and medicine had long been a respectable part of the Chinese canon of studies in spite of the pacifistic bent of Confucianism. The tradition had reconciled itself to the role of
violence in societies as they actually are. Many scholars had
busied themselves with *Sun-tzu* and other treatises on war.
It had long been recognized that the achievement of the
aims of military defense and medicine required a scientific
techne—certain rational methods, in the Weberian sense,

which enjoyed a degree of independence from the general moral code. Economics is an autonomous sphere in the same sense, and the achievement of economic ends depends on the use of rational economic means. The means can only be discovered "scientifically." With the growing acceptance of the aims of wealth and power, the prestige of the practitioner of violence—the new soldier—was rapidly rising, even among conservative literati. How could the literati object to a similar revaluation of the techne for creating wealth and of the ethos which necessarily accompanies that techne? One cannot blame the entrepreneur for thinking in terms of material gain any more than one can blame the soldier for thinking in terms of violence. On the contrary, within his area of competence it is his duty to think in terms of gain.[28]

Elsewhere Yen Fu points out that, in passing from a morality of negation to a morality which affirms the positive role of enlightened self-interest, China will by no means be unique. The true cleavage here is not so much between China and the West as between the modern world and the past. "The cleavage between 'righteousness' and 'interest' (i li) has been most detrimental to the advance of civilization. Mencius states, 'All one needs is righteousness and humanity. Why speak of interest?' Tung Chung-shu asserts, 'Act righteously and do not scheme to advance your interests. Make manifest the Way and do not calculate advantage.' The ancient teachings of both East and West all draw a sharp line between righteousness and interest. The intention was most sublime, but the effect in terms of bringing men to the Way has been negligible in all cases."[29] Yen Fu is aware of the fact that the morality of enlightened self-interest has won only a recent victory in the West, and he is able to point to this fact to assuage the cultural pride of his fellow literati. In transvaluating its own values China will simply be following a universal path of human evolution which has begun in the West. China has not been alone in regarding self-interest as demonic and in basing its morality on a negation of men's constructive energies.

Between enlightened interest and "righteousness" there is no cleavage. "Ever since the emergence of the theory of evolution it has become as clear as a burning flame that without righteousness there can be no utility and without the Way no profit, and it was the economists who anticipated this insight. Smith always maintained that, while the world is full of shallow men and ignorant men, there are no genuine 'mean men' (*hsiao jen*). The 'mean man' presumably sees only his own interest. However, if we assume that he discerns his long-term, real interests, how does he differ in his behavior from the virtuous man? . . . The process of evolution does not treat the self-intreest of the short-sighted and ignorant as true self-interest and does not treat narrowly abnegating self-righteousness or extravagant and excessive 'righteousness' as true 'righteousness.' "[30] Here we almost have a description of Weber's "Protestant Ethic." Not only do Adam Smith and Herbert Spencer allow for a self-restraining morality in realms other than the economic; they advocate a conception of self-interest which demands the presence of sober virtues. A self-interest which is channeled into constructive entrepreneurial endeavors and leads to wealth and power is divided by a yawning abyss from the degraded selfishness of the corrupt officialdom in China, which is simply a blind consumer hedonism feeding on the substance of society and giving nothing in return. In the West, man's self-regarding and other-regarding tendencies are harnessed to constructive national goals. In China both the negative "righteousness" and the hedonist selfishness of the literati lead to the society's growing debility.

There is, of course, an assumption throughout that the British path of economic growth is the only path and that Great Britain has achieved its wealth by adhering to the principles of Adam Smith. There is the further assumption that economic liberalism, political liberalism, the rule of law, and the march to democracy are all parts of one inseparable organic whole. At the end of the nineteenth century Yen Fu can as yet discern little that disturbs this image, although the somewhat divergent economic models of Imperial Germany, Tsarist Russia, and Meiji Japan are already on the scene. He does mention Imperial Germany at one point and even remarks on the spectacular advance of Germany during the last fifty years. The context is provided by Smith's discussion of the state's role in creating "institutions for the Education of the Youth." "There is no country in the modern world which has paid more attention to the education of its people than Germany, and the results can be seen. In times of peace the results are visible in industry, commerce, and agriculture. In times of war the results can be seen in their military arts . . . Thus Germany has within the space of fifty years been able to pass from weakness to power, from poverty to wealth."[31] All of this praise is, of course, directed to public education—an issue on which Adam Smith himself takes a most positive view, uninfluenced by Herbert Spencer's social Darwinist prejudices. To the extent that Germany has diverged from the British path of economic development, however, Yen Fu does not seem to be acutely aware of this divergence.

Meiji Japan's economy[32] is not mentioned; if he had turned his attention in that direction, he would have found most of the economic thinkers and industrialists of Meiji Japan, such as Taguchi and others, accepting the very assumptions which underlie his own image—the assumption that Great Britain was the model par excellence of wealth and power, and the assumption that this wealth and power had been achieved by adhering to the principles of economic liberalism. As for Russia, Yen Fu by no means shares Smith's high opinion of Peter the Great's reforms, which "almost all resolve themselves into the establishment of a well-regulated standing army."[33] The fact that Russia had simply adopted a standing army (truly free states, in Yen Fu's view, can rely on the infinitely more effective weapon of a loyal conscript army), without adopting any of the political, economic, or legal roots from which national strength draws sustenance, means that Russia was a hollow giant: "Outwardly it appears strong, but one cannot expect it to remain stable for long. It has used Peter's system to rise and as a result of Peter's system it will fall."[34] In the same passage he notes that Germany and Austria still leave much to be desired in the realm of people's rights, but they have, at least, a mixed constitution. Nothing that he observes in the world of his time is sufficient to shake his faith in Smith's economic principles.

Yen Fu's translation of the *Wealth of Nations* was widely read, according to all accounts. In retrospect, however, it would not appear that Yen Fu's effort to spread the gospel of economic individualism as an operating value was notably successful in twentieth-century China. There was, to be sure, at the turn of the century a new orientation on the part of gentry elements to such matters as railroad investments. Yet whatever may have been the actual motives of such new interests, they were probably seldom justified in terms of enlightened self-interest.[35]

However, beneath the specific doctrines of economic liberalism, there is in Adam Smith a much broader message. Smith is not only the father of the classical school, he is the great theorist of economic orientation in general. He was by no means the originator of this orientation, but he certainly was its earliest great systematizer. Dugald Stuart in a memoir[36] on the works of Adam Smith points to the "striking contrast between the spirit of ancient and modern policy in respect to the *Wealth of Nations*. The great object of the former was to counteract the love of money and a taste for luxury by positive institutions and to maintain in the great body of the people habits of frugality and a severity of manners. The decline of states is uniformly ascribed by the philosophers and historians both of Greece and Rome to the influence of riches on national character . . . How opposite to this is the doctrine of modern politicians! Far from considering poverty as an advantage to a state their aim is to open new sources of national opulence and to animate the activity of all classes of the people by a taste for the comforts and the accommodations of life."[37] He then goes on to point out that Smith was a great theoretician of this transvaluation of values: "The great and leading object of his speculation is to illustrate the provisions made by nature in the principles of the human mind and in the circumstances of man's external situation for a gradual and progressive augmentation in the means of national wealth."[38] In other words, Smith is one of the great initiators of the orientation to what is now called economic development. It is thus entirely conceivable that the main message which Yen Fu's readers derived from this work was not so much the specific message of economic individualism as the gospel of economic development in general. From Smith and from Yen Fu's commentaries on Smith one could gain a vivid comprehension of the "contrast between ancient and modern policy" mentioned by Dugald Stuart. Smith had demonstrated that a purposeful systematic application of human energies to the increase of national wealth could yield undreamt-of results whatever the ends to which this wealth was applied. With the emergence in the twentieth century of anti-capitalistic schools of economic development, the gospel of economic individualism no longer seemed to be the inevitable means to the achievement of these ends.

CHAPTER VI

On Liberty

Y E N F U ' S labors on the *Wealth of Nations* proceeded steadily during all the stormy events of 1898. As already indicated, he had remained more or less on the sidelines during the whole period of the "Hundred Days Reform." He never was to become a member of K'ang Yu-wei's inner circle in spite of his friendly relations with individual members of the group—men such as Liang Ch'i-ch'ao and Lin Hsü. There can be no doubt, nevertheless, that he was deeply disturbed by the *coup d'état* of August 1898, whatever may have been his reservations concerning the reform program. The death of the famous "six martyrs" seems to have profoundly shocked him. In a short poem written at the time he identified himself wholeheartedly with the young martyrs and bitterly complained, "To search for good government has become a crime! . . . The skies over the capital seem to be covered with a pall of darkness . . . No one can dispel my profound depression."[1] He also composed a *tz'u* (a Chinese poetical form) bewailing the sad situation of the young Kuang-hsü emperor.[2]

Furthermore, in spite of his lack of direct involvement in the Reform movement, his own position during the period of reaction was most precarious. His reputation as an advocate of barbarian thought was, of course, well known, and he was warned by the grand secretary, Wang Wen-shao, to leave the capital for the safer ground of Tientsin.[3] At Tientsin, however, he continued to occupy his position as superintendent of the Tientsin Naval Academy.[4] According to one account, he was protected from the Empress Dowager's full wrath by the famous Jung-lu, who had presumably not identified himself completely with the reactionary party in spite of his prominent role in the *coup d'état*. According to another account, the *kuo-wen-pao,* with which Yen Fu had been so prominently connected, enjoyed Japanese support and protection, and therefore to a degree Yen Fu also enjoyed the protection of Japanese interests which tended to identify themselves at this time with the cause of reform.[5]

Whatever may have been the case, the period between the *coup d'état* and the Boxer Rebellion can hardly have been a happy one for Yen Fu. The whole course of reform had been reversed, the general atmosphere was one of repression, and he himself was highly suspect to the reactionary coterie at court. It was during this dark period that Yen Fu seems to have undertaken the translation of Mill's *On Liberty.* One is tempted to speculate that the atmosphere of repression and the acute sense of deprivation of liberty (particularly the "Liberty of Thought and Discussion") may have provided an immediate motive for this undertaking. In his "Translator's Directions to the Reader," which was not written until 1903, he dwells on freedom of opinion in particular. "Freedom of opinion is nothing more than to speak the truth plainly, to search for truth . . .

One is not deceived by the ancients or cowed by those in authority. It is to accept facts as facts even if they proceed from an enemy, and falsehoods as errors even if they proceed from one's lord or father."[6] Only the proper laws can create a situation in which this fearless search for truth can go on. This, of course, reflects Mill's fervently expressed faith that only a free market of ideas can ultimately lead to truth.

Whether the motive for the translation is to be sought in immediate circumstances, or whether Mill is translated simply because he clarifies an important area within the larger synthetic structure, is not a question of great consequence. We know, of course, that a concern with liberty already formed part of Yen Fu's Spencerian outlook and that both Spencer and Smith had emphasized the absolute necessity of liberty in the all-important realm of economic activity.

John Stuart Mill's concerns in *On Liberty*, however, are to a considerable degree of a different order from those of either Adam Smith or Spencer. While Mill is an eminent economist in his own right, he concerns himself very little in this work with "freedom of enterprise" or "economic freedom." In one passage he specifically states that "the so-called doctrine of free trade rests on grounds different from, though equally solid with, the principle of individual liberty asserted in this Essay." Free trade is to be justified on the ground that it ultimately promotes the economic welfare of the greatest number, but the basic values served by individual liberty are of a different order. In the words of Barker, "From a concept of liberty as external freedom of action necessary for the discovery and pursuit of his material interest, Mill rose to that concept of liberty as free play for that spiritual originality which alone can constitute a rich and balanced society."[7] As has often been pointed out, the economic had already become for Mill precisely one of those spheres in which the interests of society were beginning to override the interests of the individual, or rather a sphere in which the interests of the individual could be promoted only by a conscious intervention of the state.

On the other hand, the whole rhetoric of "natural selection" and the "survival of the fittest" is completely absent, although the latter phrase had already been coined by Spencer. (The *Origin of Species* and *On Liberty* were both published in 1859.) Even in subsequent years, however, Mill's writings remain singularly untouched by the influence of social Darwinism in either its individual or its collective interpretation. The liberty of the individual is thus not simply the means to the achievement of economic growth nor a means of releasing or heightening men's "energy of faculty." It is an end in itself and may even involve such matters as "peculiarity of taste" and "eccentricity of conduct."[8] Mill's biographer, Packe, points out that this little work, *On Liberty*, was written in a somewhat defensive mood. Against the growing claims of society and the subtle pressures of democratic "conformism," Mill was anxious to stake out a legitimate area for the operation of individual liberty. In doing so he leans very far in the direction of rendering society its due, but his essential aim is to defend against society the value of that in the individual which is most individual. He defends the liberty not merely of businessmen nor of men of superior faculties and talents to make their way in society, but presumably even of the ineffectual and talentless to carry on their own mode of existence.

It would thus appear that Mill deals to a considerable extent with forms of liberty which are not very relevant to Yen Fu's concerns. The liberty of individuals to be hedonists or "beatniks" or eccentrics of every variety hardly seems to contribute substantially to the wealth and power of the state. Some of the modes of individual existence which Mill seems prepared to defend would certainly belong to the parasitic in Smith's system and to the unfit in Spencer's universe.

Unfortunately, the translation of *On Liberty* is not embellished with commentaries. Except for the "Introduction" and the "Translator's Directions to the Reader" we have no explicit interpretations by Yen Fu of Mill's views. However, an examination of the "Translator's Directions" as well as the text of the translation (also the superimposed marginal summaries) does throw considerable light on the framework within which Yen Fu envisages its contents. As elsewhere, Yen Fu complains bitterly of the difficulty of conveying the original text in Chinese and of his inability to translate Mill's sentences literally. The translation is thus inevitably paraphrastic, and the paraphrasing embodies striking examples of the unconscious adaptation of Mill's thought to Yen Fu's concerns; we find here good examples of interpretation by translation.

Essentially this interpretation involves the forcing of many of Mill's ideas into a framework of Spencerian categories. Spencer's name is introduced at the very outset in the "Translator's Directions," where his authority is invoked to support Yen Fu's efforts to define the word liberty. "In his discussion of 'Justice' ['Justice in Principle of Ethics'], in his *Data of Ethics,* Spencer states that liberty is necessary to human ethics, for without liberty the choice between good and evil would not proceed from oneself and one could only speak in terms of fortune or misfortune. Thus the people's virtue [moral qualities] would not evolve. It is only when the people are granted liberty that natural selection can be applied and that the good society can ultimately be achieved."[9] Now while the notion that liberty involves the concept of the individual as the source of moral choice is not foreign to Mill's view, the Spencerian-Darwinian language immediately constricts the concerns of liberty to those areas involving the "survival of the fittest"—to liberty as a tool of social efficiency and hence as an ultimate means of attaining wealth and power. Once more, it is the potential captain of industry and those who have socially useful talents who become the main beneficiaries of liberty. Liberty again is mainly to be valued because of its contribution to the famous triad of men's moral, intellectual, and physical powers as previously defined.

Mill's chapter on "Liberty of Thought and Discussion" offers no particular difficulty. It can readily be assimilated to the doctrine that men's intellectual capacities can be improved only by the free struggle for existence in the area of thought. It has already been suggested that it may have been Mill's argument in this chapter above all which prompted the translation of the whole book. The "Translator's Directions," as already noted, turns its particular attention to freedom of thought. Freedom of thought, Mill has proved, provides the only way to reach the truth, and "if the people's intellect and the people's virtue are now to be advanced, this can only be achieved by loving and treasuring the truth."[10] The truth to which Yen Fu is committed above all else is the truth of the natural and social sciences (as revealed by Spencer and Smith), and it is only within an environment of intellectual freedom that this truth can be advanced.

Does Mill's conception of the "Freedom of Thought and Discussion" lend itself to Yen Fu's purposes? On the whole it does. Mill, like Smith, is no absolute egoist, à la Max Stirner. He is not merely interested in advancing his own happiness or the happiness of the happy few but constantly speaks in terms of mankind at large or the welfare of society. The "greatest good of the greatest number" remains his goal. "Were an opinion a personal possession of no value except to the owner; if to be obstructed in the enjoyment of it were simply a private injury it would make some difference whether the injury was inflicted only on a few persons or on many. But the peculiar evil of silencing the expression of an opinion is, that it is robbing the human race."[11]

Here again, however, as in the case of Smith, whereas grounds of social utility or of the welfare of society are put forth, they are not infrequently transmuted by Yen Fu into the language of the interests of the state. Furthermore, while Mill is not consciously Darwinian, his discussion of the beneficent effects of the free and open struggle of opinion in human society bears within itself a certain resemblance to Darwinian notions. It is only when opinions struggle among themselves that the fittest survive, and there is, of course, a general notion of the growing preponderance over time of right opinion. "As mankind improve, the number of doctrines which are no longer disputed or doubted will be constantly on the increase and the well-being of mankind may almost be measured by the number and gravity of the truths which have reached the point of being uncontested."[12] This is not simply a result of the accumulation of inductive experience. "There must be discussion to show how experience is to be interpreted. Wrong opinions and practices gradually yield to fact and argument but facts and argument to produce any effect on the mind must be brought before it."[13] Even the argument that when heretic opinion is suppressed "the minds of the orthodox are bound to deteriorate for lack of mental exercise" can be readily assimilated to Yen Fu's notion that men's intellectual powers can be improved only by the "rubbing together" of men's minds. It is thus quite obvious that freedom of thought and expression is a freedom most relevant to Yen Fu's concerns.

It would appear, however, that Mill's conception of "freedom of individuality" is less tractable to Yen Fu's use. It is precisely here that Mill addresses himself to those aspects of individual freedom which seem most relevant to the individual himself and least relevant to society as a whole or, a fortiori, to the interests of the state. It is in his chapter on individuality (chapter iii) that he discusses individual spontaneity "in things which do not primarily concern others."[14] It is here that he discusses "freedom of impulse, desire and taste" and "different experiments of living." It is also here that we find his famous defense of eccentricity ("that so few now dare to be eccentric, marks the chief danger of the time").[15] It is here that we find his assertion that "it is not only persons of decided mental superiority who have a just claim to carry on their lives in their own way . . . If a person possesses any tolerable amount of common sense and experience, his own mode of laying out his existence is the best, not because it is the best in itself, but because it is his own mode."[16] All of these forms of liberty seem to be immediately valuable only to the individual himself.

Even in this chapter, to be sure, the argument in terms of the welfare of society as a whole is not absent. "In proportion to the development of his individuality, each person becomes more valuable to himself and is capable therefore of being more valuable to others. There is a greater fullness of life about his own existence and when there is more life in the units there is more in the mass which is composed of them."[17] "Where not the person's own character but the tradition or customs of other people are the rule of conduct there is wanting one of the chief ingredients of human happiness and quite the chief ingredient of individual and *social* [italics mine] progress."[18] Again there is no reference here to the interests of the state, and in the case of "individuality" one might well argue that one cannot readily translate the language of "greatest happiness of greatest numbers" into the language of state interest. The freedom to be eccentric, to live a life according to men's own tastes (even though these may not be the best), while it may enrich society by lending life variety, hardly seems to contribute anything to the strength of the state.

Actually, however, Mill's conception of "individuality" in this chapter is hardly crystal-clear; many quite different things are brought together under this rubric. At the very outset of the chapter we are confronted with a definition of individuality derived from Wilhelm von Humboldt's *Sphere and Duties of Government,* namely, that "the end of man as that which is prescribed by the eternal and immutable dictates of reason and not suggested by vague and transient desires is the highest and most harmonious development of his powers to a complete and consistent whole."[19] The idea of the "development of powers" reminds us immediately of Spencer's concept of the "energy of faculty." All this is linked throughout the chapter with the exaltation of the energetic personality. At times individuality itself seems to be identified by Mill with "strength of impulse" and "energy." "More good may always be made of an energetic nature than of an indolent and impassive one." It is not always easy to determine what Mill means precisely by his exaltation of "powers," "strong impulse," "energy as the raw material of human nature," "men of strong bodies or minds," and so forth. At times he seems to be referring to the Bohemian, the man who defies public convention in his emotional life. The words themselves, however, seem to point to the kind of individual who achieves dominance in society, or to men of unusual physical or brain capacity. Alexander Bain in his life of Mill cogently remarks in this connection, "Mill pleads strongly for energetic natures and strong impulse. But energy as such is not thwarted and the difficulty will always remain that superabundant energy is exceedingly apt to trench upon other people's rights. Mill too closely identifies energy with originality or genius and genius with eccentricity."[20]

One may well question the connection between individuality as described in some passages of Mill's chapter and the cult of the energetic individual. Mill's society by no means downgraded energy or human powers. These energies and powers were, however, flowing into activities which had no necessary connection with individuality in the sense of uniqueness of personality or spiritual originality and which were entirely compatible with the conformism which he deplored. The development of late nineteenth-century Germany and Japan and of the twentieth-century totalitarian state has amply demonstrated that the positive authoritarian state of modern times aims to enhance the physical and intellectual (technico-intellectual) powers of the individual and places a premium on human energy. It is interesting to note in this connection that Wilhelm von Humboldt's German biographer, Binswanger, makes a good case for the thesis that von Humboldt was himself never really a "liberal." He attacked the post-Frederick state in Prussia because it was a "negative," passive regime which did nothing to develop human powers. "Humboldt is in no sense prejudiced against the state just as he is not prejudiced against power. If the state had been the gathering point (*Sammelpunkt*) of energies, his decision would have been otherwise. His ideas would have sounded differently. His later career is proof of this."[21] In his later years of growing nationalism Humboldt thought of individuality (*das Individuelle*) more and more in terms of the individuality of nations, and one even finds in him the tendency to think of the released powers of the individual mainly as serving the ends of the nation.

Thus, to the extent that Mill speaks in terms of "powers" and energy, Yen Fu tends to associate this form of "individuality" with his own Spencerian conception of the "people's virtue," which, we recall, embraces all those muscular qualities of body and soul which are required to advance the wealth and power of the state. It is interesting to note that while Mill entitles his chapter "Of Individuality as One of the Elements of Well-Being," Yen Fu's translation gives the title a somewhat unexpected twist: "Explaining the principle of freedom of action (lit., 'action proceeding from self') and individuality (lit., 'one's own special mode of life') as the basis of the people's virtue."[22] While Yen Fu does not neglect those phrases in the chapter which refer to "well-being," the title shifts attention from "well-being" to "virtue." It is interesting to note that Yen Fu introduces interpretation via translation precisely in that passage in which Mill exalts the energetic man of strong impulse. Where Mill states that "it is through the cultivation of these personal impulses, vivid and powerful, that society both does its duty and protects its interests,"[23] Yen Fu translates, "Statesmen must realize that it is only by fostering superior people of this type that they can be said to have fulfilled their heaven-imposed duty. The honor of their race and the strength of the state can only be achieved thus."[24] Where Mill maintains that "to be restrained in things not affecting their good by their mere displeasure [the displeasure of others] develops nothing valuable," Yen Fu translates, "To be restrained in freedom of action (*hsing chi*) where one does not injure the rights of others simply because of their displeasure does not advance the people's virtue." In the marginal summary, he summarizes the whole passage as follows: "Where few people possess individuality, the state is bound to decline."[25] Mill nowhere implies in this passage that what is "valuable" is the type of people's virtue which sustains the power of the state. He speaks of human beings becoming "noble and beautiful objects of contemplation," of human life becoming "rich, diversified, and animating." He does indeed speak of "strengthening the tie which binds everyone to the race by making the race infinitely better worth belonging to," but race obviously means the human race. Yen Fu, however, mentions three beneficiaries of individuality—the individual himself, the national society (*kuo-ch'ün*), and the state—and the marginal comment focusses on the last.

There is only one passage in the whole of *On Liberty* in which Mill relates himself directly to the interests of the state as such. After arguing that wherever possible a state should not substitute its own action for the activities and powers of the individuals who make up the state, Mill asserts in his peroration that "in the long run the worth of a state is the worth of the individuals composing it . . . A state which dwarfs its men in order that they may be more docile instruments in its hands—even for beneficial purposes—will find that with small men no great thing can really be accomplished."[26] While one cannot help feeling that for Mill this argument for liberty is strictly marginal and simply a reinforcement for views held on quite other grounds, it is, of course, an argument which directly meshes with Yen Fu's interpretation of Spencer and Smith. So close is it to his own perspectives that he even allows a Darwinian phrase to creep into his paraphrase of the original—which is bare of all such phrases. "It [the state] deprives the people of its rights to act by itself in local affairs and substitutes its own activities for theirs. It fails to realize that in the present world of struggle for existence, the capacities of the state are in direct proportion to the capacities (*neng shih*) of the people. By consolidating the freedom of the individuals in order to achieve the freedom of the state as a whole, the prestige of the state is raised to insuperable heights."[27]

On Liberty provides us with some of the most glaring examples of interpretation through translation. While much of the original argument comes through intact, many of the expressions interpolated by Yen Fu, and the argument of his "Translator's Directions to the Reader," prove sufficient to bend Mill to his own purposes. His Chinese reader probably did not derive from it any clear sense of the differences among Mill, Spencer, and Smith on the matter of liberty. If liberty of the individual is often treated in Mill as an end in itself, in Yen Fu it becomes a means to the advancement of "the people's virtue and intellect," and beyond this to the purposes of the state.

While Yen Fu's translation was completed before 1899, he informs us that the manuscript was lost with many other papers in 1900 during the Boxer Rebellion, when he was forced to flee to Shanghai. It was found by a Western friend, who returned it to him in 1903, and in the same year he wrote his introduction and had the work published.

It might be well to pause at this point to review some of the significant events in Yen Fu's life during these years. As might be expected, he stood aside completely from the Boxer fever; in his essay "A Dialogue between a Host and his Guest" he refers to the rebellion as an "uprising of the superstitious mob and of ignorant and worthless armed bandits . . . It was certainly a disaster for our state." This sentiment, however, does not exhaust his reaction to the events. The spirit of the Boxer armies did impress him. "One cannot say that there were not patriots among them,"[28] he wrote, and in a commentary to the *Wealth of Nations* he refers to the remarkable performance of the Chinese soldiers.[29] Here again we see manifested the contrast between his low opinion of the actual state of the people and his profound faith in what might be called their potential capacities. Even the Boxers had shown some signs of the moral qualities which a true system of education could make manifest.

In Shanghai Yen Fu busied himself with the formation of a "Society for the Study of Logic." The formation of the society reflects his concern with Mill's *Logic,* which, we shall find, is not a whit more "academic" in its purpose than any of his other concerns. His readiness to turn his attention to such matters during these hectic months, however, graphically illustrates his Archimedes-like ability to assume the long-range view.

It was at this time that he finally resigned from his superintendency of the Peiyang Naval Academy. For a time in 1901 he acted as an agent of the manager of the Kaiping mines in Tientsin and evidently participated in the negotiations involving the sale of the mines to British interests. For this he has been severely attacked by his Communist biographer, Wang Shih. Yet there is no reason to assume that Yen Fu himself would have been at all ashamed of his role. He thought well of the British and probably was quite satisfied that British management of the mines was a good thing.

With the launching of the so-called "Manchu Reform," Yen Fu's credit with the establishment rose somewhat, although he never was to achieve a position of real importance. When his patron, Wu Ju-lun, became chancellor of Peking University, he was invited to occupy the post of director in its newly established Translation Bureau alongside the famous translator of novels, Lin Shu. In 1903, however, Wu Ju-lun died, and Yen Fu abandoned his post in 1904. Lin Shu reports that he lived a life of utter seclusion in this post and evidently derived little satisfaction from it.[30] In the winter of the same year he was again invited by Chang I to aid in certain litigations concerning the Kaiping mines. This matter involved an extensive trip to Europe.

Yen Fu's outer career thus continued to be marked by frustrations and uncertainty. His prestige had undoubtedly increased and the establishment treated him with a certain deference even while holding him at arm's length. Although this deference was to become more marked in the years immediately preceding the revolution, he never seems to have occupied a position of real power in spite of his wholehearted support of the reform effort.

The Chinese biographer, Chou Chen-fu (and he is followed by others), professes to see in Yen Fu in the years immediately following the Boxer Rebellion, a steady evolution, or rather devolution, from the radical "all-out Westernization" outlook of the pre-1900 years to the traditionalist reactionary outlook of old age through a period of "compromise between China and the West"[31] roughly corresponding to these years. This, of course, neatly fits the usual stereotype concerning the radicalism of youth and the conservatism of old age.

One of the items of evidence used to support this view is provided by Yen Fu's own handling of the *On Liberty* translation in 1903. There is first of all the matter of the title. It would appear that he had originally entitled it simply *On Liberty* (*Tzu-yu lun*). In 1903, however, he insists on the cumbrous title *On the Boundaries of the Rights of Society and of the Individual*. In actuality this is nothing more than an abbreviation of his translation of the title of Chapter IV of the original ("Of the limits of the authority of society over the individual").[32] The obvious explanation of this shift seems to be a concern to emphasize the limits on individual liberty and the rights of society. Again, his preface written in 1903 seems to be directed quite as much against "lovers of the new who think of liberty in terms of unbridled license, and recklessness" as against the reactionaries who think of it as a heretical doctrine "of raging floods and ferocious beasts." Finally, in a letter written to his young disciple, Hsiung Ch'un-ju, during his bitter old age when he was inclined to blame the chaos of China on the revolution, he states that he had translated *On Liberty* in order to teach the radical youth that the new Western ideas had their own built-in limits and could not be applied in "a stupid and destructive fashion."[33]

One may well doubt this retrospective account of his motives in 1899. It is, however, quite likely that in 1903 Yen Fu was indeed anxious to stress the limits on individual liberty. What had changed, however, was not so much Yen Fu as the milieu within which he now moved. Since the Boxer Rebellion, the party of revolution had come to the fore as a leading force, particularly among the younger members of the literati, and even many of those who called themselves constitutional monarchists were pushing forward to reduce the power of the monarchy to a shadow. One may, of course, attribute Yen Fu's reaction to all this to a temperamental conservatism (which had, however, been there from the very beginning), or to his sense of stake in the regime (actually not very great). However, it is entirely possible to explain his position in strictly intellectual terms, without departing a hair's breadth from the Western premises of his thought. There is no evidence whatsoever that a traditional sentiment for the dynasty as such or even for the monarchic institution as such plays any role.

As already indicated, Yen Fu had been effectively inoculated against the mystique of revolution by Spencer, Huxley, and even by Mill himself. They all had taught him to believe in the evolution of the human race as a long, hard, slow, cumulative process. There could be no miraculous skipping of stages. By every criterion, China was in a backward stage of development (in his own view—a hybrid "patriarchal-militant society" stage), and both Spencer and Mill believed that authoritarian-despotic government was necessary in this stage. Mill does not hesitate to state that "despotism is a legitimate mode of government in dealing with barbarians provided the end be their improvement and the means justified by actually effecting that end. Liberty as a principle has no application to any state of things anterior to the time when mankind have become capable of being improved by free and equal discussion."[34] The utilitarian Mill firmly rejects the notion of natural right and sees liberty linked to the slow process of human enlightenment.

Yen Fu has been taught by his Western mentors to reject all the possible grounds in terms of which a republican revolution might be justified in the China of his day. The idea of natural right is anathema to both the Darwinists and Utilitarians. "The principle stated at the beginning of Rousseau's *Social Contract,* that man is born free, has been rejected by later thinkers (*hou-hsien*). They assert that a baby when born is no different from any other animal. He has no control over his own life or death or whether he starves or is fed . . . The higher the level of evolution of civilization the larger the scope of liberty and independence . . . Liberty can be enjoyed only by those whose power of self-mastery is already great."[35]

It need hardly be added that Yen Fu has no faith whatsoever in anything like the native rationality or the uneducated common sense of the average man posited by a Jeffersonian outlook. The people do, to be sure, have an infinite capacity for absorbing enlightenment, but the enlightenment must be brought to them from outside. Certainly one cannot rely on the "general will" of a people whose physical, intellectual, and moral powers remain completely undeveloped.

Even if Yen Fu had accepted a Marxist theory of evolution (Wang Shih reproaches him for not knowing Marx), he would probably not have found much satisfying evidence that China was ripe for even a bourgeois revolution. It must, of course, be stressed that it was generally assumed before 1911 by the leading revolutionaries, such as Sun Yat-sen, that a revolution would be a democratic-republican revolution; it was precisely this assumption that China was ripe for a democratic republic which probably seemed most unacceptable to Yen Fu. We cannot know what he would have thought of the authoritarian elitist revolutions of the twentieth century, which harness the energy of popular resentments to their purposes.

We have, in this connection, an interesting record of conversation between Sun Yat-sen and Yen Fu during the latter's trip to England in 1905. Yen Fu is quoted as saying that "the quality of our people is inferior, their knowledge (*min chih*) is at a low state . . . What is most urgent in our present situation is that we turn our efforts to education. Perhaps we shall then make some progress."[36] Sun is alleged to have replied, "How long can a man wait for the river to clear? You, sir, are a thinker, I am a man of action." The basic sentiment underlying Sun's reply is that "on s'engage et puis on voit." What was required, in Yen Fu's view, was to create the conditions of progress, and one had to begin where one found oneself. In China one would have to begin with the Manchu state. Inasmuch as this state was finally beginning to show a disposition toward reform in the overwhelmingly crucial areas of education, economics, military organization, and legal reform, one ought to do everything possible to assure the success of these reforms. If Yen Fu cherished any doubts whether the demoralized and corrupt element of the Manchu leadership would be able to convert themselves into "enlightened despots," he suppressed them in the interest of his larger hopes. Under these circumstances, reckless talk of revolution, of "racialism," and of the immediate achievement of total freedom was utterly irresponsible and would only impede the orderly effort of reform.

In none of this does one detect the slightest movement from the "Western" pole to the "Chinese traditional" pole. As a matter of fact, his "Letter to the Editor of the *Wai-chiao-pao* on Education" of 1902 is as uncompromising a statement of his commitment to the West as one can find anywhere in his writings. Of all the evils which confront China, ignorance is the most dire, since it is only knowledge which can overcome all of China's ills, and more specifically it is only Western knowledge which can overcome the particular forms of ignorance from which China suffers. Here is an uncompromising acceptance of the West as the model of China's future and a total repudiation of anti-foreignism of any variety.[37]

It is in this context that we must view Yen Fu's treatment of Mill's text in 1903. The change of title and the attack on the reckless innovators may indeed reflect a shift in his view of Mill's message. As against the reckless young revolutionary advocates of the outdated notions of Rousseau, he must emphasize the limits within which liberty should operate. If such limits exist even within the advanced civilization of England, how much more must this be the case in backward China! As we have already noted, Mill makes very generous concessions to society and even to the state. The contrast between Mill's "liberalism" (in the twentieth-century sense) and Spencer's doctrinaire anti-statism is quite marked. Yen Fu thus notes in passing that Mill's view on the state's role in education is in marked contrast to Spencer's; indeed, one cannot but feel that he supports Mill as against Spencer, since Spencer's doctrinaire anti-statism had never penetrated deeply. There was, in short, nothing in Mill to encourage the notion that one should concede to the revolutionaries the liberty[88] to destroy the state precisely at a point in China's evolution when a strong and aggressive authority was more urgently needed than ever.

CHAPTER VII

The Spirit of the Laws

W E D O N O T K N O W precisely when Yen Fu began his labors on Montesquieu's *Spirit of the Laws*. Wang Ch'ü-ch'ang[1] surmises that it was probably after his completion of the *Wealth of Nations* in 1902. The first part of the manuscript was completed in 1905, but the whole manuscript was not published until 1909. In terms of Chou Chen-fu's biographical scheme it thus belongs to the period of "compromise between China and the West," that is, of compromise with Chinese traditional thought. Whether Yen Fu's commentaries on Montesquieu do indeed substantiate this hypothesis is a question which will be treated later. The translation is excellent and adheres rather more tenaciously to the original text than most of the translations. It is, furthermore, copiously interlaced with some of Yen Fu's most thoughtful commentaries.

Yen Fu does not provide us with an account of his reasons for this undertaking. The introduction, in fact, is actually a biography of Montesquieu, with only occasional clues to Yen Fu's views on the significance of Montesquieu's magnum opus.

In speculating on the implicit reasons for this mammoth undertaking, one is aware in the first instance of the obvious fact that Montesquieu is, after all, concerned with the law in the specific legal-juristic sense. *The Spirit of the Laws* is vastly more than a treatise on the laws, but it is a treatise on law among other things. The author is concerned with the whole range of law from the civil up through the constitutional (in both the broad and narrow sense), and it is at the latter end that his concern with law blends into a concern with political structure in its broadest sense (which is then associated with a concern for social structure and culture). Furthermore, in his concern with law Montesquieu plays a somewhat ambivalent role. He is already the "detached" social scientist in the nineteenth-century sense, but he is also still the "enlightened" vicarious legislator of the eighteenth century, interested in the improvement of the laws—in what the laws ought to be. His conception of the arena of action of the enlightened legislator is indeed far more modest than that of many of his contemporaries. The legislator can operate only within the confines of a given socio-political framework, but within this framework he can act to improve matters. "The laws which the legislator makes ought to be relative to the principle of government," reads the title of Book V. Here we see enunciated simultaneously the limits within which the legislator acts as well as the injunction to act. Each of the three "principles of government" which form the range of Montesquieu's typology is subject to its own corruption.[2] It is the legislator who attempts to prevent this corruption, and it is the legislator who makes it possible for the given type of polity to realize its finest inherent potentialities.

Yen Fu's concern with the law is unmistakable, and in

his concern he shares the ambivalence of Montesquieu. He too is concerned with both the limiting conditions within which legislation must take place and with the changes which can be effected by the legislator. We will find, indeed, that he has a far broader conception of the role of the legislator than can be encompassed in Montesquieu's rigid categories. Beyond his interest in law as an instrument of change, however, he is enormously preoccupied with the legal systems and legal outlook of the West as one indispensable ingredient in that synthesis of factors leading to the West's Promethean explosion.

These are, of course, the years in which the Manchu government itself was turning its attention to the modernization of China's legal system and the creation of a constitutional framework. Shen Chia-pen and others had begun to occupy themselves with the introduction of Western legal codes, and the discussion of constitutional monarchy was well under way. Yen Fu was no longer a single voice in the wilderness. Unlike many of his contemporaries, however, his conversion to a Western "impersonal" conception of law and his appreciation of the role of law in the whole complex of Western (particularly British) development was by no means new. It is, in fact, in a commentary on Montesquieu's discussion of the English constitution that he recalls his conversation of years gone by with Ambassador Kuo Sung-t'ao during his first trip to England:[3] "When I first travelled in Europe I always visited the law courts to observe the administration of justice and after returning to my lodgings I would spend days in a sort of trance. I once remarked to Ambassador Kuo that the reason why Great Britain and the other countries of Europe are wealthy and powerful is because the principles of even justice are daily extended. This is the ultimate root. The Ambassador heartily agreed with me."

Montesquieu and Yen Fu share a common enthusiasm for England as the land par excellence of the independent judiciary and the "rule of law." In his introductory biography Yen Fu relates that "Montesquieu spent over two years in London observing English legal institutions (*fa-tu*) and proclaimed that only the people of England could be called free."⁴ Montesquieu loves England for what he considers its profound concern for liberty grounded in law. Yen Fu, living in the twentieth century, sees fruits of this liberty grounded in law of which Montesquieu could hardly have dreamt. The same England which had already enjoyed liberty under law, an independent judiciary, and a vigorous class of lawyers during Montesquieu's lifetime was subsequently to undergo the industrial revolution and become the wealthiest and most powerful nation in Europe. These subsequent developments not foreseen by Montesquieu (although he did perceive a relationship between the prosperity of commerce and the concern for liberty⁵) were certainly not unrelated to the excellencies of which he was already aware. The extraordinary economic accomplishments of the English were a result of the release of the energies of the individual. It was the environment of liberty which made this possible, and Montesquieu graphically demonstrates that liberty is grounded in England's system of laws (the "system" in its most comprehensive sense—including the constitution of the state).

Already in the translation of the *Wealth of Nations* there are many passages in which Yen Fu points to the close connection between the excellence of England's laws and its wealth and power. It is actually in a commentary in the *Wealth of Nations* that we find it proclaimed that "the point on which the political systems of East and West are most irreconcilable is in the matter of law."⁶ Yen Fu has a very sharp sense of the legal environment within which Adam Smith writes and he can, of course, discern in Smith, as well as in Montesquieu, a faith in the potency of legislation, in the possibility of bringing about change in society through changes of law. Smith is also a man of the enlightenment who believes that matters may be improved by legislative action. One of the main purposes of his book is legislative—to obtain a modification of those forms of legal restraint which continue to inhibit the creation of a "natural" economy. In the apt words of Dugald Stuart: "to direct the policy of nations with respect to one of its most important classes of its laws—those which form its system of political economy—is the great aim of Mr. Smith's inquiry."[7] Smith is not Marx. The politico-legal structure of society is not to him simply a "superstructural" reflection of economic processes. The system of laws has the power to restrain the economic processes, and proper legislation may serve to propel the process. Smith also is a potential, vicarious legislator. Yen Fu, who must desperately hope that state legislation may foster the economic, educational, and political development of a poverty-stricken China, cannot help sharing within limits the eighteenth-century faith of Montesquieu (circumscribed as this may be) and Smith in the power of the legislator to influence the course of human affairs.

What is more, Montesquieu helps to crystallize in Yen Fu's mind the fundamental notion that the impersonality and universality of Western law are two of its essential values. Here again, he places himself in sharp and explicit juxtaposition to Confucian values. He draws a stark and striking contrast at one point between a state in which the administration of justice depends on the virtue of the judge and a state in which justice depends on a universal, impersonal system of laws. In China all law is a matter of the "noble ruling the mean." "When they are benevolent they may be like fathers and mothers to the people. When they are cruel, they may be like wolves."[8] A moral system embodied in impersonal law is stable and unchanging. In China laws can be changed by rulers.[9] When law is based on the goodness of rulers, it is built on a capricious and unstable foundation. Here we have what almost amounts to the quintessential critique of a "government of good men" from the point of view of a "government of law," and as such it represents a frontal assault on the whole Confucian philosophy of government. Yen Fu even goes so far as to praise the famous, reputedly "legalist" minister of the ancient principality of "Ch'i," Kuan Chung: "I have always stated that among the many thinkers of the Spring and Autumn period none was closer in his thought to the thought of the nineteenth century." Kuan Chung was hardly a liberal in any sense, but he had seen the relevance of an impersonal, universal system of laws to the wealth and power of the state. In the West, however, the concept of an impersonal, universal law was associated with the most exalted virtues—with public spirit, patriotism, liberty, and equality.

In the first instance, therefore, Montesquieu is a teacher of the Western philosophy of law, and what China needs is not merely new laws (penal, civil, and constitutional) but above all the new values which lie behind the Western English conception of the law, values which represent nothing less than a repudiation of fundamental Confucian views.

Beyond this, however, Montesquieu also appeals to Yen Fu in his capacity as "social scientist"—as a pioneer in the field of comparative sociology. Durkheim, in his essays on Montesquieu and Rousseau,[10] hails Montesquieu as the forefather of modern "scientific" sociology. He strongly emphasizes that Montesquieu's three "ideal types" of polity—despotism, monarchy, and republicanism—are really integrated social systems in which law, government, religion, economics, and social psychology are all bound together by necessary "functional" relationships. Yen Fu's own appreciation of this side of Montesquieu is made amply clear in his introduction where he rapturously exclaims, "In the vast forest of human events and vicissitudes, in the patterns underlying the mesh of events, he has sought out the causes and consequences of all the mores, customs, political systems, and religious beliefs of all the five continents."[11] The ideogram here translated "sought out" is the ideogram used by Yen Fu to refer to the procedure of induction. Montesquieu had attempted to derive a knowledge of reality by basing himself on human experience, and, while in Yen Fu's view many of his inductions were wrong and based on faulty information, he belongs to that honorable company, including Smith and Spencer, who derive their knowledge of the world from the facts. To the method of induction he also adds the method of comparative socio-political analysis —a method which Yen Fu as a pioneer in comparative studies from the Chinese side cannot help appreciating.[12]

The fact remains, however, that Yen Fu does not need Montesquieu to teach him the doctrine that socio-political systems are structures all of whose parts are linked together by determinate laws. This had already been clearly demonstrated by Spencer. Nor does he need Montesquieu to reinforce the "conservative" strain in his thought—the notion that the only social changes which are feasible are those which correspond to the possibilities provided by the given socio-political structure (although he does use him for this purpose). Spencer's teachings were indeed much more nearly complete in this respect. While Montesquieu is, on the whole, concerned with socio-political structures as static types, Spencer adds the evolutionary time dimension. The reformer must concern himself not only with the possibilities of the given social-political structure but also with determining the stage of evolutionary development. As a pioneer sociologist, indeed, Montesquieu suffers from the grievous inconsistency already pointed out between belief in the power of legislators and sociological determinism. His nineteenth-century interpreter, Durkheim, while claiming him as a precursor, deplores his eighteenth-century naïveté. Like Spencer, Durkheim fancies himself the completely detached scientist examining the impersonal forces

of social development from the outside. He does not prescribe legislation. Montesquieu, however, cannot refrain
from interlacing his social analyses with advice to the legislator.[13] He very often attributes to the statesman the power
to shape society. The legislator in a monarchy must act
within the framework of conditions which pertain to the
monarchic "ideal type." He is hedged in by all sorts of
unwritten mores, climactic factors, and other limiting conditions. Within the area bounded by these conditions, however, he can practice his art and attempt to raise his society
to its highest possible level of attainment. Durkheim scorns
this naïveté. Montesquieu, we learn, fails to realize that
"laws [framed by legislators] are nothing more than well-
defined mores." Men, including legislators, are themselves
products of the impersonal forces of social development.
Montesquieu's view that legislators can shape society to
conform to certain ethical ends is a symptom of the fact
that he still "preserves the antique confusion of art and
science."[14]

One reason, of course, for the complacency with which
Durkheim and Spencer (and also the later Marx) were
able to banish the conscious will of men as a factor in
shaping the socio-historic process was their faith that "the
forces of progress," the whole socio-historic process, was
moving in the direction of their hopes. They could view the
process ostensibly *sine studio et ira* because the process was
remarkably responsive to their aspirations.[15] In Montesquieu, however, there is no clear notion of progress as an
impersonal process; Durkheim states quite explicitly that the
"lack of the notion of progress"[16]—is one of his most glaring
defects. Montesquieu's ideal types of monarchy, despotism,
and republicanism are static, self-contained structures without any inbuilt principle of change and evolution. "He does
not know the process by which society even while remaining always faithful to its nature continually becomes something new,"[17] and presumably something better. It might

be added here that, precisely because he does not share such hopes in an impersonal scheme of progress, Montesquieu must hope that improvements in human affairs can be brought about by the conscious will and intention of intelligent legislators.

Now Yen Fu's situation is such that he must share both the optimistic determinism of Spencer and Durkheim and the faith of Montesquieu that the conscious will of men may affect the course of events. As the disciple of Spencer he is thoroughly impregnated with the conception of evolutionary progress and is extremely conscious of the defect in Montesquieu of which Durkheim speaks. The historic-evolutionary, optimistic determinisms of the nineteenth-century social philosophers are of an entirely different order from the static, depressing determinism of Montesquieu, and Yen Fu is able to criticize Montesquieu most effectively from the platform of nineteenth-century notions of evolutionary progress—particularly Montesquieu's implication that China must forever remain immured within the prison-house of "despotism." It is by no means accidental that Yen Fu completed his translation of the obscure little work of Edward Jenks, *History of Politics*,[18] even while working on the *Spirit of the Laws*. What Jenks does, in effect, is to provide a short account of historic evolution in terms of socio-political stages, each growing organically out of the other. As against Montesquieu's static "ideal types," he provides a unilinear, universal scheme of progress from the past into the future. To the extent that Yen Fu accepts Montesquieu's typology he attempts to locate all of Montesquieu's types along a time-continuum corresponding to Jenks's scheme of savage, patriarchal, military, and industrial societies. Democracy to Yen Fu is not merely a description of a state of affairs which happened to exist in the ancient city-state and might never recur. It is rather the inevitable "wave of the future" —the culmination of human progress corresponding to the

Spencer-Jenks stage of industrial society. "It is the very highest point of human development. It will be democracy which will one day bring about good government on all five continents."[19]

As against Montesquieu, Yen Fu fervently embraces the promise for the future embedded in the evolutionary determinism of Spencer and Durkheim. As a Chinese, however, he cannot entirely share their optimistic quietism— their reliance on the "spontaneous" forces of history. He must face the brute fact that Chinese development has not, after all, corresponded to the laws of social evolution as outlined by Spencer and Jenks.[20] In his preface to Jenks, he will speculate on why this was the case, but, whatever the reason, he must hope that conscious human effort—on the part of those who know—will again set in motion the stalled motor of Chinese history. To this extent he cannot but sympathize with Montesquieu's "confusion of art and science." As a vicarious legislator profoundly concerned with "changing the laws" he must be concerned with the question, What to do? and cannot accept *in toto* Durkheim's fanatical sociological determinism or Spencer's hatred of the meddling legislator who dares to tinker with the machinery of social evolution. If Montesquieu is a precursor of sociology, his sociology is centered in the political, and in the area of politics he continues to hope that men may make decisions which will shape the course of human affairs. Yen Fu obviously must share his hope.

In fact, the combination of a nineteenth-century deterministic scheme of social evolution with the eighteenth-century faith in the power of the legislator makes a most formidable mixture. Unlikely as the comparison may seem, Yen Fu can be compared here with Lenin and many intellectuals in the more "undeveloped" parts of the world. The notion of a predetermined path of social evolution moving inexorably from a known past into a known future is enormously attractive and inspiring. At the same time one is painfully aware that one's own society has not been moving satisfactorily along the path indicated.[21] One must therefore hope that the human conscious will—the "legislator," as it were—will be able to push one's society onto the prescribed path. To Spencer and Durkheim the movement to the appointed goal is carried forward by the vast impersonal socio-historic forces. To Yen Fu (and to Lenin) the stages of social history (at least at the latter end) have become in fact a kind of static, clearly indicated path or pre-established series of steps, but the dynamic principle pushing mankind forward along the path must be sought in the conscious will of men who know the way and are able to guide their societies from the past into the future.[22] As Yen Fu had stated long before, the sage himself is a factor in destiny. From Spencer's scheme of social evolution, Yen Fu derives his high hopes for the future. From Montesquieu he derives a faith that an elite of legislators and educators may take action to realize these hopes.

As in his treatment of Huxley, however, Yen Fu's stance toward Montesquieu is often highly critical. By and large, we find that his criticism is directed precisely against the type of depressing, hope-restricting determinism which he finds in Montesquieu, particularly those forms of naturalistic and static-sociological determinism which seem to deny a priori the hope of further development for China.

Thus Yen Fu refuses to accept Montesquieu's classification of China as the prototype of despotism. Here Montesquieu's views not only limit the future; they also caricature the past. One might suppose that this represents a revulsion of national pride against Montesquieu's highly unflattering account of the Chinese state. While this motive is undoubtedly present, Yen Fu by no means rejects all of Montesquieu's strictures on the Chinese state. On the contrary, he finds many of them astonishingly perceptive. What he feels he must reject is the notion that China really fits Montesquieu's ideal type of despotism. He must reject it not only because it does not accord with the facts but precisely because it fails to get at the heart of what is really wrong with the traditional Chinese polity.

He cannot, in the first place, reconcile Montesquieu's crude image of the despotic state with his own perception of the complexities of Chinese history. Montesquieu asserts that while the "principle" or moral cement of republicanism is virtue, and that of monarchy, honor, the moral cement of a despotic polity is fear. "The immense power of the prince passes entirely into the hands of those to whom he entrusts it. People capable of estimating themselves very highly might be in a position to bring about revolutions. Fear must therefore be used to beat down courage and crush the slightest feeling of ambition."[23] Yen Fu refuses to concede that the Chinese state has rested on nothing but fear. As against the Jesuits in China who speak of its admirable government which "combines the principles of fear, honor, and virtue,"[24] Montesquieu cries out, "What is honor among people who can only be made to act by bastinadoes?"[25] (Montesquieu in his polemic against the Jesuits appeals, incidentally, to the testimony of "our traders.") He also refers to the brutal action taken by the Yung-cheng emperor against his brothers and goes on to imply that the Jesuits have a peculiar affinity for despotism.

In reply Yen Fu points out that in China it had always been assumed that gentlemen were governed in their behavior by the rules of propriety, while "mean men" depended on punishments. He also points out that even in the European lands of "honor" cruel punishments were not unknown.[26] To Yen Fu it is patently obvious that fear of punishment has not been the only motive of action of the Chinese ruling class. If monarchy in the West is based on the principle of "honor" as the guiding ethos of the ruling class, then it is obviously clear that the whole "system of rites" (*li*—'the norms of proper behavior') has been the

Chinese equivalent of the principle of honor. "Democracy is governed by virtue, monarchy by *li*, and despotism by punishment. *Li* places great emphasis on rank and title and takes great delight in honor, while punishment exercises restraint through fear."[27] Yen Fu finds both of these principles operative in Chinese history,[28] and therefore cannot take seriously Montesquieu's sharp distinction between monarchy and despotism. "According to Montesquieu a despotic state is one which is based on the spirit of fear and in which the arbitrary (*wu tao*) will of the prince is the constitution. I strongly doubt whether there has ever existed for long anywhere, whether in Asia or Europe, a political system of this type."[29] Even evil rulers in China have had to claim some moral basis of legitimate authority transcending their own individual wills and the machinery of terror. "They have had to say, I have received my authority from heaven and I model myself on my ancestors,"[30] and the extent to which they have relied on fear or the moral sanctions of *li* has varied with the ruler and with the circumstances.

In contradistinction to Montesquieu, Yen Fu recognizes only two fundamental polar types of polity—monarchic and democratic. "In monarchic government the authority of the state proceeds from the one and is diffused among the many. In a democracy it proceeds from the many and converges on the one."[31] Despotism is simply a perversion of the monarchic type and, to this extent, China has indeed known despotism under evil rulers. When Montesquieu states—"A monarchy is a government in which one man governs through fundamental laws. I have spoken of intermediate, subordinate, and dependent powers. Actually in a monarchy the prince is the source of all political and civil power. These fundamental laws necessarily suppose mediating channels through which the power flows, for if there is nothing in the state but the momentary and capricious will of one man, nothing can be fixed and consequently there can be no fundamental law"[32]—Yen Fu sees in this a good description of the traditional state in China when it operated at its best. "When one had a hard-working ruler above and reflective, diligent ministers below, they all stressed the fixed institutions of the preceding reigns. When this was the case, the divergence from what Montesquieu describes in this passage [on despotism] was enormous . . . if, according to Montesquieu, any government which has long-established, fixed, fundamental laws is constitutional, then the Chinese state was constitutional for four thousand years."[33] The real difference, however, is between states in which the ruler is above the law, and modern constitutional states in which the ruler himself must obey the constitution. Where the ruler is above the law, instances of despotism are always possible.

This is not the place to attempt an assessment of Yen Fu's critique of Montesquieu's concept of despotism. Yet one might perhaps note that Yen Fu underestimates the factor of power. In Montesquieu's conception of monarchy, the power of the king is actually limited by that of the estates—the "intermediary powers"—whom he tends to regard "in some sense, as tribunes of the people."[34] At one point Yen Fu seems to acknowledge this difference, but implicit in his whole argument is the view that the scholar-official class in China, animated as it was by its own principle of "honor" embedded in *li*, also acted as a kind of intermediary power. The question of whether this class was simply the servile tool of despotic power, or whether it represented in some sense an intermediate power, remains an open matter of discussion among students of Chinese history to this very day. Whatever may be the case, Yen Fu will not acknowledge that the Chinese state has for thousands of years corresponded to Montesquieu's crude notion of despotism. Whatever may have been its divergences from the European model of monarchy, it was a form of monarchy and as such could be placed within the stream of socio-political evolution. China was a monarchy, and the universal militant-monarchic phase of human history was one which China could also transcend.

Yen Fu's rejection of Montesquieu's predilection for explanations in terms of climatic-geographic determination is, of course, closely linked to the rejection of the effort to squeeze China into the despotism category. Montesquieu himself becomes involved in enormous self-contradictions on this whole matter of the climatic-geographic factor, on which he leans most heavily in his treatment of Asia ("On the Climate of Asia"). Asia, we are informed, has no temperate zone, properly speaking. "Areas located in a very cold climate are in immediate contact with areas in a very warm climate—that is, Turkey, Persia, the Mogul (Empire), China, Korea, and Japan."[35] From this "fact" it follows that in Asia nations confront each other in terms of strength and weakness. Brave and active peoples are in immediate contact with lazy, timid, and effeminate peoples. It is inevitable that the weak should be conquered by the strong, thus leading to a spirit of servitude. In temperate Europe, peoples "who are in contact have approximately the same degree of courage."

Yen Fu decisively rejects the notion that China has no temperate zone as simply false and points to the fact that there are many temperate areas of the world which have remained uncivilized. Again, he rejects the notion that the great despotic empires of Asia are a result of the fact that Asia consists of broad plains with few internal barriers. Yen Fu points out that although Germany occupies the central plains of Europe it has only recently achieved national unity. In the past it was made up of small principalities. The unification of Germany has been more the effect of the laws introduced by Stein and Scharnhorst[36] than of its geographic fate.

In the end Yen Fu must refuse to climate and geography the enormous role which Montesquieu assigns to them. "In accounting for the relative strength of the two races, one must take into account climate, geography, and man. No one of these factors can be neglected or ignored."[37] "Religion, philosophy, literature, and art all have a most subtle effect on the minds of men. If the people of Europe had not had the guidance of Greece, then carried forward by Rome, and if this had not been mediated by the Christian and Mohammedan religions, Europe could not have reached its present state. The fact that China and India have not been destroyed by foreign races is due to their millenial culture."[38]

The stress on the cultural factor is, of course, entirely consistent with Yen Fu's whole outlook, and we will see it further emphasized in his commentary on Jenks. It is entirely consistent with his own conception of social evolution. On the other hand, the static, naturalistic determinism of Montesquieu is unacceptable to him. Like most of the Chinese Marxists of a later period, he cannot accept those forms of social theory which lean heavily on geographic determinism. He cannot believe that China has been doomed by geographic fate to remain fixed in the mold of the patriarchic-monarchic-despotic stage of socio-political evolution.

All this does not mean that Yen Fu has become an apologist for the Chinese traditional state. Actually he responds most readily to some of Montesquieu's most critical observations on that state. The charge of despotism, in his view, hardly touches the heart of the matter. It is not that this state was much more arbitrary or capriciously cruel than most other states in the militant-monarchic stage of human development. It is rather its debility and passivity which arouse his exasperation. The authoritarianism of the Chinese state has been negative. Instead of fostering human energies and capacities, instead of propelling the evolution from a homogeneous simple society to a highly developed, highly differentiated and articulated society, it has done everything possible to inhibit that process. By attaching all social prestige to government service, all the intelligence and talent of the empire have been channeled exclusively in this direction, and the division of social labor has been inhibited.[39] "Even our students who now go abroad specialize for the most part in law, politics, and finance, and very few turn their attention to medicine, engineering, or biology."[40] It is only when China has a new constitution guaranteeing equal prestige and honor to all lines of human endeavor that this situation will be remedied.

When Montesquieu points out that, in China, religion, mores, laws, and manners are all confounded under the category of "rites,"[41] Yen Fu finds himself completely awed by such penetrating perspicacity. It is not only the social division of labor which has been inhibited in China but also the differentiation among the various spheres of culture. "Not only did the statesmen of China fail to differentiate between 'rites' and laws but even confounded religion and learning. I have heard that the more advanced the stage of evolution, the greater the degree of heterogeneity and the clearer the distinctions among things; and with the less advanced, the opposite is true. The situation in our country can be taken as a clear demonstration of this."[42] The pervasive and paralytic hold of this all-inclusive system of rites, however, reminds Yen Fu much more of Spencer's description of patriarchal society than of Montesquieu's ideal type of despotism. "The people and even the sages were circumscribed by their habits. They knew only the patriarchal stage of human development and were unconscious of the ulterior stages of human development."[43] The system of rites is not evidence of despotism but of arrested development.

Finally, we again meet the charge that the Chinese state had done nothing to foster the "people's virtue." When Montesquieu waxes dithyrambic over the close connection between equality and patriotism in the idealized democratic city-states of the ancient world, this, of course, reinforces Yen Fu's insistence on the close connection between equality and the strength of the state. When Montesquieu states that in spite of their rites the Chinese people are the "craftiest people in the world," Yen Fu is not overly inclined to quarrel with him, embittered as he is by his fellow-countrymen's narrow absorption in their private lives. The Chinese state had done nothing to develop a sense of "public spirit"—a sense of citizenship. "In the West, people are free in matters which involve their own individual affairs and others cannot interfere. In matters involving the whole society all men may be concerned. In China it is not so. The affairs of society are confined to the state and only the sovereign and officials can concern themselves with them."[44] Thus the "small men" naturally concern themselves exclusively with their own narrow private interests which they never identify with the interests of society. Essentially we find here a reiteration of the charges made in the early essays. The patriarchal-monarchic state of China has negated the moral, physical, and intellectual energies of the Chinese people. Its essential earmark has not been ferocity and demonic power but a craven yearning for security and tranquillity above all else.

If Yen Fu must reject Montesquieu's account of despotism, he is also highly critical of Montesquieu's excessively high-flown view of the prerequisites of democracy. His conception of democracy as an ideal type is, of course, based on an extreme idealization of the Greek and Roman city-state. The fact that he was unable to find any actual example of democracy in the contemporary world (Venice, of course, was an oligarchic republic) facilitated this idealization of antique democracy. In the first place, he finds his prototype of the republic (consisting of the two types, aristocratic and democratic) only in the city-state. From this he concludes that "it is the nature of a republic to possess only a small territory. Otherwise it can hardly survive." For this he provides numerous reasons. "In a large republic there are large fortunes and, as a consequence, little moderation of spirit—interests become particularized. A man feels that he can be happy, great, glorious without his fatherland . . . In a small republic the public welfare is better perceived, better known, closer to each citizen."[45] These and many other considerations lead him to the view that the only political form appropriate to the modern, extended nation-state is some form of monarchy.

Here Yen Fu believes himself in a position to contradict Montesquieu flatly from the vantage point of the twentieth century. "Montesquieu's contentions may be true of ancient states. As applied to the present world, they are almost completely untrue . . . The area covered by the United States is of the order of China. France is about half the size; yet they are both genuine democracies."[46] Montesquieu had completely failed to foresee the advances in the technology of communications. "The effect of ships, railways, postal systems, and telegraph has been to shrink the five continents into provinces and counties; what was impossible in ancient times is now no longer difficult."[47]

This emphasis on the positive correlation between technology and democracy leads to a much more serious objection to Montesquieu's conception of democracy. A democracy according to him rests on the moral cement of "virtue," and virtue is described in terms of antique austerity. Virtue implies nothing less than a "renunciation of self"—a total devotion to the interests of the fatherland. "This love [of the laws and the fatherland], demanding a continual preference for the public interest over one's own, establishes the virtue of the individual."[48] Furthermore, virtue also involves an ideal of frugality and of the simple life. "The love of democracy is again the love of frugality. Everyone must have the same advantages, enjoy the same pleasures, and form the same hopes—something which can be expected only where one has a general frugality."[49] To Montesquieu democracy, equality, and the simple frugal life form part of one inextricable whole. It is not only that he does not foresee the possibility of a general economic development which will enrich all simultaneously, but democracy (direct democracy) requires the immediate public virtue of each citizen. Today the notion that democracy and industrial development are "functionally interdependent" has become such a widely held cliché that we often forget that some of the most ardent democrats of the eighteenth century shared Montesquieu's view concerning the relationship between democracy and the frugal life. Thomas Jefferson's dread of the effects of "manufacture" on democracy is a good case in point.[50]

It must, of course, be added that Montesquieu does not find a necessary link between personal liberty and democracy. On the contrary, he finds that they do not necessarily go together. "Democracy and aristocracy are not free states by their nature. Political liberty can only be found in moderate governments."[51] "It is true that in democracies the people seem to do what they wish, but political liberty does not consist of doing what one wishes. In a state, in a society where there are laws, liberty can only consist of doing what one ought to do."[52] Here we have in Montesquieu an intimation of Rousseau's notion of the "general will" of the people standing in conflict with the will of individuals. The liberty of the individual, on the other hand, is found most fully realized in the constitution of England, which is a liberal monarchic state. Unlike democracy, liberty and wealth may go hand in hand, as is clearly proven by the case of "the English, who are a people who more than any others in the world have known how to make religion, commerce, and liberty prevail."[53]

With the example of the United States, Great Britain, and France before him, Yen Fu finds that he can reject a large part of Montesquieu's image. He finds that liberty, equality (of opportunity), and economic dynamism are all part of one syndrome. He had not rejected the anti-economic bias of Mencius in order to exalt it in ancient Greece and Rome. He had not translated the whole of Adam Smith with its exaltation of enlightened self-interest in order to re-embrace the morality of "renunciation of self." The facts of history have shown that liberty and democracy have gone along with enlightened self-interest and that all three have led to the enormous wealth of the modern industrial world. Dalembert, he points out, had already refuted Montesquieu's exaltation of "renunciation of self" as the moral base of democracy. Montesquieu's democratic virtue, states Dalembert, is another name for patriotism. Patriotism may require a suspension of self-interest, but in the end the interests of the individual are served. When the country enjoys well-being, its citizens will also be well off. Thus the virtuous citizen has his own long-term interests in view. Yen Fu might have added that the industrious citizen serves his country not only when he sacrifices for the state, as in war, but even in the very course of pursuing his own enlightened self-interest. Democracy and wealth are mutually reinforcing. Where the people enjoy prosperity they will prize their freedom and equality and hence be filled with patriotic fervor. On the other hand, democracy itself is a basic cause of economic advance. "The perfect organization of European and American commercial companies is practically the same as democracy . . . Despotic-monarchic peoples have no idea of equality. Thus China has never come close to anything like the company organization."⁵⁴

When Montesquieu draws a distinction between two modes of poverty—"the poverty of those who have been rendered poor by the harshness of government and are incapable of almost any virtue because their poverty is part of their servitude" and of "those who are only poor because they have disdained or not known the comforts of life,"⁵⁵

Yen Fu refuses to accept this sharp distinction. Undoubtedly Montesquieu would class the degraded poverty of China as belonging to the former class. Yet Yen Fu claims that if he must assign weights, 70 per cent of Chinese poverty belongs to the latter class. Chinese thought has also exalted frugality and simplicity. If these are virtues, China has known virtue. It is a type of virtue, however, which he rejects, whether it be Roman or Chinese. The nineteenth century has demonstrated that all good things go together. Liberty and equality, the rule of law and democracy, wealth and power are all poured out of the same cornucopia.

It remains to inquire whether Yen Fu's interpretation of Montesquieu is a manifestation of a liberal or conservative tendency. If by conservative tendency one means an orientation to the traditional Chinese, enough has been said to indicate that there is no evidence for this. Yen Fu remains imbedded in his Western premises. Montesquieu does serve, however, to reinforce a conservative strain which had already been amply fed by Spencer. Social and political reform are enormously difficult because they cannot be implemented in a socio-historic vacuum. They must relate to the nature of the environment in which they are inaugurated. Art must be based on science. One need not accept Montesquieu's theory of "once a despotism always a despotism" in order to concede that a people formed in a "patriarchal-monarchic-despotic" environment cannot be transformed overnight. When Yen Fu reads Montesquieu's description of the education of the people under a despotism, "he cannot help weeping . . . Our laws must be changed but it is not easy to change them!"[56] One can only begin at the beginning. One must first educate the legislators and only then can the legislators educate the people and gradually create a new constitution. To promulgate new laws without creating the "spirit" within which they must operate is labor lost.

At a time when the clamor for a constitution and an

effective representative assembly was soaring even among constitutional monarchists, Yen Fu finds that "we ought not to create a national assembly immediately." He has no confidence in the quality of legislators who will emerge. What he does favor, however, is the creation of local district representative bodies, elected by qualified persons, to carry on deliberations with the ministers of state. Not only will this create a basis for local self-government, but it will be above all else an educational device. "If the people can be made to concern themselves with the strength of the race and the survival of the state, their enlightenment will proceed rapidly."[57] The people will finally learn to identify their interests with the interests of the state. Like Mill, Spencer, and Huxley, Montesquieu lends no support whatsoever to any belief in the innate wisdom of the people. The wisdom of the people is strictly potential and can be made manifest only by a long and arduous process. "The equality of the people must have its *raison d'être* and cannot be forced. When they are truly equal in knowledge, strength, and virtue, then the rule of democracy can be achieved."[58]

Thus far, Yen Fu is simply reiterating a long-held view. However, one can also find in the commentaries an unexpected, ominous crack in his liberalism. Montesquieu has forcefully called to his attention a distinction of which he had not been clearly conscious hitherto—the distinction between democracy and individual liberty. Montesquieu's conception of antique democracy is that since laws were made by all, by a sort of "general will," the individual could not have any liberty as against the city. The liberty of the ancient democracy was only the liberty to participate in making the laws of the state. "The people seems to do what it wants, but political liberty does not consist of doing what one wants."[59] In Yen Fu's translation this somewhat vaguely expressed distinction appears as the "freedom of the nation-society (*kuo-ch'ün chih tze-yu*)" and "the freedom of the individual (*hsiao-chi chih tze-yu*)."[60] In the past he had regarded both of these freedoms as complementary. Now we are suddenly informed that "when we view the situation of China, we realize that the liberty of the individual is not yet a matter of first urgency. It is rather the matter of maintaining ourselves against the aggression of other nations which will brook no delay. The freedom of the nation-society is more urgent than the liberty of the individual. In seeking the freedom of the nation we must consolidate the counsels and energies of our society. Such a consolidation can be attained only if everyone is made to love his country and if every one is made to feel a sense of duty toward it. If we wish to instill in the people a sense of duty and create a love of country, we must induce them to concern themselves with national affairs and to familiarize themselves with foreign affairs."[61] It is on these grounds that Yen Fu proceeds to make his plea for local assemblies. It is not entirely clear what types of "individual liberty" are here being pushed into the background. It is probably not the liberty of the entrepreneur to pursue commerce and industry, or of other men to pursue other socially useful careers. All the modes of liberty which involve the "energy of faculty" are themselves vital parts of the social power which must be mobilized. One cannot help feeling that it is those forms of "liberty from society" which pertain more exclusively to the individual himself which are being assigned second priority. If this is a sign of "growing conservatism," it also foreshadows a very similar point of view expressed by Sun Yat-sen in his later years when he was also to maintain that what China required was not the liberty of the individual but the freedom of the state. It is the first intimation by Yen Fu that not all forms of liberty may be relevant to wealth and power and as such points to the future more than to the past.[62]

In spite of this crack, however, the *Spirit of the Laws* does not mark any essential retreat from his basic commitments. It is here that he acclaims democracy as the very highest point of human development. It is here and in the Jenks translation that he asserts, as against Montesquieu, his fervent faith in a unilinear progressive evolution of mankind toward democracy. Here he affirms the morality of enlightened self-interest against the morality of "renunciation of self," and it is here that he fervently espouses in opposition to the whole Confucian tradition the impersonal "rule of law" against any form of "rule of good men."

CHAPTER VIII

A History of Politics

THE TRANSLATION of Edward Jenks's[1] *History of Politics* in 1904 may be viewed as a kind of pendant to the *Spirit of the Laws*. Yen Fu refers to it throughout his commentaries in the latter work, and, as already pointed out, Jenks seems to have served the function of correcting the static,[2] "nonprogressive" nature of Montesquieu's analysis. Yen Fu had, of course, become a fervent convert to a progressive, evolutionary account of human history as early as his first contacts with Darwin and Spencer. It was Spencer who had taught him to think of human history in terms of the organic growth of socio-political systems over time. It was precisely the static nature of Montesquieu's analysis which impelled him to cast about for a manageable tract which would serve as a corrective by providing a succinct account of human history in terms of a universal, unilinear scheme of social development.

Jenks's scheme corresponds in the main to Spencer's views of social evolution but diverges from them in certain interesting respects. In his simple, unilinear scheme of periodization, Jenks proceeds from savage "totemistic" society through "patriarchal" society to the "state" or "political society." Like Spencer he traces the rise of the state (the modern nation-state) to its defensive-military function. It is interesting to note, however, that the distinction between the "military stage" and the "industrial stage" which is so clearly marked and essential in Spencer is blurred, or rather, invisible in Jenks. As a political scientist he is naturally concerned with political institutions. The fact remains that the center of attention in Jenks's account is the emergence of the modern, "rationalized" state, and not the industrial revolution. To Jenks the crucial fact of "political society" is that "all communities in the purely political stage will be found to be varieties of a single type, the type, namely, which is distinguished by *sovereignty*. Somewhere in all communities of this type there resides an authority which, in the last resort, controls absolutely and beyond appeal the actions of every individual member of that community."[3]

While Jenks tends to imply that the British constitution represents the highest form of human polity, he is more fascinated by the features shared by all modern nation-states than by those which divide them. By the same token, he by no means shares Spencer's fanaticism on the question of the role of the state in modern societies. While sharing his view that the state was "in origin a military organization"[4] he does not seem to feel that the state will wither away in industrial society (which is never discussed as a separate category). He has, to be sure, not departed in any essential respect from the liberal tradition and is unenthusiastic about "the unlimited extension of state administration"[5] and "the much governed countries of continental Europe,"[6] but he asserts nevertheless that "it would be the

worst kind of pedantry to lay down hard and fast lines
for the limits of state administration."[7] He seems to be
entirely unconscious of Spencer's distinction between the
"spontaneous" modes of cooperation represented by the
modern industrial system and the "artificial, coercive" organizations of the state.

All of this reflects the shifting currents of social thought
in England at the turn of the century when Spencer's viru-
lent brand of antistatist liberalism was rapidly receding.
It is interesting to note that Yen Fu nowhere betrays any
awareness of the difference between Spencer and Jenks.
As already indicated, Spencer's sharp distinction between
the "military" and "industrial" stages had never made any
deep impression upon him in the first place. He had responded to Spencer's positive exhortations that the energy
and initiative of the individual be given full play, but he
had never absorbed the dogma that this could be achieved
only by subtracting from the power of the state. Since he
had never been particularly sensible to Spencer's message
on these matters, he is not sensible to the difference between Spencer and Jenks.[8]

Fundamentally, the Jenks work provides Yen Fu with an
opportunity to underline his profound commitment to an
organic conception of social evolution. In his introduction
he forcefully reiterates the analogy between the growth of
mankind and of the biological individual. The human race
passes through certain determinate stages of growth just as
surely as the individual passes through "infancy, youth, maturity, and old age."[9] Above all, this is a universal, unilinear pattern common to all mankind. "Examining the
stages of evolution of all human societies we find that they
all invariably begin in the totemic stage, pass through a
patriarchal stage, and develop into the stage of the state."[10]
Yen Fu is as profoundly committed to a unilinear, universal account of the evolution of the human race as are
the Communist historians of a later period.[11] Like them, he

passionately accepts the view that the historic evolution of the West represents the normal path of human evolution, for he is ardently committed to the goals to which that path presumably leads. Like them also, he must inevitably confront the dilemma of China's undeniable failure to pass through all the stages of what is supposedly a universal pattern of development. In terms of the very criteria of progress accepted by both himself and orthodox Communist dogma, China has fallen short. We have already grazed this problem at many points. It is in his introduction to the Jenks translation, however, that Yen Fu finally confronts it head on.

The Communists have met this problem with the *deus ex machina* of imperialism. China would have passed through its normal stages of historic evolution had it not been for the intervention of the inhibitory forces of Western imperialism which had blocked the forces of evolution. This explanation is not available to Yen Fu. He constantly deplores the effects of Western imperialism on China, but the imperialism of the West is in his view a normal result of the unhampered processes of the struggle for existence. China's inability to participate in this struggle must be explained in terms of its own debilities as an organism. He will not stand in moral judgment on the Faustian dynamism of the West. The real question is, Why has China proved unfit to survive? "How strange is our Chinese society!" Yen Fu exclaims at the beginning of his introduction. "All human societies have in accordance with the stages of evolution begun in a totemistic stage, passed through a patriarchal stage and evolved into the state . . . This sequence has been as certain as the sequence of the four seasons in nature or as infancy, youth, maturity, and old age in the individual."[12]

He then goes on to point out that there have, however, been great differences in the pace of development. While the West pursued a relatively slow course of development through the end of feudalism (treated as a transitional stage from patriarchal to "political" society), its pace of development in the last two hundred years has been breathtaking. "On the other hand, when we observe the history of China our most reliable records show that during the period from T'ang Yü until Chou—a space of over 2,000 years—we already had a feudal stage, and so-called patriarchal society had already achieved its full development. Its sages were the sages of a patriarchal society. Its institutions and prescriptions were patriarchal institutions and prescriptions. Now when things have reached the limits of their actualization, change must ensue." As a matter of fact, change did indeed occur. With the rise of the universal Ch'in empire under the leadership of Ch'in Shih Huang-ti, one does have something which looks very much like the transition from a patriarchal to a centralized, bureaucratic, "military state." Yet, having completed what appeared to be the passage to the military state, the habits, customs, and thought patterns of the Chinese people have remained those of a patriarchal people. "With them the beginnings were slow and the end was fast. With us the beginnings were fast and the latter end has been slow."[13]

Yen Fu is shrewd enough to realize that this is a descriptive, not an explanatory, formula. There must be some reason why progress in China had come to a halt. Why had "patriarchalism" established its strangle hold on Chinese society? Yen Fu has rejected Montesquieu's geographic determinism and his formulas concerning the distinct nature of despotism. The Communist "imperialist" explanation would undoubtedly have seemed shallow and unconvincing to him, since he would probably have asked why a China which had passed over the brink of the "military state" stage as early as 221 B.C. had been unable to achieve sufficient wealth and power over a period of two millennia to be able to meet Western imperialism on its own terms.

The fact is that one can find scattered throughout Yen

Fu's works occasional adumbrations of what might be called a subsidiary circumstantial explanation. The very fact that China had achieved speedy unification and had remained unchallenged by any superior external power had atrophied its capacity for struggle. His essential explanation, however, remains a cultural-spiritual explanation. The doctrines of the sages had frozen and absolutized the ideas of a patriarchal society. The sages had been all too successful in imposing these ideas on posterity and thus inhibiting the march of evolution. The ideas of the sages had had socio-historical roots within a given historical-social formation, and yet they had attained a kind of autonomous potency of their own. We return again to the fatal cultural decision mentioned in Yen Fu's early essay. The Chinese ruling class had opted for the peace, harmony, and stasis assured by a patriarchal state of affairs. The outlook of the sages, which had over the centuries congealed into a fixed habit of thought, had acted as a kind of inhibiting enzyme stunting the plant of social evolution, while the emerging thought of the West had acted as a growth hormone giving free vent to the forces of natural evolution. At what point, however, had this crucial divergence of cultural paths taken place? In his early essays Yen Fu had tended to see Darwin, Smith, Watt, and Spencer as the great culture heroes—in other words, to find the intellectual origins of Western progress in a period no earlier than the enlightenment era. However, in the commentaries on *The Spirit of Laws* and *A History of Politics* we discern a new tendency to seek the origins of the great cultural divergence at a much earlier point in time.

Here we find a serious qualification to Yen Fu's unilinear conception of human history. The general morphology of social evolution had indeed been the same in East and West, yet important cultural divergences had made themselves manifest as early as the patriarchal stage of human history. Montesquieu had turned Yen Fu's attention most forcefully to the fact that a concern for something like liberty, equality, and democracy had already emerged in the Greco-Roman city-states. Yen Fu, however, has been thoroughly convinced by Jenks that the Greco-Roman world was still in the patriarchal stage of human development. When Montesquieu extols the power of paternal authority in Greece and Rome as a support to democracy, Yen Fu rebukes him, pointing out that Greece and Rome were in fact patriarchal and that this factor "really has nothing whatsoever to do with a democratic system."[14] Yet if the city-states of Greece and Rome were patriarchal, they were patriarchal with a difference. At least two of them, Athens and Rome, had injected the ideas of liberty, equality, and democracy into the bloodstream of Western civilization. These ancient ideas were in themselves not a sufficient cause of the rise of modern democratic states, since the kind of direct self-government possible in the city-state was completely inappropriate to the modern territorial state, as Montesquieu had clearly pointed out. What was required was the invention of the institution of representative government.

In his *Lectures on Politics* of 1906 Yen Fu states that it was the Europeans who realized that "the excellent laws and beautiful ideals of the ancient city-states could be applied to the large territorial state and that the key lay in the system of representation."[15] The system of representative institutions grew painfully over the centuries in the very teeth of the dogma of Aristotle and of the seemingly clear lesson of Greek and Roman history—namely, that self-government was possible only within the confines of the city-state. It was only over a period of a thousand years that Europe had painfully developed this system which gradually flowered into democratic self-government.

When Jenks points out that in its origin parliament had had nothing to do with democracy but had been a device for collecting taxes,[16] Yen Fu remains unimpressed. "The author traces the origins of parliament to its tax-paying

function and not to any notion of conferring the enjoyment
of rights. It cannot be pointed to as the origin of people's
rights. This is certainly correct and can hardly be ques-
tioned. Yet in my view it is precisely here that we must
seek the basis of the growth of popular rights among the
Aryan people of Europe and the reason why our race could
not achieve these rights. In the very midst of the dark ages
when the founders of these states were still wild, brutish,
and unrestrained they nevertheless realized that the wealth
to be taxed belonged to the people and that if they wished
to use this wealth it was insufficient merely to state that
one needed officials to maintain order or soldiers to protect
the people. One required the assent of the people. Even
though summoning the people from all over the nation was
a highly costly matter and sometimes led the people to
complain, the trouble could not be avoided. Without consent, taxes could not be imposed and wealth could not be
obtained. Now if one were to seek this principle in China,
one could ransack our sacred classics and commentaries
without finding anywhere the assertion that there can be
no taxation without popular consent. Han Yü in his *On
the Way* goes so far as to state that if the people do not
pay their taxes, they shall be punished."[17] However limited
the interests represented in the first medieval parliaments,
however circumscribed their purposes, they represent a
living link between the democracy of ancient Greece and
Rome and of the modern world. They reflect the assertion
of rights on the part of those taxed and thus already give
evidence of that active, self-assertive, resistant psychology
of the European race which is in such striking contrast to
the passivity and inertia which have held the Chinese race
in thrall since the beginning of its own patriarchal stages.

Thus, in spite of his strong commitment to a unilinear
scheme of human history, Yen Fu is nevertheless inclined
to seek the roots of the difference between East and West
in divergences of cultural orientation which extend deep

into the past. In none of this can one possibly discern any sign of a more kindly assessment of Chinese culture. It is, on the contrary, precisely China's culture which has stunted its evolutionary growth.

We can find, however, in one of the commentaries on *A History of Politics* an uncharacteristic note of unrestrained optimism—almost ebullience. It had been the West's ability to effect a marriage between the large territorial state and democracy which had accounted for the extraordinary wealth and power of modern Europe. China was far from the achievement of democracy, but did it not, after all, possess many of the elements of a strong territorial state? In a passage on modern forms of polity, Jenks discusses the weaknesses of the federal types of government. "It is less likely than national or centralized governments to awaken profound enthusiasm or to gather round it that halo of patriotic sentiment which is one of the great safeguards of a state."[18] Observations such as these on states which are, as it were, "composite" in nature suddenly call Yen Fu's attention to the fundamental homogeneity of the Chinese people. "On translating this passage, I felt full of ardor. Why? The prospects of the yellow man may not be so unhappy after all!" The Chinese people are of one race and its numbers are vast. The concept of "race" as an important factor is, of course, very prominent in Spencer, and Yen Fu had always tended to identify the yellow race with the Chinese nation. "Its customs, mores, and geography make it easy to consolidate and difficult to separate." Whatever may have been the defects of Chinese culture, it has brought about an amazing degree of homogeneity in this vast population. If China can overcome its old practices and the incubus of obsolete customs, if it can attain knowledge, strength, and virtue, "once it becomes aware that its old laws can no longer be followed, once it realizes that its fixed views and evil customs are harmful, and once it sweeps away its corruption and pursues power earnestly, there will be no nation on the five continents like it!"[19] This uncommon note of euphoria may reflect the comparative hopefulness of the author during the early period of the Manchu reform movement. It reflects above all, of course, the constant, underlying, and unremitting preoccupation with the search for national power.

If Yen Fu's hopes are now strongly tied to the modernization efforts of the Manchu regime, he is deeply hostile to anything which interferes with these efforts, and here again he finds in Jenks a somewhat unlikely crutch for certain strongly held views. In Yen Fu's eyes the anti-Manchu racism fostered by Sun Yat-sen, Wang Ching-wei, Chang Ping-lin, and other revolutionaries represented a willful sabotage of the hopes for reform, in the interests of a revolution which could only result in hopeless chaos at the current stage of China's evolution. What was more, it represented a reactionary revival of one of the most patriarchal features of Chinese society—clan or tribal exclusivism. When Jenks points out that in a tribal society "the rule was gravely admitted that each man is entitled to be judged by the law of his race or folk no matter where he might be,"[20] this immediately reminds Yen Fu of the efforts to maintain and even exacerbate the differences between the Manchu and Han peoples. A careful reading of the passage in question would indicate that it is directed as much against the efforts of the Manchus to cling to their prerogatives as against the Han racism of the revolutionaries: "Chinese society is a combination of a patriarchal and military state. Its laws are still based on the tribe and not on the state. The Manchus established their dynasty some 300 years ago and yet the separate spheres of Manchu and Han are still maintained . . . While our parties are divided in terms of the old and the new, on the matter of racial nationalism (*min-tsu-chu-i*) they see eye to eye." The phrase *min-tsu-chu-i* used by Sun Yet-sen and the other revolutionaries was, it is true, expressly designed to point to the cleavage between the Han and the Manchu. Yen Fu was by no means incorrect in ascribing to the *tsu* of the *min-tsu* phrase a kind of racial-tribal meaning in this sense. At a time when, in his view, China required above all else a strong "military" state, in which all citizens would owe loyalty only to the state, certain obscurantist elements among the Manchus themselves, and certain revolutionary demagogues, were prepared to revive a divisive, retrograde, tribal habit of thought.

It is interesting to note that this commentary roused the particular animus of the revolutionary party, which was not prepared to find itself accused of turning back the clock of history. Hu Han-min in a rather judicious and interesting article borrows Yen Fu's own social Darwinist categories to prove that the Manchus are simply an inferior people and that China can flourish only when the superior Han race prevails,[21] while the choleric Han racialist Chang Ping-lin insists that the righteous hatred of the Manchus by the Han people is a manifestation of a genuine nationalism and not a throwback to any "tribalism."[22]

In all of this we are made acutely aware of Yen Fu's overwhelmingly intellectualistic approach to political realities. The passions, resentments, and hatreds which occupy the foreground of the political scene are irrelevant or even obstructive to the tasks imposed by political science. The growing hostility between Chinese and Manchus which was beginning to color the whole atmosphere of the times had not been created by the revolutionaries; the revolutionaries were, however, prepared to harness this emotional force to their revolutionary purpose in a fairly self-conscious way. Yen Fu, as we have seen, had emphatically rejected revolution. The development of the people's intellectual, moral, and physical powers was a painful uphill task. As has already been pointed out, nothing he had learned from Spencer, Huxley, Mill, or Montesquieu lent the slightest support to the Jeffersonian notion of an untutored, innate wisdom or common sense in the people which would make itself manifest on the morrow of a revolution. Far from propelling progress, a revolution would probably give free rein to the retrograde patriarchal habits of an ignorant people. What was required was a "scientifically" guided reform promoted by an enlightened elite, and such reform could be effected only through the power of a state in being. While the Manchu state was by no means the ideal vehicle, it was the only vehicle available.[23] The irrational hatred of foreigners which had manifested itself in the Boxer Rebellion and the mutual hatred of Manchu and Han peoples could be viewed only as a destructive force. Yen Fu himself, to be sure, wished to foster a patriotic nationalism in the Chinese masses. This was the fundamental content of the phrase "people's morality." The fostering of this sentiment would have to go hand in hand, however, with a host of other transformations: the creation of a healthy sense of economic self-interest, the technical and scientific education of the masses, and, above all, the creation of the organs of a rationalized national state. All of these considerations, when added to a temperamental conservatism, are perhaps sufficient to explain Yen Fu's indifference or rather hostility to the use of popular passions and resentments as an instrument of politics.[24]

Once again, it must be stressed that this conservatism can emphatically not be equated with the slightest turn away from the West. The *History of Politics* commentaries rather constitute the final epitome of a creed of progressive evolution which seeks the image of man's future in the modern West. The values of Confucianism are not merely wrong. They are the anachronistic reflection of a stage of societal development which should long since have receded into oblivion.

CHAPTER IX

Mill's *Logic*

IN A SENSE, the translation of Mill's *Logic* is the very keystone of Yen Fu's synthesis. We have spoken of his intellectualism. The problem of China is, in his view, above all a problem of science. He had, of course, laid great weight on the role of science (both natural and social) in accounting for the wealth and power of the modern West. Newton, Darwin, Smith, Mill, and Spencer had all helped to lay the scientific foundations for the Promethean dynamism of nineteenth-century Europe. In the West, however, the scientific revolution had been anticipated by certain attitudes, certain spiritual orientations, which had preceded the rise of science itself. The spirit of self-assertion, struggle, and the forces which lay behind Western legal and political development had emerged before the scientific revolution. In China, however, the experience of the West could be assimilated only through the medium of science—only as knowledge.

In his *Lectures on Politics* delivered before the Shanghai Young Men's Association (Shanghai Ch'ing-nien hui) in 1906[1] Yen Fu insists on the rigorously scientific nature of the political principles which he espouses. China's traditional literature is, of course, very much concerned with the area of politics, but in the West "politics has become a science."[2] This science is based on a study of the laws of history, and the knowledge of these laws has been derived inductively. "Heaven, in giving birth to man, endows him with consciousness. It does not equip him at birth with any a priori (*yü chü*) intuitions. If one wishes to acquire knowledge, one must derive it by induction from that which is on the surface and close at hand . . . In induction one must rely on facts."[3] The laws of politics derive from the facts of history. Luckily the great thinkers of the West have already done much of the work. They have already derived by induction some of the fundamental laws of socio-political evolution, and these laws can now be used as deductive laws so that the modern Chinese no longer needs to recapitulate all the arduous work of induction undertaken in the West. It is only when the Chinese statesman is thoroughly equipped both with the methods of Western political science and with the knowledge of the laws derived by these methods that he can know what to do. There can be no "art" (*shu*) of politics without a correct science of politics. "The reason why [our] methods are unsatisfactory is because our knowledge is not clear."[4] What we note here is not only a burning conviction that for China salvation lies in knowledge, but also definite views on how accurate knowledge is achieved. Behind the scientific accomplishments of the West there looms that science which "Bacon has called the law of all laws and the science of all sciences"[5]—namely, the science of logic.

Yen Fu's concern with this "science of sciences" was, of course, not new. We have already noted his symbolically significant effort to form a "Society for the Study of Logic" in Shanghai during the very year of the Boxer uprising. It would appear that his translation of Mill's *Logic* was a direct outcome of this effort. The work on the first half of the *Logic* went forward during the years 1900 to 1902 even while Yen Fu was working on the translation of Spencer's *Study of Sociology* and Montesquieu's *Spirit of the Laws*. It was not published until 1905. In 1909, in his introduction to Jevon's *Primer of Logic*,[6] he expresses his regrets at not completing the second part of the work and complains that his intellectual energies are no longer equal to this enormous undertaking. (The *Primer* itself was designed to serve the purpose of a handy summation of Mill's basic teachings.) The *Logic* is indeed the most taxing of all of Yen Fu's undertakings from the linguistic point of view, and strains the resources of Yen Fu's classical Chinese vocabulary to its very limits.

Yen Fu's concern with the logic of science may have begun during his early days at the Foochow Arsenal School when he first came in contact with Western science. As already noted, as early as 1881 he had been deeply impressed with the chapter on "Discipline" in Spencer's *Study of Sociology*. In his magisterial classification of the hierarchy of sciences Spencer had stated that "unshakable belief in the necessities of relations is to be gained only by the study of the Abstract Sciences, Logic and Mathematics." If sociology is a science "in which the phenomena of all other sciences are included," logic and mathematics are the necessary foundation of social sciences as well as of the natural sciences. While Spencer's views on logic are by no means as clear as those of Mill, it is Spencer who has shown the link between the most abstract sciences and the sciences most immediately relevant to wealth and power. Logic relates itself in a twofold fashion to Yen Fu's central concern. It is the foundation of the sciences of "matter and force" (*chih-li*), as well as of the highest and most concrete science—sociology.

It must, however, be noted that Yen Fu has not committed himself to logic in general. He is not simply concerned to bring to China a vital discipline in which China
has been peculiarly weak.[7] He is committed precisely to
the logic of John Stuart Mill, which is a most particular
brand of logic. It is a brand of logic which wars against
the main tradition of logic and which has itself come under
severe attack by later logicians. It represents an attempt
to construct a logic wholly on the basis of the associationist-
empiricist tradition from which Mill derives—to base all
knowledge of experience strictly on induction. "The foundation of all sciences, even deductive or demonstrative sciences, is induction."[8] The only materials which logic has
to deal with are discrete sense impressions and "states of
consciousness," and all the sciences are constructed out of
this material wholly by induction.

There can be no doubt whatsoever that Yen Fu is
deeply committed to Mill's fanatical inductionism. He is
committed to it above all because he sees in it the specific
corrective and antidote to certain vicious tendencies of
Chinese traditional thought which are, again, closely linked
in his mind with the passivity, inertia, and rejection of
energetic effort which are the primary diseases of Chinese
culture. Mill's inductionism represents among other things
an assault on any notion of a priori or innate knowledge. In
Yen Fu's mind, the belief in a priori knowledge, in intuition, is closely linked with what he regards as one of the
most deplorable tendencies of Chinese thought. In his
essay "On Our Salvation" he had already opened his attack
on all schools of Chinese thought which stressed intuitive
knowledge. The whole vicious tendency was epitomized in
Mencius' assertion "that all things are stored up in me."[9]
This delusion of innate knowledge was carried forward by
Lu Hsiang-shan, the subjective idealist of the Sung dynasty,
and Wang Yang-ming of the Ming, who had denied that
the expression "investigation of things" (ko-wu) in the

Great Learning referred to the "external things" of nature, and encouraged the notion that "one could know the world without stepping outside one's door." Unfortunately, "later scholars rejoiced in this easy short cut. It suited their indolent and arrogant temper."[10] Here we note a direct association between the refusal to go into the world and rub against its stubburn factuality and that indolence, inertia, and self-complacency which is the ultimate root of China's debility.

Chinese thought had, to be sure, discerned the principle of induction. The *Great Learning*, the Appendices to the *Book of Changes*, and, above all, the philosophy of Chu Hsi had understood the principle of induction. "Chu Hsi has explained the phrase to achieve knowledge by the investigation of things as meaning to probe out the principles from things, but he applied this probing out of principles to the reading of books . . . Thus in Chinese learning one must seek out ancient interpretations. If the ancients are wrong, their errors cannot be exposed. Even if they are right, one does not know why they are right."[11] The principle of induction had been discovered but had been misapplied to the classical literature as a primary datum. To sit in one's chamber leafing and annotating books whose ultimate data may themselves be pseudo-facts is not much better than sitting with folded hands contemplating one's own intuitions. Induction is a form of activism. It involves the value of struggle. One must struggle with the brute discrete facts in order to wrest from nature its immutable principles.

One may, in fact, understand the principle of induction within a Darwinist framework. When Mill points out that "we may reason from particulars to particulars" without the intervention of general propositions, as when a child avoids thrusting his hand into fire without setting up a general maxim, "Fire burns," Yen Fu adds that the evolutionists regard this simplest kind of learning, which forms the basis of induction, as a function of the struggle for existence. Animals and children are conditioned by their struggle with brute facts to avoid that which is harmful to them. In the case of man, as Huxley points out, language has made it possible for humans to embody all these separate inductions in general propositions which are a kind of shorthand of science.[12] What science does is to consciously and systematically extend man's exposure to the whole realm of natural fact and thus enormously increase his advantage in his struggle with nature.

The commitment to a wholly inductionist account of science is already clearly hinted in the early essays, and the attack on innate knowledge, on intuition, on a priori knowledge and what might be called pseudo-facts not based on observation, is repeated throughout Yen Fu's commentaries. When Mill points out that, while all science is originally inductive, as a given science advances it becomes more and more reduced to a set of simple deductive principles (the sciences become "more and more deductive" but are "not thereby less inductive"), this leads Yen Fu to a dithyrambic exclamation. "The process of learning is from induction of fact to deduction. However, the mere fact that knowledge has become deductive does not mean that it no longer has any connection with induction. What this deductive law embraces is indeed comprehensive! By seizing hold of the one, one can control the rest. This is truly a most profound discernment! This is why Western science is so accurate, why its revelations increase day by day, why the knowledge of the people constantly grows, and why all their knowledge is useful! The reason why the older [Chinese] learning was so ineffectual was that, while it possessed the principle of deduction, its deductions were based on theories spun from the mind . . . When one examined the basis of these principles one found that many of them were based on falsehoods."[13] For centuries deductions were made from propositions involving such notions as the five elements and the astrological relations of the nine planets, which were "based on nothing but trumped up fantasies and not on generalizations inferred from facts."

Here Yen Fu seems to be attacking the arbitrary imagination, but he also shares Mill's aversion to any notion that mathematical truth is based on a priori deduction. When Mill attacks Dr. Whewell's contention that mathematical axioms are perceived a priori "by the constitution of the mind itself without any necessity for verifying them by repeated trials,"[14] Whewell's view immediately reminds Yen Fu of Wang Yang-ming's notion of intuitive knowledge (*liang-chih*). "Whewell maintains that such principles as geometric axioms are rooted in the human mind, are uniform for all, and require no verification by the experience of the senses. This view is the same as that of the 'intuitive knowledge school' in China."[15] Mill's insistence that all mathematical truth is derived inductively is, in Yen Fu's view, a devastating refutation of all Chinese intuitionism.

Another reason for his sympathy with Mill's effort to demote mathematics from its privileged status as an a priori, purely deductive science whose truths are necessary and independent of experience is the fact that the claims of the mathematicians are somehow linked in his mind with the claims made in China for the symbols of the *Book of Changes*—which, in the apt words of Needham, was regarded "as a depository of concepts to which almost any natural phenomenon could be referred."[16] He is, of course, aware of the numerological element in the science of the *Book of Changes* and the role which numerology has played in Chinese speculation in general. Any hint that the terms and relations of mathematics lie beyond experience (as conceived of by Mill) immediately sets up a disagreeable train of association with centuries of Chinese effort to derive conclusions about reality from speculations on numbers and symbols. "There are those who in speaking of Western science praise mathematics as the foundation of this science. The truth of this statement is more apparent than real. One can speak of mathematics as a great instrument."[17] He then goes on to discuss the Chinese effort to use "number" as a foundation of science—the sixty-four hexagrams, the five elements, and other sources of futile speculation.

It may seem absurd to compare Chinese numerological speculation to Western mathematics. To Yen Fu, however, there is at least one common denominator lying behind Chinese numerology and Western schools of mathematics which stress its purely deductive nature. They both tend to deduce truths about the world of events from a world of pure concepts.[18] One might say that he is completely overlooking the enormous difference between the arbitrary or purely suggestive nature of numerological speculation in China and the role of logical implication in Western mathematics. Mill had, however, assured him that the rationality of Western mathematics is based on the fact that it, like all the other sciences, is derived from an observation of experience and does not rest on grounds differing from those of the other sciences. It derives from experience and it is a handmaiden to the other more useful sciences which also derive from experience.[19] Mill does not provide a crumb of comfort to those in China who are seeking something in Western science which will allow them to continue sitting with their hands in their sleeves spinning truths out of their own heads rather than rubbing against the harsh world of fact.

It might be noted at this point that Yen Fu seems to have implicit faith that the essential truths which he has found in the writings of Spencer, Smith, Mill, Darwin, Montesquieu, and Jenks have all been the fruits of the inductive methods. Montesquieu, more than the others, is occasionally accused of not basing himself on the facts, while Smith is excused for not knowing facts which were not to emerge until after his death. By and large, however,

Yen Fu regards them all as men who have wrested their truths from the world of experience by the canons of the method of induction.

While he accepts this method, however, as the salutary medicine for China's intellectual ills, he does not seem to accept the positivist "anti-metaphysical" assumptions which presumably underlie Mill's whole work. Here again we note his ability to seize upon what he finds congenial and to reject the rest. Mill's *Logic* was, after all, designed to provide his own phenomenalistic empiricism with a logical arm. Mill claims never to depart from experience, which, in his conception, ultimately embraces only states of consciousness and sensations. Aggregates of sense data happen to be related in certain ways in our experience; this is really all we can say about them. Mill consistently refuses to commit himself to any belief in what Morris Cohen calls "the objectivity of the relational structure of the real world."[20] To Mill, the area of experience is the state of consciousness and its contents. "As body is understood to be the mysterious something which excites the mind to feel, so mind is the mysterious something which feels and thinks."[21] In the *Logic,* at any rate, he steadfastly refuses to concern himself with these "mysterious somethings," comfortable in his assurance that the sphere of the phenomenal will yield all that man requires to know. The causal hypothesis so necessary to induction rests ultimately on nothing but a mental habit—a habit of association.

Are we then to suppose that Yen Fu's decision to translate *Logic* signifies a break with the grandiose metaphysical scheme he had derived from a combination of Spencer's synthesis and Taoist mysticism? The fact is that his profound piety vis-à-vis the realm of the inconceivable, which he continues to identify with Lao-tzu's Tao, Buddha's Nirvana, and the Great Ultimate of the Neo-Confucians, remains untouched by Mill's subjectivist positivism. The language of unknowability in the usual sense does not shake him, because it is the agnostic language of mysticism everywhere, which refuses to use the language of ordinary experience to describe ultimate reality. When Mill defines the body as the unknown external cause of our sensations, this immediately reminds Yen Fu of the Buddhist tenet that everything which has dharmas is unreal, or the non-dualist doctrines of Vedanta, or the definition of the "Tao" in the Shuo-wen (an ancient Chinese etymological dictionary). To Yen Fu in his religious orientation, that which Spencer calls the "Unknowable" and which Mill calls "the unknown external cause" may be the most real and important realm of all. He is willing to concede to Mill that the world of the "ten thousand things" may be phenomenal and relative. "I have always maintained that the substance (*pen-t'i*) of the ten thousand things cannot be known and that all that can be known is the sensations."[22] "The human mind finds its limit in the absolute and inconceivable."[23] But his fundamental attitude toward the inconceivable is separated by an unabridged abyss from the *Logic's* studied indifference to the realm of the "mysterious noumenous."

What is more, it is doubtful whether Yen Fu accepts Mill's agnosticism concerning the "objectivity of the relational structure of the world." Spencer had indicated in his *First Principles* that the world of the knowable could not be as sharply divided from the world of the unknowable (or in his own language, the inconceivable) as Mill would have us believe. On the contrary, the world of the knowable, as Spencer had pointed out, could be understood only in terms of such categories as space, time, and natural laws, which are conceived of as both objective and universal and yet incomprehensible in themselves. The flux of phenomena is organized in a rational order which itself emanates from the ultimate inconceivable—the Tao. It is thus Spencer rather than Mill who remains Yen Fu's philosophic mentor.

The main animus which Yen Fu shares with Mill is the

animus against all notions of innate ideas, a priori subjective categories of thought, and intuitive knowledge. He has no compelling objection, however, to the notion of an objective rational order lying behind the flux of phenomena, and he fails to discern the philosophic difficulties involved in any attempt to derive such an order wholly by sheer induction.

In the end, what Yen Fu obtains from the Mill of *Logic* is a program of action—a plan for conquering nature (including man's nature as embodied in his social history) through the method of induction. Bacon, the father of inductionism, had proclaimed that knowledge is power. Only by assaulting the "brute, disconnected manifold" of the world of fact could the inexhaustible storehouse of the universe be made to yield its treasures. The method of induction itself is the ultimate weapon in the struggle for wealth and power. To the extent, however, that Yen Fu continues to feel deep religious and metaphysical needs, the sober, restrictive positivism[24] which underlies Mill's *Logic* leaves him entirely untouched.

CHAPTER X

Meditations on the Tao

AT FIRST GLANCE, one could hardly conceive of two products of the spirit more alien to each other than Mill's *Logic* and Lao-tzu's *Tao te ching*. Yet it was in 1903, scarcely a year after the completion of his translation of the first three books of the *Logic*, that Yen Fu was persuaded to write a series of marginal commentaries on a new edition of Lao-tzu's classic, prepared by his student-disciple Hsiung Chi-lien (Ch'un-ju).[1] This was also the year of the publication of Yen Fu's translation of Spencer's *Study of Sociology*, as well as of *On Liberty*, and the year of the completion of his translation of Jenks. The translation of Montesquieu was also steadily forging ahead.

It has already been observed that Yen Fu's universe had never been neatly divided into the two incommunicable spheres of "Chinese tradition" and "modern West." The commentaries on the *Logic* themselves furnish some indication of the perspective which is able to accommodate John Stuart Mill and Lao-tzu within the same universe. The marginal commentaries on Lao-tzu do not, in fact, represent the slightest departure from any of the basic premises which underlie Yen Fu's synthetic philosophy of these years. If the commentaries on Huxley, Mill, and Montesquieu contain laudatory references to Lao-tzu and Chuang-tzu, the marginal commentaries on Lao-tzu contain unambiguous affirmations of Yen Fu's complete commitment to Darwin and Spencer. What the marginal commentaries do, in fact, is to provide a thumbnail sketch of Yen Fu's general conception of human destiny and of his basic positions in the areas of religion and philosophy as they had developed during the whole previous decade.

The fact remains, however, that Yen Fu had chosen in the very midst of his most feverish translation activities to call attention to the hoary, semi-mythical figure of Lao-tzu. There is even some reason to think that Hsiung Ch'un-ju's very act of preparing a new edition of *The Way and Its Power* had been prompted by Yen Fu's frequent assertions that "only the views of Lao-tzu are compatible with the views of Darwin, Montesquieu, and Spencer."[2] The young Hsiung, whose education had been primarily traditional and who had ardently been seeking new orientation within the familiar frame of reference provided by Chinese thought (he had been an extreme enthusiast of Wang Fu-chih), was probably enormously excited by Yen Fu's assertion of affinities between Lao-tzu and the sages of the West.

All of this would tend to support the view that Yen Fu's primary motive is to salvage national pride—to save his own sense of self-esteem and that of his countrymen in the face of what he himself regards as the obvious superiority of modern Western thought—by once more asserting that "we had these things before you (at least in embryo form)." On a lower level one might even suspect that this gesture in the direction of the traditional culture was designed to protect his own security against the traditional-minded forces which were still powerfully entrenched. The latter suspicion would, however, seem to be without foundation. The traditional-minded elements of officialdom were not committed at this point to the abstract category of "tradition." They were committed to official Confucianism. Now, the fact is that Yen Fu's single reference to Confucianism in his marginal commentaries is extraordinarily harsh. Commenting on the potentially democratic bent of Lao-tzu's principles, he contrasts this most sharply with Confucianism. "Authoritarian states cannot use Lao-tzu. The Taoists of the Han dynasty could accept him only by distorting him. Only the methods of the Confucianists could serve as a tool for authoritarian rule!"³ Official traditionalism is interested in saving Confucianism. Yen Fu's apologia for Lao-tzu is expressly directed against Confucianism.

There can be no doubt, however, that one of the preoccupations of the marginal notes is to find in Lao-tzu, in particular, intimations of "democracy" and "science" as Yen Fu understands these terms. He is insistent above all on the beautiful compatibility of Lao-tzu's metaphysic with that of Spencer. The effort to find anticipations of Western thought in the thought of the Chou period was, of course, not new. The preface to the translation of *Evolution and Ethics* had already found intimations of the procedures of induction and deduction in the *Book of Changes* and the *Spring and Autumn Annals*. Lao-tzu's philosophy had already been praised in "In Refutation of Han-yü" for its democratic proclivities, and the question of motivation remains as difficult in 1903 as it had been in 1895. We recall that in the preface to *Evolution and Ethics* Yen Fu had expressly stated that present-day Chinese have little cause to pride themselves on the fact that the ancients had had intimations of modern Western truths. Again it must be noted that his praise of Lao-tzu is directed to Lao-tzu as an individual. He does not praise him as a representative of the "national heritage" but as a unique source of wisdom. While he is undoubtedly delighted by the equivalences which he believes he finds between the insights of Lao-tzu and the sages of the West, there is ample evidence that the ultimate ground of his attraction to Lao-tzu lies elsewhere. Indeed the effort to find equivalences, we shall see, actually breaks down at certain crucial points and, when this occurs, Yen Fu candidly deserts the ancient Chinese sage.

All this would suggest that, at least in the case of Yen Fu, the motive of salvaging national pride by finding Chinese precedents for modern Western ideas may not be dominant, even in his dealings with Lao-tzu. From Montesquieu and Jenks he had derived the view that at least some of the characteristics of the modern West had their roots in the ancient Greco-Roman and medieval worlds. He was thus no longer committed to the notion of absolute discontinuity between the modern and pre-modern world in general. Since he was firmly committed to a unilinear account of human history there was no reason for asserting, a priori, that an ancient Chinese thinker might not also have anticipated some of the thoughts of Spencer. He might draw pride from this belief, but the pride might be a consequence of the belief rather than the reverse. The validity of the belief is, of course, another matter. On the whole, the grounds for finding "democratic" and "scientific" beliefs in the *Tao te ching* seem to me to be quite tenuous, although they do anticipate by several decades the similar claims and even the line of argument of Joseph Needham in his *Science and Civilization in China*.[4]

Science, as Yen Fu understands the term, must be identified with nothing less than Spencer's whole metaphysical system, just as Needham tends to identify science quite unproblematically with what he calls the "philosophy of organism." Mill may have spelled out the logical method of science, but he had not shaken Yen Fu's conviction that Spencer's synthetic philosophy had been derived by the strictest canons of inductive logic. As we have seen in the essays of 1895, Yen Fu had already identified Spencerianism with the monistic-pantheistic mainstream of Chinese metaphysics. What he does in the marginal notes is to identify Lao-tzu as the fountainhead of this Chinese philosophy. There can be little doubt that Yen Fu shares the traditional view, expressed in Hsia's preface, that Lao-tzu preceded Confucius and the other "hundred schools" in time and that his book is therefore the first expression of abstract philosophy in China. Thus the whole central image of Chinese thought which sees the "ten thousand things" as generated out of some original ground of reality, continuing somehow to abide in it and constantly returning to it, is here attributed to Lao-tzu. This image is indeed a constant substratum of Chinese metaphysical and cosmological thought. Whether it originated with Lao-tzu, and whether all forms of Chinese thought which share this common image are mutually consistent in other respects, is a question which can hardly be considered here. To Yen Fu, the image is readily assimilated to Spencer's world of the heterogeneous and complex which emerges out of the homogeneous and the simple (Lao-tzu's *p'u* or 'uncarved block').

Furthermore, like Spencer's Unknowable, the ultimate ground of reality cannot be described and yet it is the cause of all things. At one point, in fact, Yen Fu insists on identifying the Tao with the First Cause of Western philosophy as well as with the Great Ultimate of the Neo-Confucianists and the Unknowable of Spencer. The question of whether the concept of a First Cause is indeed identical with the sort of genetic metaphor ("The Progenitor of the Ten Thousand Things . . . Generated by I Know Not What")[5] which dominates Lao-tzu's gnomic phrases is one which does not bother Yen Fu, who is at best a somewhat crude metaphysician. It does, however, serve to create a link between Lao-tzu and the world of science, which, of course, is notoriously concerned with the search for causes.

Again, Yen Fu finds that, like Spencer in the *First Principles*, Lao-tzu stresses the "relativity of the world of the Manifold."[6] The ten thousand things are all relative, only this [the Tao] stands alone." Again, the famous statement we have met before in the commentary to Huxley's *Evolution and Ethics*—"Heaven and earth are not benevolent, they treat the ten thousand things like straw dogs"—is claimed as a support of the teachings of Darwinism concerning the lofty indifference of nature to the fate of its individual creatures.

One of the most far-fetched examples of Yen Fu's "scientific" interpretations can be found in his note on chapter 48 of the text, which reads, "Practice learning and there is daily increase, practice the Way and there is daily decrease." Here Lao-tzu is used to support the teachings of Mill's *Logic*. The phrase "daily increase" is presumably a reference to the inductive method with its cumulative methods of acquiring knowledge, and "daily decrease" a reference to the process of deduction which gathers together the results of the cumulative process into one reductive formula. In faithful adherence to Mill's view on the relations between the processes of induction and deduction, Yen Fu goes on to assert that "one increases daily in order that one may decrease daily."[7] To the candid reader this passage, like so many similar ones in the *Tao te ching*, would seem to involve a typical attack on the learning which attaches man's attention to the world of ten thousand things and draws him away from the quiet emptiness of the Tao. Far from involving the advocacy of inductive logic, it would seem to involve the depreciation of "knowledge" in general. In the main, however, Yen Fu's claims for Lao-tzu as a philosopher favorable to science rest on the assumed affinity of his thought to that of Spencer.[8]

Again like Needham, Yen Fu finds in Lao-tzu propensities toward democracy, although here the grounds are quite different. Unlike Needham he does not seek the prototypes of Taoist democracy in the Levellers and other types of "collectivist" thinkers but in Montesquieu's description of antique democracy. Montesquieu had found the principle of antique democracy to be an austere, self-abnegating "virtue." Was this not the same as Lao-tzu's "virtue" and "effortlessness" (*wu wei*)? "China has never had a democratic system and, while Lao-tzu had never seen it, one can find the concept of it here." When Lao-tzu speaks of his utopia as consisting of a "small country with few inhabitants" is he not making the same point as Montesquieu, that true democracy is possible only in the confines of a city-state? When he insists that in this society people will not prize sweet food and beautiful clothes, is he not making the same point as Montesquieu—that true democracy is possible only where an austere and simple life prevails?[9] Elsewhere he makes the more conventional comparison to Rousseau's primitivism.[10] One may pause at this point to wonder whether there is indeed any affinity between the antique "virtue" of Montesquieu with its deadly seriousness and strained civic consciousness and the completely relaxed and unpolitical "virtue" of Lao-tzu, just as one may wonder whether there is any real affinity between the pathos of the *Lao-tzu* and the puritanical purposiveness of Needham's Levellers. What Needham and Yen Fu are able to draw on is the negative element—the attack on culture and the association of oppressive government with high culture.[11] Both the *Lao-tzu* and *Chuang-tzu* devalue the contemporary social order as they devalue technology and all other manifestations of "high culture." Lao-tzu, however, has no "constitution" to propose as an alternative to the political structure of his times. On the contrary, he seems to take the political structure for granted. What he calls for is not democratic government but minimal government and minimal social organization.

Yen Fu thus clearly sees the link between the elements which he regards as favorable to democracy in Lao-tzu and the theme of primitivism. Has he then become a sudden convert to primitivism even while gnashing his teeth over the sluggishness of historic evolution in China? The very fact that he links Lao-tzu's democratic utopia to Montesquieu's vision of antique democracy is an indication that such is not the case. As we have seen, Yen Fu had in the end rejected Montesquieu's vision of antique democracy. He had rejected the view that austerity, self-denial, and smallness of territory are in any way necessary prerequisites of democracy in the modern sense. On the contrary, in the modern world large-scale representative democracy has become an engine producing wealth and power. What the ancient Greco-Roman world had provided were certain bare notions of democracy, and it is on this level that Lao-tzu can be spoken of as their Chinese counterpart.

In the end, however, Yen Fu admits that on the issue of primitivism, which is probably the most fundamental issue of all, he is divided from Lao-tzu by an unbridgeable abyss. At this point he displays a lack of evasiveness not readily discernible in Needham's treatment. When he confronts chapters 18–20 of the *Tao te ching* he feels forced to acknowledge that beneath all the presumed equivalences between the thought of Lao-tzu and that of the modern West there lies the fundamental cleavage. "When the Great Way declines," states Lao-tzu, "there is 'humanity' and 'justice.' When cleverness and knowledge appear there is the great artificiality (*ta-wei*) . . . Abolish 'sageness' (sheng) and reject knowledge, the people will benefit a hundredfold. Abolish 'humanity' and 'justice,' the people will return to filial piety and maternal affection. Abolish skill and reject profit, thieves and robbers will disappear . . . Display natural simplicity (*su*) and cling to artlessness (*p'u*); decrease selfishness and diminish desires. Abolish study and you will be free from care . . . Let all men have a purpose, I alone am ignorant like a boor; I alone am different from others because I prize feeding on the 'Mother.' "[12] It is precisely in passages of this sort that we find that which is most characteristic of the Lao-tzu–Chuang-tzu brand of "philosophic Taoism." Whatever may be the metaphysical propositions which Lao-tzu may share with later varieties of Chinese "perennial philosophy," it is here that we find that which is specifically and uniquely Lao-tzu.

To Yen Fu, however, this passage involves nothing less than a repudiation of the whole human cultural enterprise —the repudiation in advance, as it were, of the whole process of human evolution. "We cannot help noting," he remarks, "that in these three chapters Lao-tzu's philosophy parts ways with modern philosophy. It is a natural tendency for raw simplicity (*chih*) to turn into a patterned culture (*wen*), for the homogeneous (*ch'un*) to turn into the heterogeneous (*tsa*), for the static condition of heaven and earth (*ch'ien-k'un*) to pass over gradually into that which is capable of achieving completion but which is not yet complete (*wei chi*).¹³ Lao-tzu's notion of 'returning to the pure and reverting to the simple' is very much like trying to force the waters of a stream back to their source in the mountain. Now, Lao-tzu is right when he condemns forcing the primitive into the patterns of culture, but he is certainly wrong in attempting to force an [attained] culture back into a state of simplicity. Both of these methods are alike in that they go against nature and violate the 'Tao.' In present-day civilization there is nothing more exalted than freedom. Where freedom exists, everything may achieve that to which it can attain, while the function of natural selection is to preserve that which is most fit. In this way, the flourishing state of the Great Peace will inevitably come into being."¹⁴ Lao-tzu has made, in a most radical form, the fatal cultural decision made by the Chinese sages in general. Instead of welcoming the actualization of all the potentialities of man which emerge from the inexhaustible storehouse of the cosmos—potentialities which realize themselves through the process of cosmic and human evolution—he would drive the stream back to its source in "Non-being." Instead of welcoming the unobstructed thrust of human energies embodying themselves in ever more complex and "higher" patterns of human organization by gradually passing through the purifying crucible of natural selection, he yearns for the quietude of the "Mother"—an image which almost suggests Freud's conception of the return to the womb (a conception applied in this case, however, to the whole human race).

Yen Fu has here returned to the grand theme first broached in his essay of 1895 on "The Speed of World Change."[15] If Lao-tzu and Chuang-tzu had decided against freedom conceived of in terms of a maximum realization of men's "energy of faculty," if they had turned their backs on energy, dynamism, self assertiveness, and fierce struggle and had sought the ultimate escape into the womb of the nameless Tao, Confucianism also had attempted to stop the further flow of the stream by freezing and idealizing the "patriarchal" stage of human development. To the Taoists, the early Chou social order which the Confucianists attempted to idealize had already gone too far. It already embodied violence, injustice, anxiety, fuss, and falsehood. To the Confucianists, on the contrary, it embodied peace and harmony as necessary ingredients of all "high culture." Thus both Taoists and Confucianists had rejected the further liberation of human physical, intellectual, and moral energies. Both had rejected the systematic and purposive pursuit of wealth and power as a conscious ideal. The West had demonstrated that precisely by flowing along with the river of evolution, precisely by riding the current, as it were, one might ultimately arrive at the ocean of the Great Peace. There is also, to be sure, a passing attack on the "Left." The reference to those who attempt to force the pace of evolution may well be meant for the revolutionary party, who are oblivious of the necessity for knowing at what point in the stream one finds oneself.

Essentially, however, this passage would indicate Yen Fu's awareness of the yawning gulf of existential attitudes which divides Lao-tzu from Spencer, whatever may be the formal resemblance between their metaphysical presuppositions. The realization that Lao-tzu's ultimate views on "science" and "democracy" are in the end qualitatively different keeps breaking through the effort to find equivalences. When Lao-tzu exclaims, "Abolish learning and you will be free from care,"[16] Yen Fu cannot interpret away the anti-intellectual nature of this utterance, in spite of his effort elsewhere to find in Lao-tzu intimations of Mill's *Logic.* "The kind of freedom from care which comes from abolishing learning," he observes, "is not true freedom from care . . . The African ostrich when pursued buries his head in the sand in order not to see the harm which may befall him, believing that in this way harm will not befall him. Is this very different from Lao-tzu's teachings concerning the abolition of learning?"[17] To the extent that one may argue an ideal of freedom in Lao-tzu, it is obviously not Yen Fu's ideal. It is freedom from purpose, freedom from the effort to "achieve that to which one can attain." Finally, if there are "democratic" thoughts in Lao-tzu, they are the counterparts of the principles of "antique democracy" described by Montesquieu. The principles of antique democracy may have been one of the necessary conditions lying behind the dynamic, powerful democracies of the modern West, but they were certainly not a sufficient condition. The sages of antique democracy, like Lao-tzu, had recognized that the people can take care of itself, but neither Lao-tzu nor the ancient democratic city-states had recognized the enormous evolutionary potentialities of the people.

Yen Fu is willing to concede Lao-tzu's point that "high culture" leads to injustice and corruption, and he willingly admits that both may be found in the modern West. "The varieties of deceitfulness in modern Europe did not exist before the emergence of civilization." Elsewhere he even remarks that Lao-tzu would have considered "what we now call civilization not very different from the culture of robbing and arrogance" described in his 53rd chapter.[18] "That is why the ranks of the socialists and nihilists grow daily."[19] This recognition of the reverse side of modern Western civilization is not new. We recall the passage in his "On Strength" in which Yen Fu remarks on the enormous inequalities of wealth in the Western world but then proceeds to treat this inequality as a stratagem of natural selection. He had before this pointed to the socialists' response to this situation. However, he is not a convert to socialism and remains committed to civilization. These are the historic prices which must be paid to achieve wealth, power, and the ultimate Great Harmony. These are the eggs which must be broken to make the omelette of the powerful democratic state.

In the end, Yen Fu's interest in Lao-tzu does not rest simply on the case he is able to make for him as the Chinese precursor of democracy and "science." In the end he is more valued for the religio-metaphysical core of his teachings. That side of Yen Fu which had from the very outset sought to establish an equivalence between Spencer's Unknowable, Lao-tzu's Tao, the Nirvana of the Buddhists, the Advaita of Vedanta, and the Great Ultimate of Neo-Confucian philosophy is very much in evidence. Here the contrast with Needham's treatment of Taoism is most striking and enlightening. Not only does Needham attempt to minimize the mystical element of Taoism (he achieves this aim in part by constantly translating the term "Tao" as "order of nature"), but he vehemently insists on the absolute difference between Buddhism and Taoism. Yen Fu himself does not equate the two, to be sure; at one point he even makes the interesting observation that "Lao-tzu asserts that there is no death, while Buddha asserts that there is no life."[20] Taoism is marked by an affirmative attitude to those aspects of the world of the ten thousand things which are characterized by purposelessness, effortlessness, and spontaneity. These aspects of the phenomenal world abide in the Tao. This observation, however, does not prevent Yen Fu from asserting an absolute identity between Lao-tzu's nameless Tao and the absolute of Buddhism. The ultimate ground of reality in both is identical: "The Eternal Way, the Eternal Name, refers to the Absolute; that is why it cannot be described in words and hence is the inconceivable."[21] "Lao-tzu calls it the Way. The *Book of Changes* calls it the Great Ultimate, the Buddhists call it the Self-existent (*Iśvara*), the Western philosophers call it the First Cause . . . It alone neither comes into being nor perishes. It neither increases nor decreases. The Ten Thousand Things are all relative. It stands alone. The Ten Thousand Things are in flux. It does not change."[22] "Lao-tzu's description of the Tao is, in its broad outlines, the same as Buddha's description of Nirvana."[23]

Thus we are again confronted with the problem already posed as early as 1896 in Yen Fu's comments on Huxley. Why does the Chinese apostle of social Darwinism feel this strong need for the sense of some ultimate, unchanging, higher reality lying behind the evolutionary stream? If he is already a Chinese nationalist primarily engrossed in the task of lifting China from its present humiliation to a position of wealth and power, if he is, beyond this, committed to a firm belief in the values of a certain brand of liberalism as providing the only means for achieving these goals, why are these new commitments not sufficient to provide a center of meaning to his life?

There is, of course, no pat answer to these questions. It should be pointed out once more that we are not dealing entirely with the personal idiosyncrasy of Yen Fu. His preoccupation with Taoism and Buddhism is one which he shares with some of his more illustrious contemporaries, such as Liang Ch'i-ch'ao, Chang Ping-lin, T'an Ssu-t'ung, Yang Wen-hui, Hsia Tseng-yu, and others. The young T'an

Ssu-t'ung had claimed to be a Confucianist but had raised the Confucian notion of *jen* ('universal love,' in this case) into a kind of metaphysical absolute readily assimilable to the ultimate reality of Buddhism. On its negative side, this turn to the "non-orthodox" traditions of Chinese thought may have represented a deep revulsion against the Confucian absolutization of a determined social and political order. Buddhism and philosophic Taoism both point to an ineffable, inconceivable, ultimate ground of reality which transcends and relativizes all determinate orders and structures of reality. Precisely because the transcendant reality lies beyond all determinate orders, it can, in the words of T'an Ssu-t'ung, become an inspiration for efforts to "break out of the enmeshing nets" of orthodox Confucianism. The ultimate reality lying beyond all determinations is a storehouse of infinite possibility. As Yen Fu states in his marginal notes, the Confucianists did not realize that the Tao is inexhaustible. Viewed in this light the Tao and even the absolute of Buddhism can be detached from the specific life views of Lao-tzu and the Buddha and become the source of an expansive romanticism.[24] Yen Fu himself, to be sure, is no romantic. For him the ten thousand things evolve out of the womb of the Tao in strict obedience to the laws of physics and the mechanisms of evolution as laid down by Darwin and Spencer. The evolution of human society from the past into the future follows a clearly demarcated, well-defined course. Yet there can be no doubt that the inexhaustible void is more hospitable to the possibility of an evolution of the ten thousand things to ever higher levels of heterogeneity, complexity, and organization than is a Confucianism which attempts to absolutize and freeze a given social and political order.

Beyond the fact, however, that Taoist mysticism is more hospitable to the emergence of new possibilities than Confucian "rationalism," Yen Fu is in the end also drawn to the Tao as the "inconceivable" and the "void." He maintains his Janus-like attitude. That side of him which is concerned with his aspirations for China—with wealth, power, and Prometheanism—looks to the West. Somehow, however, his personal needs remain unsatisfied by the religion of evolution and progress. He still feels a profound need to view the whole process "under the aspect of eternity." If this is so before 1911, when his hopes for China's future still run high, one may imagine how much more it is so in his later years of growing despair. Yen Fu does not approve of Lao-tzu's efforts to force the stream of evolution back to its source in the mountain of the primordial Tao. It remains a matter of supreme importance to him, however, to be able to look back for reassurance to the source even while drifting down the stream.

CHAPTER XI

The Later Years

AN ATTEMPT has been made to reconstruct Yen Fu's image of the world from a body of writings which roughly spans the period from 1895 to 1908.[1] Contrary to Chou Chen-fu, who professes to discern in these writings a gradual, steady backsliding from the "all-out Westernizer" of 1895 to the "reactionary traditionalist" of the later years, my own impression is that of a persistence of underlying preoccupation and of a substantial inner coherence of thought during this period. To the extent that one can speak of a fundamental break with traditional values, this is as evident in the commentaries on the *Spirit of the Laws* and in the marginal notes on the *Lao-tzu* as in the essays of 1895. To the extent that one can discern a conservative political bent, this is already visible in the early essays and is simply made more obvious by the circumstances of the post-Boxer period; nor is this conservatism in any way to be identified with the "return to tradition." To the extent that there is a favorable orientation to certain strands of traditional thought, this is already discernible in the commentaries on Huxley's *Evolution and Ethics*.

The basic concern of this study has been with the image of Yen Fu's creative period, and we shall return again to this image and to some of its broader implications. At this point, something must be said about the circumstances of Yen Fu's later years and the vicissitudes of his thought during the somber decade which followed the 1911 revolution.

In the years immediately preceding the revolution Yen Fu's reputation as a sage in Western matters was already firmly established, although he had incurred the hostility of the revolutionary party. The court was by now prepared to treat him, with a degree of cautious respect, as a "safe" constitutional monarchist. In fact, we note a modest rise in his fortunes during the years after 1905. In 1906 he was invited by En-ming, governor of Anhui, to be the superintendent of the Anhwei Higher Normal School.[2] During the same year he was invited by T'ang Shao-i, the Minister of Foreign Affairs, to act as chief examiner for Chinese students who had returned from abroad. In 1908 he became Chief Reviser of the Committee for the Compilation of Technical Terms[3] within the Ministry of Education, a position which he held until the revolution of 1911. The position did not arouse any great enthusiasm in Yen Fu; according to Chang Shih-chao, who later saw some of the work papers written by him, his soul was not in it.[4] In 1909 he was appointed Second Rank Advisor to the Committee for Drawing up Regulations for Constitutional Government, Advisor to the Committee for the Reorganization of the Financial Affairs of the Empire, and Advisor to the Province of Fukien.[5] During the same year, however, he refused to accompany the princely naval minister, Tsai-hsün, on his naval inspection tour of Europe. In 1910 he was appointed, with the rank of "Illustrious Scholar," to the newly created

Legislative Council (Tzu-cheng yüan); he was also made a rear admiral in the Navy and in 1911 was appointed to the Naval General Staff. In 1909 he was finally awarded the degree of *chin-shih ch'u-shen,* which, symbolically as it were, brought an end to his "outsider" status. Yen Fu himself, however, greeted this honor with a wryly ironic poem.[6]

While many of these positions brought Yen Fu modest emoluments and honors, they did not bring him to the centers of power. Again one may raise the question whether he really desired power, whether he really enjoyed the routines and responsibilities of administration or the moral atmosphere within which power was exercised in China at this time. There is a fairly well substantiated report that the redoubtable Yüan Shih-k'ai, whose power in the Manchu government before 1908 was most formidable, had attempted to attach him to his inner circle.[7] While Yen Fu admired Yüan's accomplishments in the crucial area of military modernization, he refused to be enticed because, in the words of Hou I, "their temperaments were not compatible." Yüan Shih-k'ai himself is reputed to have remarked, "Mr. Yen is the reincarnation of a saint; I don't dare to use him again."[8] Social Darwinism in the abstract had not conditioned Yen Fu's sensitive nose to the smell of the ingredients of power in the concrete.

It cannot fairly be maintained that Yen Fu remained profoundly committed to the monarchy because of a deep personal stake in its perpetuation.[9] Even his hostile critics do not raise this charge. As a matter of fact, his immediate response to the revolution of 1911 was not entirely hostile in spite of all his profound theoretical objections to revolution in China. We have a poem from his hand, written some time after the Wuchang uprising and before the establishment of the new government, in which he compares the situation so that of an ardent lover eagerly listening for the sounds which will signal the arrival of her beloved.[10] For one moment of hopeful suspense, he was ready to believe against his own better "scientific" judgment that revolution itself might be the vehicle of evolution, as his revolutionary opponents insisted. Perhaps the revolution was itself the outcome of large impersonal forces of evolution which might lead China more rapidly than he had had reason to expect to the level of a modern wealthy and powerful state. This mood was to pass very quickly, but it is important to note that the favors he had won from the Manchus did not prevent the mood from arising.

As a matter of fact, Yen Fu's political situation was by no means adversely affected by the revolution. Yüan Shih-k'ai's swift rise to power actually placed Yen Fu in a most favorable position. In spite of his own strong aversion to Yüan's character, in spite of Yüan's recent expression of disdain for the finicky intellectual, Yen Fu nevertheless enjoyed the new president's respect. In 1908 when the Manchu cabal at the court had forced Yüan's resignation, Yen Fu had openly praised him, and in 1912 when all his transient hopes for the revolution had again given way to what he regarded as his sounder earlier judgment, he threw his moral support behind the strong man who in his view now constituted the only block to total anarchy. As a result, at the beginning of 1912 he was made Head of the College of Letters at Peking University (probably the most responsible position he had ever held), only to resign this position in November of the same year because of "backbiting."[11] In the same year he became Chief Reviser of the Naval Ministry's Translation Bureau and supervised the translation of foreign naval documents. In 1913 he was made an advisor on international law to the President's office. In 1914, after the collapse of the Second Revolution, he became a member of Yüan's State Council.[12] He had thus clearly associated himself with the cause of Yüan Shih-k'ai and it was, perhaps, only natural that those who sponsored Yüan's movement to make himself emperor should seek his support. According to Yen Fu's own account (which will be con-

sidered below) he did not support Yüan's monarchic ambitions, and the use of his name as one of the sponsors of
the "Peace Planning Society" (a committee of notables
which was to smooth the way for the restoration of the
monarchy) had not really been authorized. The association
of his name with the monarchic effort was to damage his
reputation most severely during the period of the Third
Revolution and in the official histories of both the Nationalist and Communist parties. In June of 1917 after Li
Yüan-hung's assumption of the presidency he was even in
some danger of arrest as a supporter of Yüan's restoration
movement. His old friend Lin Shu urged him to flee
Peking, but Yen Fu replied that his conscience was clear
and that he would accept any punishment with equanim-
ity.[13]

It was after these events that he finally withdrew from
all participation in public life. He spent the remaining
years of his life observing the growing chaos, Cassandra-
like, from the sidelines. Looking back over his career in a
letter to his disciple Hsiung Ch'un-ju, he bitterly observes
that all that he had won from his effort to make a name
for himself was hatred, without obtaining either wealth or
high office.[14]

Yen Fu spent most of his remaining years in Peking,
making occasional trips to Shanghai and his native province,
Fukien, primarily for reasons of health. While he was by
no means wealthy, the royalties from his translations and
his investments in the Commercial Press[15] proved sufficient,
though barely so, to provide for his own needs and the
education of his children. His increasingly dark view of
China's fate was no doubt intensified by the usual infirmi-
ties of old age. His health had never been robust and after
1911 his asthmatic condition became progressively worse,
finally leading to his death in 1921. The rapid disappearance of friends and contemporaries—one of the perennial
tragedies of old age—was felt with peculiar intensity in a

society where the cleavage between generations within the
intelligentsia ran deep. In one of his letters to Hsiung
Ch'un-ju, he bemoans the loss of old friends who, "while
they were all equipped with new knowledge, were at home
in the old tradition." In the usual manner of the elderly,
he finds that they were head and shoulders above "the so-
called new personalities" of the younger generation. There
is, however, more here than the usual lament over the new
generation. There is recognition on the part of Yen Fu
that he belongs to what might be called the watershed
generation within the Chinese intelligentsia. He and his
literati contemporaries had spent their youth within the
framework of the older culture, and the habits and style
of that culture had left an indelible mark upon them. The
older culture is, as it were, in their bones, and their personal style of life is entirely molded by it. They are as much
at home within the patterns of the older family system as
they are in their long gowns. They are, nevertheless, the
first generation which looks abroad for new wisdom and
which, on the intellectual level, is willing to question some
of the basic values of the old society, without, on the other
hand, ever seeing the issue in terms of any clear-cut dichotomy of traditionalism versus antitraditionalism. The generation of Ch'en Tu-hsiu and Hu Shih had drawn youthful
inspiration from Yen Fu. An analysis of their early writings
in *Hsin ch'ing-nien* (*La Jeunesse*) and elsewhere would
indeed reveal that a considerable part of their bold new
thinking is already present in Yen Fu's synthesis of the
1895–1908 period. Yet they and he are divided from each
other not merely by age but by a difference in life experience
which lies deeper than the level of conscious intellectual
attitudes.[16]

One of the last images we have of Yen Fu is that revealed
in his letters to his children at school. The genre itself is
highly traditional and the image which emerges is that of
the traditional kindly but firm pater familias sedulously

guiding the education of his children. Characteristically, however, while the framework is traditional, the educational program of both son and daughters is decidedly Western and the paternal advice is by no means entirely traditional.[17]

When we turn to the evolution of Yen Fu's intellectual attitudes after 1911, we find that there is indeed some ground for the assertion that he "repudiated the West and returned to the tradition" during his last decade. The turn away from the West was, however, by no means as precipitous nor as total as some of his biographers would imply. "After the 1911 revolution," states Wang Shih quite flatly, "Yen Fu went the way of reaction,"[18] while Chou Chen-fu discusses the whole period under the rubric of the "return to the ancient."[19] While I am not particularly interested in defending Yen Fu against the charge of being a "reactionary" after 1911, the assertion that his whole image of the world suddenly collapsed after the revolution bears some examination.

Having experienced his moment of wistful hopefulness in 1911, Yen Fu soon returned with renewed conviction to his view that a republican revolution in China was an enormous mistake. Indeed, what had previously been an intellectual conviction grounded mainly on his readings of Spencer, Mill, and Jenks was now being sadly corroborated, in his view, in the laboratory of experience. Life itself was vindicating the correctness of his theory. The Chinese people was decidedly not ready for republicanism or democracy. However, most of what he has to say on this subject during the years immediately following the revolution is actually firmly imbedded in the categories provided by his Western mentors. "The reason why I was so deeply worried over the prospect of revolution in the past was not because I was one of the inner officials of the court nor because I love the Aisingoro clan; what I argued was that the level [of civilization] of our masses could not be

forced."[20] "Here we see how the principle of natural selection applies to the facts. Only when the selection has been
made is there a chance for survival. Westerners say that
China will become strong only when China has been thoroughly rid of certain evil dispositions and certain inveterate
habits which make her unfit for survival."[21]

Again, after the Second Revolution, when his disciple
Hsiung expresses the hope that China will finally achieve
unity, he quickly disabuses him: "I dare not hope that this
is so. Our previous situation was caused by the moral state
of our people (min te), and since the cause has not changed
what reason do we have to expect that the results will be
different? If the state wishes to make certain fundamental
plans (as in the realm of tax unification or the improvement of education), it must make infinite preparations,
but people now wish to attain the goal at one fell swoop."[22]
The "people's morality" (min te), a category with which
we are now familiar, may refer to anything ranging from
the masses' lack of national consciousness to the intellectual irresponsibility of the new politicians. The basic
thinking here has no connection whatsoever with traditionalism. Evolution cannot be forced. It is a slow cumulative process and can only be fostered by an enlightened
elite which knows the requirements of modernization. "Even
if a sage were now to arise, he could do nothing better
than expand our communications, stabilize our legal system, and foster education in order to make it possible for
the people to take care of themselves. There is no escape
from the laws of the struggle for existence and natural
selection. The intelligent will follow the course of evolution
and the stupid will oppose it. In the struggle between the
superior and inferior, one side must die. If we follow the
path of evolution, those who survive will be the fittest. On
the other hand, if we set ourselves athwart the path of evolution, only the unfit will survive, and since they are unfit
they will also not survive in the end, and the destruction of

our state and the extinction of our race will finally take place."[23] In this case it is, of course, clear to which category the revolutionaries belong. They have no idea of the priority of tasks imposed by evolution.

There is nothing new in all this, nor is there any novelty in Yen Fu's notorious "Critique of *The Social Contract*,"[24] which is cited by biographers as clear proof of his departure from both Westernism and liberalism. As a matter of fact, Yen Fu had never been favorably inclined toward Rousseau, nor were any of his spiritual mentors in the West. "Yen Fu had attributed the superiority of Western culture wholly to liberty and equality," states Chou Chen-fu. "Now Rousseau's *Social Contract* must be considered the most influential and penetrating work on the theory of liberty and equality."[25] The fact is, however, that Yen Fu, like Spencer, Huxley, Mill, and Jenks, had never shared Rousseau's views of the foundation of liberty and equality. There is, to be sure, in Spencer a certain vacillation, already pointed out by Barker,[26] between his strictly social-evolutionary account of human development and the notion of an innate "respect for the rights of others." This is reflected in Yen Fu's own earlier essays. Yet the main thrust of Spencer and Darwin is toward a denial of the meaningfulness of any notion of innate "rights" or of any equality not brought into being by the "objective" processes of social evolution. John Stuart Mill, who states in *On Liberty* "that I forego any advantage which could be derived to my argument from the idea of abstract right as a thing independent of utility,"[27] draws his views from a combination of Benthamism and nineteenth-century historicism, traditions which are both highly hostile to Rousseau.[28]

Yen Fu had always been quite clear concerning his rejection of Rousseau. In his "Translator's Directions" to *On Liberty* he had already stated explicitly that "Rousseau's view that men are born free has been rejected by later authorities who maintain that when a child is first born he is like a beast."[29] In his *Lectures on Politics* of 1906 he had sharply contrasted the historic-inductive approach to politics with Rousseau's approach. Before the eighteenth century, there were those who spoke of politics without relying on history. Men like Plato in ancient Greece, and in modern times Rousseau, have based their discussions of the state on psychology or attempted to deduce their views from natural law.[30]

The "Critique" of 1914 marks no major departure from Yen Fu's previous views on Rousseau except perhaps in its vehemence of tone. The authorities to which he appeals are all Western, and he quotes with particular relish Huxley's comments on the famous statement that "men are born free." Huxley had seen many infants in the course of his medical practice, and he had seen no evidence that they were in any way free. There is no natural equality among men. "Freedom and equality are based on law. One cannot say that people are free and equal by their very nature (*min-chih*)."[31] Law, on the other hand, is a product of a long historic development. The knowledge of the conditions within which freedom and equality actually emerge in human history can only be derived inductively from the study of history, not deductively from "a priori" propositions about human nature. On of the more interesting aspects of Yen Fu's article is its attack on socialism, which, of course, had by now become one of the mottoes of some elements among the political parties (Yen Fu sees Rousseau as the ultimate inspirer of socialism). The emphasis is new but the argument is not. Socialism denies the role of conflict[32] in human progress—that fact that "all the most fundamental issues of society are settled through conflict." Rousseau, in brief, is the godfather of all those who believe that liberty, equality, and democracy can be achieved in any time and place without the slightest regard for the historic circumstances which prevail. As for China in 1914, it is absolutely obvious that what "is most urgent at present is not freedom but the willingness of everyone to curtail freedom in the interests of the state and for the benefit of society."[33]

While nothing here is absolutely new, we do note a much more decided disassociation in Yen Fu's mind between the immediate tasks of modernization, or what Max Weber would call rationalization of society, and the values of liberty and equality. Even before 1911, Yen Fu had assigned priority to science and education—to the creation of modern industrial, military, bureaucratic, and legal systems. In the West "rationalization," liberty, equality, and democracy had grown together, had mutually reinforced each other and produced enormous yields of wealth and power. In China, however, first things would have to come first. Nevertheless, Yen Fu had committed himself before 1911 to a gradual "feeding in" of liberal (in the broadest sense) reforms. He had argued in his introduction to On Liberty for the freedom of speech and thought. In his discussion of legal reform he had related himself to the rights of the individual and he had approved of the government's cautious movement toward constitutionalism and parliamentary government. With the disappearance of the monarchy as a center of authority, however, it now appeared obvious to him that what China needed first was precisely those aspects of modernization which required organization, consolidation of forces, and direction from above: enlightened despotism was more necessary than ever. "It is my personal opinion that China must continue to be guided by a despotic government. Otherwise it will be impossible to restore order, let alone attain wealth and power."[34] The slogans of liberty, equality, and democracy under such conditions could only lead to further disintegration and anarchy. Under prevailing conditions, the only effects they could produce would be counter-revolutionary.

Whatever may be the "non-rational" substratum of Yen Fu's post-revolutionary political outlook, it is this type of thinking which provides the conscious, rational framework for his attitude toward Yüan Shih-k'ai during the years of his overlordship. Again we note that the rational framework is thoroughly consistent with the Western image of the world developed in previous years.

The attitude toward Yüan which emerges from Yen Fu's letters to Hsiung Ch'un-ju, while by no means simple, is fairly consistent. On the one hand, he does not have an excessively high opinion of Yüan's genius as a statesman. He certainly does not admire his moral character. On the other hand, in his view Yüan is the only strong leader China has. If he cannot immediately achieve measures leading to wealth and power, he can at the very minimum prevent complete disintegration. Yen Fu's response as a *chün-tzu* to many of Yüan's more sordid political acts is one of instinctive repugnance,[35] but his fundamental objection to Yüan does not lie here. "The most essential requirement of our policy," Yen Fu states in one of his letters to Hsiung, "is the achievement of strength abroad and order at home. The question of what methods are to be used is of secondary importance. I regret very much that you are unable to read the books of Machiavelli and the modern writer Treitschke. If you could read them, your views might be slightly different. Mencius states that if one can win the empire at the cost of one unrighteous act or by killing one innocent person, one should not do so. This is an extremely exalted opinion but one which can hardly prevail in the world. What I hold against Yüan Shih-k'ai, besides the fact that he performed many unrighteous acts and killed many innocent people, is that he did not even dream of achieving strength abroad and order at home. When one surveys the four years in which he was in power, one finds that the disunity of our armed forces and the confusion in our finances, which it was presumably his immediate aim to overcome, remained as they were. As for the other basic problems, such as education and the legal system, we need hardly speak of them."[36] Yüan Shih-k'ai had manifested all the unsavory aspects of the Machiavellian ruler without possessing any real ability to achieve Machiavellian goals.

Elsewhere, in speculating on Yüan Shih-k'ai's ability to cope with the crisis created by Japan's Twenty-One Demands, he states, "Our president has been a hero for a time, but his abilities do not go beyond those of a capable viceroy or governor under the old imperial system. He does not have the scientific knowledge required for contending with the rulers and ministers of the great powers, and he has no world view."[37] China has not been blessed with a truly modernizing enlightened despot. On the other hand, as against the Kuomintang politicians and ideologues, Yüan at least represents the principles of order and centralized authority. "Who is there, either in the new or old party, who is more fitted to be the head of state than Yüan Shih-k'ai?"[38] Finally, after the failure of Yüan's effort to establish a dynasty, Yen Fu in opposing those who are clamoring for his resignation concedes that Yüan has done some unforgivable things but insists that "we must forgive him because the level of our people is so low, because we are so drastically lacking in talent, and because our material power is so negligible—added to all of which are our foreign troubles. From the point of view of our survival, it would be just as much a mistake to force Yüan's resignation now as it formerly was to destroy the Manchu dynasty."[39]

It is into this context that we must place Yen Fu's much discussed role in Yüan's monarchical movement. In the first place, it is assumed almost as an axiom throughout his correspondence with Hsiung Ch'un-ju that the destruction of the monarchy had been a mistake and that there was no evidence that China had as yet passed beyond its "patriarchal-monarchic" stage of evolution. "Even a babe in arms must know that our country is best suited to monarchy."[40] The essential reasoning underlying this view has already been considered at length and probably differs in no essential respect from the reasoning of Yüan Shih-k'ai's American advisor, Frank J. Goodnow. The figures of Herbert Spencer and the other apostles of evolutionary thinking loom behind both the American political scientist and the Chinese literatus. If there lies beneath this "rational," theoretical level a profound traditional sentiment for the imperial institution as part of China's immemorial "Way," this does not become evident in any of Yen Fu's overt utterances, which always present the matter in coldly "political-scientific" terms.

On the other hand, if Yen Fu believed that the "ejection of the Ch'ing government like straw dogs"[41] had been a fatal error, this does not mean that he had thought of Yüan Shih-k'ai as the possible founder of a new dynasty. The main evidence we have concerning Yen Fu's role in 1915 is derived either from his own account or from that of Hou I, a former student who participated in the events. While these sources may not be unimpeachable, none of Yen Fu's Chinese biographers, including those who take a most dim view of the aging Yen Fu (for example, Wang Shih, Chou Chen fu) feel any need to raise questions concerning the credibility of these accounts. The fact is that both Yen Fu and Hou I maintain that Yen Fu had not really consented to the use of his name as a sponsor of the Peace Planning Society but that the use of his name had been the result of extraordinary pressures.

Hou I's circumstantial account relates that Yang Tu, the central figure in the whole monarchic movement, called upon Yen Fu one evening in August 1915 and asked him if he had read Mr. Goodnow's treatise on the unsuitability of republican government in China. When Yen Fu replied that he had, Yang Tu then asked, "Well, what do you think of our present political structure as compared to that of the Ch'ing dynasty? Do you really think that a republic can lead China onto the road of wealth and power?" To this question, which was clearly designed for Yen Fu's particular benefit, Yen Fu replied "Alas, this is a question which is now very difficult to answer. At the time of the 1911 revolution when the Ch'ing court proclaimed the nineteen articles of the draft constitution and swore never to violate them, I advocated the adoption of a system of titular monarchy (*hsü-chün*). If this could have been managed, the Manchu court, out of fear that the dynastic line might be cut off, would certainly have adhered to the nineteen articles and not dared to violate them. Since the prestige of the state had not yet been completely destroyed and the sentiments of the people not completely alienated, the deterioration in our national affairs might not have reached its present point. We might have had something like the British system where the monarch is inactive (*wu wei*) yet all political affairs proceed in their proper groove."

Whereupon Yang Tu replied, "This being the case, some of my colleagues and I have been planning the formation of a society which we are calling the 'Peace Planning Society'. It will explore the question of whether our country is best suited for a republican or monarchic form of government. Goodnow has opened up the subject and we intend to pursue it. Now among our scholars you, sir, are the man from whom we must seek direction.[42] Would you be one of our founders?" Yen Fu was taken aback by this proposal and changed color. He replied, "What I have just been talking about is the past. Once a revolution has occurred within a state, the political order cannot readily be brought back into its groove. A monarchic system depends on the majestic authority (*wei yen*) of the monarch. At present this sense of majestic authority has been swept away, and, if we rashly attempt to restore it, we may actually aggravate our present disorder. You all know that it has been my firm opinion that when a change in state is carried out too precipitously, the loss in vital energy may not be restored for decades. That is why I did not approve of what is now vulgarly called a 'revolution,' whether the intention was to introduce a democracy or a monarchic system, so long as this would lead to an abrupt overturn of the whole status quo. How similar the affairs of state are to a chess game where one error follows another! As for the question whether our country ought to have a monarchic form of government, even a babe in arms would know the answer to that question. The difficult point, however, is who shall be the monarch. As things now stand, even a sage could not decide. In my view, this is a most fearsome problem!"

Yang Tu then proceeded to assure him that the society would devote itself only to the theoretical question of whether China was best suited for a monarchy, not to the actual practical steps for creating a monarchy. Yen Fu tried to elude his grasp by asserting that such a society was unnecessary. The candidates for emperorship in the past had simply relied on their own powers. Yang Tu, continuing to press the point that a theoretical justification of monarchy was absolutely essential, grew more importunate. He even urged that if the society should decide against monarchy, the whole idea would be dropped. Finally Yen Fu agreed that he might be willing to join such a discussion group later.

The next evening, Yang Tu invited Yen Fu to a meeting of the future founders of the society, but the latter refused to attend on grounds of illness. After midnight, however, he received a letter from Yang Tu stating that Yüan Shih-k'ai was insisting that the new society would be inconceivable without the sponsorship of Yen Fu and that the names of the founders would be listed in the newspapers the next day. Yen Fu himself states that he was finally forced to give his assent. He did not, however, participate in the meetings of the society, nor did he accede to Yüan Shih k'ai's demand that he reply to Liang Ch'i-ch'ao's famous attack on the monarchic restoration movement.[43]

Whether this account of Yen Fu's relationship to Yüan's

monarchic plans represents the entire truth is not our main concern here. It is quite conceivable that, in addition to failing to discern in Yüan the qualities of the great founders of dynasty, Yen Fu was suffering from his life-long fear of assuming responsibility for large political decisions. If he had indeed been pressured into lending his name to the movement, certainly he had not insisted that his name be removed. Probably he would have given his wholehearted support to a Yüan dynasty if it had proved successful; his political sense, however, seemed to warn him that the movement would not succeed.

Our main concern here is with the views on monarchy expressed in the interview with Yang Tu. The stress is wholly directed to what might be called the symbolic authority of the monarchic institution. Yen Fu is essentially concerned with the question of the bases of political authority. Within a "patriarchal monarchic" society the monarchy could be used as a focus of "majestic authority" around which the modernization effort could proceed. Given such an ongoing, traditional, universally understood center of authority, one might even hope that power could actually be separated from authority and that China might in the course of time achieve as much democracy as Great Britain. However, the spiritual foundations on which the authority of republics rested were as yet totally lacking.

It is thus highly debatable whether Yen Fu's expressed political opinions of the 1911–1915 period can be offered as solid evidence of "the return to tradition." Viewed in terms of their inner logic, his ideas are perhaps more prospective than retrospective. His essential critique of the effort to establish a democratic republic in China in 1911 is still very much with us. The notion that certain tasks of "rationalization" in the spheres of education, industry, technology, and state administrative organization must precede the achievement of democracy (however understood) is imbedded in numerous contemporary ideologies, as well as in the reasoning of economic development theorists and others. Yen Fu does not, to be sure, anticipate the potent twentieth-century blend of enlightened elitism with radical "populist" or "proletarian" theories of legitimation—the notion that the same enlightened elite which assumes the essential tasks of modernization also incarnates the general will of the people or the proletariat. In seeking sources of legitimation for elitist government in 1911 one would naturally look to the forms of legitimation of authority provided by the past. After all, even Imperial Germany and modern Japan, which were the most successful cases of "modernizing" authoritarian regimes, derived their ultimate authority from traditional monarchy. In 1911 the notion of popular sovereignty still implied political democracy—not the "dictatorship of the people."

Until World War I, Yen Fu did not seem ready to abandon the belief that "liberty, equality, and democracy" in their Anglo-American interpretation were ultimately indispensable elements in the syndrome of factors leading to wealth and power. If his particular form of liberalism was inherently vulnerable from the very outset to the demonstration that there might be swifter and more direct ways of achieving wealth and power, nothing Yen Fu himself had observed before World War I shook his conviction that liberalism was an indispensable element in the ultimate achievement of national power. He had been aware that Prussia and later Imperial Germany and Japan had been able to tap the energies of their people with something far less than a fully liberal constitution. As already pointed out, he was acutely aware of their accomplishments in those realms of "rationalization" which had no necessary connection (at least at the outset) with liberalism. In the *Wealth of Nations* he had spoken in high praise of Germany's accomplishments in the realm of education—accomplishments which had made it possible for Germany to "pass from weakness to power in the space of fifty years."[44]

Until World War I, however, Yen Fu's image of Germany and Japan was that of states which were also moving in the direction of "people's rights." "In Germany and Austria people's rights still somewhat counteract the power of the sovereign."[45] When he read Ito's commentaries on the Japanese constitution, he was impressed with the evidence offered of Japan's movement toward people's rights. "The Japanese constitution differed widely, to be sure, from European constitutions, but this was because Ito realized that constitutions must be based on the people's degree of advancement . . . The law can be constantly improved in order to keep abreast of the people while the people are transformed by the law, until both law and people advance together and a most rational government can be achieved."[46] Yen Fu was thus convinced that Japan itself was riding the universal wave moving toward the establishment of "people's rights."

As for Russian Tsarism, which had carried out a narrow program of military modernization and neglected all other aspects of modernization, and which was fiercely resisting the universal trend toward people's rights, Yen Fu was contemptuous, in the main,[47] of its claims to real power and actually predicted its defeat in the Russo-Japanese War. When Adam Smith presumes to praise Peter the Great for establishing a well-regulated standing army, and even argues that the standing army is a means by which "a barbarous country can be suddenly and tolerably civilized,"[48] Yen Fu declares from the vantage point of subsequent history that this is not so.[49] A narrow policy of military modernization within an arbitrary despotism cannot lead to real strength. (Yen Fu disagrees, in any event, with Adam Smith's praise of professional standing armies; he favors conscription.) "While Russia is strong abroad, its regime cannot long endure. It used Peter's system to rise to its present position, and it is by Peter's system that it will meet its ruin."[50] Yen Fu's views of the ingredients of wealth and power are not crass. Nothing less than a total, integrated program of modernization ultimately including "people's rights" can achieve true wealth and power.

It is during World War I, however, that his views begin to vacillate. The word "vacillate" is appropriate. Yen Fu by no means completely abandons his former outlook. The overriding conviction that the Allies will win in the end seems to be linked to the view that they—particularly his first love, Great Britain—enjoy abiding strengths not available to the Germans. Indeed, at the very outset of the war, at a time when German power was rolling across Belgium and northern France, he assures his protégé, Hsiung, that the Germans will not prevail in spite of the fact that "since 1870 they have risen to brilliant heights." In spite of their impressive accomplishments in military affairs, medicine, commerce, philosophy, physics, and education, "they live under an arrogant sovereign" who "lightly uses his people to make war against four or five world powers."[51] The archetypal image which comes to his mind is that of Hsiang Yü and Liu Pang after the fall of the Ch'in dynasty. Hsiang Yü is portrayed by Ssu-ma Ch'ien as the protagonist of sheer brute military power who hopes to win the kingdom wholly by the sword. Liu Pang is the shrewd statesman[52] who knows that the sentiments of the people and the ability to influence men have more to do with final victory than sheer ability to wield the sword. The British polity embodies these intangible "Liu Pang" elements of power. If the Germans are to win, Yen Fu asserts, they must win quickly.[53]

As the war proceeds, however, this view comes to contend with other views and sentiments which are colored as much by his Chinese preoccupations as by his observation of European events.[54] The enormous staying power of the Germans against overwhelming odds, the brutal assertion of Japanese power in China during the Twenty-One Demands episode, and the growing fiasco of the republic in China all affect his sentiments. "The power of Germany," he asserts at one point, "is something which has never existed since the beginning of the human race."[55] The ability of Germany to sustain a prolonged war on several fronts, to lose untold numbers of men and sacrifice untold treasure, overwhelms him with awe. The British were indeed responding to the challenge, but the war had demonstrated that Germany's emphasis on military affairs and dictatorial government had put her in a favored position. After all, "democracy is not suited to military planning." England and France had had to reorganize themselves along more authoritarian lines[56] in order to prosecute the war. The Japanese had modelled themselves on Germany rather than England, not simply because they felt that this was more in keeping with the level of civilization of the Japanese people, but also because they realized that if they modelled themselves on Great Britain and France "it would have been difficult to achieve national power."

Yen Fu here departs significantly from his usual unilinear, evolutionary line of argument, hinting that there may, after all, be quicker and more direct routes to national power than that provided by the British example. What now impresses him far more than the difference between "democratic and despotic" states is a common characteristic of all states in the West which he has long admired—the incredible "people's virtue" which has made possible this unheard-of sacrifice of men and treasure. "While there are differences among Western states, in their ability to educate the people to the service of the state they are all more or less alike."[57] The most bitter expression of the tendency to downgrade liberal values can be found, however, in a passage in which Yen Fu notes that the vast and swift changes now occurring in the world are leading to the disintegration of theories which have in the past been considered sacred truths. "As for the various doctrines of equality, liberty, and people's rights [democracy] which have been considered a second gospel during the last hundred years, their limitations are now apparent."[58] The British and French have been forced to modify these doctrines in order to avoid destruction. Meanwhile, the Turks, the Chinese, and the Russians (immediately after the February Revolution) were treating as a sacred treasure the very principles which were being abandoned in the land which had given them birth. "China is already on the road to destruction and Russia will not avoid disaster if it attempts to implement republicanism." Here we finally meet the explicit avowal that liberalism may not be so much premature as obsolete (even in the West).

Even here, however, one cannot really speak of a repudiation of the West unless one equates the West with liberalism. What we find, rather, is a radical reassessment of the role of liberal values in the syndrome of factors leading to wealth and power. Military, bureaucratic, and industrial "rationalization" in the Weberian sense, which is symbolized in Yen Fu's mind by the Legalist strain in Chinese thought —by Han-fei-tsu and Shen Pu-hai—still commands his adherence. Authoritarianism is not out of date in the modern world. It must, however, be a dynamic, positive authoritarianism.

Commingled with this intertwined tangle of confused sentiments, however, we can also find bitter statements of outright repudiation of the West and of all its works. The last few years of Yen Fu's life are years of black despair, at least as far as his public hopes are concerned.[59] He belongs to a generation whose life-span occupies a most unfortunate sector of time. As a patriotic Chinese fated to die in 1921, as a man of not particularly sanguine temperament, he sees a China descending ever more deeply into the abyss. The forces of evolution have not simply bogged down in China. They seem to have deserted it entirely. His letters abound in laments and outcries. He sees no signs of hope and refuses to be comforted.[60] Added to this, one of the strands in his complex reaction to the war is a genuine sense of shock. His social Darwinism had prepared him for the more limited wars of the nineteenth century, such as the Boer War, but the enormity and scale of destruction of World War I fill him with alternating moods of awe and horror.

One of the acts of Yen Fu which is often cited as a clear indication of his turn away from the West and his return to tradition is his adherence as early as June 1913 to the Society for Confucianism[61] and his endorsement of the Society's petition that Confucianism be recognized as China's state religion. But even this gesture is not as conclusive as it might seem. Do we have here an act of authentic, profound commitment, or are we still dealing with the calculations of the vicarious statesman? It is interesting to note that "The Program of the Confucian Society" is itself a sort of statesman's document. It argues (as K'ang Yu-wei had been arguing for several years) that a state cannot exist without some commonly shared faith. Some have claimed that the French Revolution abolished religion, but what it abolished was France's "old faith." Confucianism is compatible with everything good that the West has to offer, but in addition it offers the Chinese people a focus of "religious" devotion. It is because the Jews and Indians possess such a focus that they may some day hope to recreate their political power. On the other hand, the ancient Mexicans, who lost their religion, also lost their national identity.[62]

Yen Fu adds his own characteristic perspectives to the argument of this manifesto. In a letter to Hsiung, who was engaged at this time in educational activities in Kiangsi, we find him advising the younger man that "reading the classics" should form part of his school's curriculum but "should not occupy too much time." Traditional values should, however, be inculcated, for "it is in the nature of evolution that one should proceed gradually in the transition from a patriarchal to a military society. Changes cannot be forced by human effort (jen-li)."[63] Here Confucianism is clearly identified as the ethos of a passing stage of human history. Confucianism has a role to play as a moral preservative until the preconditions of a fully "military society" come into existence. Here we met again a kind of reasoning which has little to do with any authentic commitment to Confucian values. Yen Fu is still operating within his evolutionary categories.

It is only after the outbreak of the war that we finally meet assertions which express an explicit repudiation of the West. "Such has been the effect on the human race of civilization and science! When I look back on our sacred wisdom and culture, I find that it foresaw this even at that early date and that what it valued was not the same as what these nations [of the West] value."[64] "As I have grown older and observed the seven years of republican government in China and the four years of bloody war in Europe —a war such as the world has never known—I have come to feel that their [the West's] progress during the last three hundred years has only led to selfishness, slaughter, corruption, and shamelessness. When I look back on the way of Confucius and Mencius, I find that they are truly the equivalent of heaven and earth and have profoundly benefited the realm. This is not my opinion alone. Many thinking people in the West have gradually come to feel this way."[65] The sages may, after all, have been right in shrinking back from the Promethean enterprise of the West.

It is quite difficult to gauge the depth of this latter-day conversion to Confucius and Mencius.[66] Yen Fu was certainly at home in the Confucian family morality and comfortable with the principle of authority in general. It is exceedingly doubtful, however, whether he had been reconverted to the Confucian-Mencian faith in "government by virtue," or to the Confucian-Mencian optimism concerning what might be called the spiritualization of politics. On the contrary, his praises of Confucius are intermingled with his invocation of Legalism and of the "tough men" of Chinese history (Ts'ao Ts'ao, T'ang T'ai-tsung, and so forth), as well as with praises for Machiavelli and Treitschke.

In the end, Yen Fu's deepest commitment within the world of Chinese culture probably remains what it had been in the past—the commitment to the mystical strain in Lao-tzu and Chuang-tzu. At the end of 1916 he reports to his disciple that his thoughts are now being drawn more and more to the thought of Chuang-tzu, who had demonstrated more clearly even than Lao-tzu the relativity, transiency, and fundamental unimportance of all purposes and principles within the world of the ten thousand things. The ancient kings, states Chuang-tzu, had treated the Confucian principles of "benevolence and righteousness" like straw huts in which one can lodge for the night but hardly take up permanent residence. If Chuang-tzu were alive today, he would have said the same about liberty, equality, and fraternity.[67] The world of the ten thousand things is indeed an inconstant flux in which there can be no fixed principles for all times and places. Evolution does take place but probably does not matter. His face is now turned to the Void. "Idling in my little pavilion," he writes after returning to his native village in 1921, "I watch the clouds and listen to the rain . . . or else kill time by practicing calligraphy. I cannot look at the books on history and philosophy of which I was formerly so fond and do not care to talk of current affairs. I lie here like a dry stick and cold ashes, all but dead.[68] Of what avail is it to live longer this way in the world of men? My heart is now at peace. I am resigned to the Great Transformation."[69]

CHAPTER XII

Some Implications

TURNING BACK from the discouragements of old age to the vision of the younger Yen Fu (while noting that the discouragements themselves throw some light on the nature of the vision), we return to the central question. What does the West have which China lacks? Where does the crucial difference lie? The question is, of course, not raised in a spirit of disinterested inquiry. It is thrust forward by an urgent, overriding concern with the woeful debility of the Chinese state—its lack of wealth and power. This does not mean that Yen Fu does not have perspectives which lie beyond this immediate preoccupation. Like Herbert Spencer himself, he discerns in the golden future a state in which struggle will have ceased (Taiping) and in which welfare, freedom, and every other value will prevail in a utopian equilibrium. I would urge again, however, that this "ultimate" perspective is by no means as significant in shaping the nature of his vision as the preoccupation which occupies the foreground.

While the preoccupation itself may seem narrowly political, in seeking out the ultimate sources of the West's power Yen Fu finds himself driven far beyond the domain of the political to an inquiry into the very essence of modern Western civilization. Unlike some of his more superficial successors he does not find the crucial difference in the conventional dichotomy between the materialist West and the spiritual East.[1] He is too keenly aware of the role of the spiritual-intellectual component in the Promethean surge of the West. He is deeply conscious of the fact that the whole machinery of industrialism, of modern state bureaucracy, modern legal systems, and military organizations could not have been the creation of men exclusively interested in immediate material pleasures. As already indicated, he tends to find more "materialism" (in the ethical sense) among his Chinese contemporaries than in the modern West. The crucial difference is not a question of matter but a question of energy. The West has exalted human energy in all its manifestations—intellectual, moral, and physical. It has identified spirit not with passivity and withdrawal but with energy and assertion. The West has discovered the unlimited nature of human capacities and has fearlessly proceeded to actualize human potentialities undreamt-of in traditional Chinese culture. The terms which come to mind as key-value terms are dynamism, purposive action, energy, assertiveness, and the realization of all potentialities.

These are, after all, terms which are valued by the most diverse modern Western ideologies and which cut across all their divergencies. One is indeed tempted to describe that to which Yen Fu responds, in the first instance, as the Faustian character of Western civilization. Without necessarily endorsing Spengler's total treatment of this notion, or his effort to find its origins in the primeval forests of

Germany, the term is useful as a designation of that quality of Western civilization which is probably primary in the perception of Yen Fu and of many others in the non-Western world. Like his master Herbert Spencer and unlike some romanticists, he sees in the increasingly complex machinery of modern Western civilization an embodiment of, not an impediment to, the West's Faustian energy. The Faustian nature of Western culture has led to the Promethean conquest of external nature and the enormous growth of social-political power within human society. It is obviously the Faustian-Promethean nature of Western civilization which has produced the West's enormous output of wealth and power.

Viewed in this light, Darwinism as interpreted by Spencer emerges not simply as a scientific hypothesis concerning the nature of biological evolution, but as a singularly appropriate cosmic myth epitomizing and supporting all the values of a Faustian civilization. Energy, action, assertiveness, struggle leading to the actualization of human potentialities on ever higher levels of heterogeneity, complexity, and organization—all these values are clearly realized in a Darwinian universe. In sharp contrast to many sensitive spirits in Victorian England, the younger Yen Fu accepts the Spencer-Darwin image of the universe because he ardently wishes it to be true.

If the Faustian character of the West is crucial, the strictly liberal aspects of Yen Fu's vision must be considered as a part of the whole—as a means to an end. Herbert Spencer, Adam Smith, and, to a certain extent, John Stuart Mill have convinced him that the energies which account for the West's development are stored up in the individual and that these energies can be realized only in an environment favorable to individual interests. Liberty, equality (above all, equality of opportunity), and democracy provide the environment within which the individual's "energy of faculty" is finally liberated. From the very outset, however,

Yen Fu escapes some of the more rigid dogmatic antitheses of nineteenth-century European liberalism. Precisely because his gaze is ultimately focused not on the individual per se but on the presumed results of individualism, the sharp antitheses between the individual and society, individual initiative and social organization, and so on, do not penetrate to the heart of his perception. His more detached eye sees in the modern industrial corporation a triumph both of individual enterprise and of social organization. Prometheus is no more favorable to rugged individualism per se than to social organization per se, and will use whatever means are appropriate to the achievement of his ends. While the individual may be the ultimate source of energy, the consolidation of individual energies in bureaucratic organizations does not inhibit or diminish these energies. It rather enhances and channels them toward constructive goals.

If Yen Fu thus escapes the dogmatic features of Spencer's individualism, the real question which confronts us is, How profoundly rooted is his variety of liberalism? In the final analysis one may assert that what has *not* come through in Yen Fu's perception is precisely that which is often considered to be the ultimate spiritual core of liberalism—the concept of the worth of persons within society as an end in itself, joined to the determination to shape social and political institutions to promote this value. Yen Fu's concept of liberalism as a means to the end of state power is mortally vulnerable to the demonstration that there are shorter roads to that end. Spencer has given him the conception of the individual as a unit of energy, as well as the notion that this unit is valuable only in proportion to its efficiency. What if it can be demonstrated that these useful energies can be called forth in states which completely negate the values of liberty and political democracy? What if it can also be demonstrated that a social organization has been as essential to the enhancement of social

energies as individual initiative? The positive authoritarian-
isms of the twentieth century have not inhibited the physical, moral, and intellectual (that is, technico-intellectual)
energies of the energetic individual. These authoritarian
states have in fact been deeply interested in enhancing
these energies. Spencer's ideal "happy" man (see note 34
of Chapter III)—"the healthy man of high powers, conscious of past successes, and by his energy, quickness, resource made confident of the future"—can function as well
as a *Gauleiter*, commissar, or Soviet industrial manager as a
capitalist tycoon, particularly if he is endowed with the
requisite lack of moral imagination and reflectiveness.

Spencer's concept of individuality allied to a preoccupation with state power can only lead to a deformation of the
values of liberalism. Even in its original "individualistic"
form, this concept had little to do with the spiritual core
of liberalism as defined above. What it involves is not the
assertion of the intrinsic value of individuals but the exaltation of wealth and power on the individual rather than
the collective plane. The cult of "the man of high powers"
on the individual plane is likely to be just as contemptuous
of the "ill-endowed" person as any totalitarian philosophy.
It was, after all, this demonic strain in Spencer which
aroused the profound antipathy of the elderly Huxley.

The possibility of this type of deformation is by no means
confined to liberalism. The cluster of notions which hover
about the word "socialism" are, if anything, even more
vulnerable to deflection in the service of power goals. There
is an element of surface paradox in Yen Fu's efforts to prove
that the ethic of economic individualism can serve the
collective interests of the state. On the surface, at least, the
"ethic of socialism" seems much more directly available to
the collective ends of state power. In the Stalinist development of Marxism-Leninism one has a classical instance of
how socialism (defined in terms of state ownership and
planning) can become a means to the end of power.[2] The

argument that socialism in this sense is superior because it leads to higher rates of economic growth, superior technology, and national might has become a central feature of current Soviet apologetics, although it would have seemed most strange to Marx and many other nineteenth-century socialists.

Yen Fu's English liberalism was not to prosper in China after the May Fourth period. However, his preoccupation with wealth and power and his response to the Faustian element in Western civilization have remained fundamental features of the consciousness of the Chinese intelligentsia, underlying and becoming entangled with all the separate ideological currents which have since emerged, whether they have been labelled socialist, liberal, or even neo-traditionalist.[3] This generalization does not, of course, apply to many individual thinkers, poets, and literary figures whose concerns have been quite unrelated to the goals of national power. But it remains, it seems to me, true in the aggregate.

One might indeed broaden the scope of this observation to include many of the emerging intelligentsia of the non-Western world at large. As in the case of Yen Fu, one discerns in their "response to the West" something which lies below all the explicit social, political, ideological commitments. On the one hand, they profoundly resent the failure of their own cultural traditions to reveal man's limitless Faustian capacities. On the other hand, they profoundly resent the West, which has used its Faustian power to humiliate those who lack this power. The latter *ressentiment* is, to be sure, not particularly present in Yen Fu. His special brand of social Darwinism will not allow him to blame the "fittest" for asserting their powers. Yet in his essential concern with the crucial, humiliating difference between East and West, Yen Fu may well represent a universal, underlying element in the response to the West everywhere. It would nevertheless be quite wrong to dispose of Yen Fu's treatment of Western ideas as a distortion of modern Western thought in a non-Western mind. If social Darwinism and liberalism are linked in his thought, it is because he already finds them entangled with each other, in a somewhat different way, in the writings of Herbert Spencer. The unsolved problems of nineteenth- and twentieth-century Western thought must themselves be brought into the arena of discussion. *De nobis fabula narratur.*

Broadly speaking, it seems to me that one can distinguish two strands of modern Western development in Yen Fu's writings: (1) the Faustian-Promethean strain—the exaltation of energy and power both over non-human nature and within human society, involving the "rationalization" (in the Weberian sense) of man's whole socio-economic machinery; (2) what might loosely be called the stream of social-political idealism. The latter strand, represented by terms such as freedom, equality, democracy, and socialism, has been concerned with the nature of relations among men within the larger macroscopic structures of political and social life and with the shaping of those structures to promote these social-ethical ends. It represents one particular variety of ethical thought. Much of the ethical passion of Western man in recent centuries has been directed toward such social-ethical ends and has been involved in conflicts concerning the relations of these various ends to one another. Some, no doubt, would object violently to any effort to distinguish these strands even conceptually; it is indeed true that in "life" they are hopelessly intertwined. Historic simultaneity is not, however, a proof of immanent logical ("functional") relationship, and we may distinguish in analysis that which comes together in life.

The vast issues raised here can hardly be dealt with in the space of a few pages. Some questions may, however, be raised. The notion that the two strands are "functionally" related comes to the fore in many complex forms in the ideologies of the nineteenth and twentieth centuries. Before the nineteenth century, the relationship was by no means so obvious, and it is by no means certain that the two strands spring entirely from the same sources. Many serious historians have sought the roots of the concern for liberty, equality, democracy, and socialism in impulses rising, intentionally and unintentionally, out of the Reformation (combined with other strands of ancient and medieval thought), coming into confrontation with the concrete historic circumstances of the seventeenth and eighteenth centuries. On the other hand, some aspects of the Faustian growth of the West—the emergence of the modern bureaucratic, military, legal, and even industrial machinery—are clearly linked to the emergence of the absolute nation-states and the conflicts of these states. We are forcefully reminded that Jefferson, Rousseau, and many other patron saints of libertarian and democratic views during the latter half of the eighteenth century perceived no necessary functional relationship between liberty, equality, and democracy and the machinery of industrialism, let alone the machinery of power. Halévy makes a good case for the proposition that the democratic and utilitarian movements (the latter most clearly associated with Adam Smith's economic orientation) in England were in origin quite separate and only gradually became fused at the end of the century.[4]

It is only in the early nineteenth century that close functional relations come to be perceived between the expanding machinery of wealth, in particular, and the social and political ideals, even though the question of the nature of the relationship remains a matter of dispute. One can find it argued, on the one hand, that the teachings of Locke made possible the industrial revolution, and on the other, that the industrial revolution brought liberty, equality, and democracy into being. For Karl Marx it was obvious that we are borne to socialism on the wings of the forces of production. Common to Spencer, Saint-Simon, and Marx is the belief that the machinery of industrialism will automatically realize their most cherished political and social ideals. Also common both to economic liberals (such as Spencer) and to Marxists is a tendency to think of the industrial age as marking the end of the age of the nation-state and of its power goals. There is a common assumption that while the expanding machinery of wealth is a functional prerequisite for the achievement of either liberal or socialist goals, the machinery of state and military power is either already obsolete or about to become so.

In fact, a candid, retrospective glance would indicate that at no time in the history of nineteenth-century Europe, even at the height of Manchester liberalism, was economic development ever completely divorced from the machinery and goals of state power, even though its immanent economic end may be defined as the ultimate achievement of general economic welfare.[5] It can hardly be claimed that this "mercantilist" factor has diminished in the slightest in the middle of the twentieth century, when the two world super-powers confront each other in terms of the balance of terror. Here again, Yen Fu's old Chinese formula permits him to perceive more clearly than many Western thinkers confined by their ideological commitments the fact that the machinery of industrialism and the concerns of national (or super-national) power are never divided by an iron wall. If the values of liberalism and/or socialism are a by-product of the "rationalization" of modern society, then they must be related to this rationalization in all its aspects—political, military, and economic. The growth of state and military power is as relevant as the march of industrialization.[6]

One need not deny all claims of positive relation between the political and social values mentioned above and the machinery of wealth and power. I would suggest, however, that the relationship between them is much more accidental, equivocal, haphazard, and mutable than is generally assumed in the bland religion of modernization. The more "liberal" state structure of eighteenth-century England may have provided a more favorable environment for the first breakthrough of industrial capitalism than the bureaucratized states of the Continent. The machinery of wealth and power does require the expansion of its ruling elite and—up to a point at least—a stress on achievement is inherent in the process of modernization. This does imply a growing area of equality of opportunity. One will thus find a growing equality of opportunity in societies as diverse as Meiji Japan, Nazi Germany, the Soviet Union, and the United States. The freedom to choose among career opportunities and to develop one's physical and intellectual powers (when these are safely technical in the broadest sense of that term) are equalities and freedoms which have been fostered within both democracies and the modern, positive authoritarian states. These authoritarian states have been quite able, however, to dispense with civil rights involving the physical inviolability of individuals, with spiritual liberty, with political democracy and social equality. If the word "socialism" involves a concern with human equality and not simply a "planned" and centrally organized society, it has been amply demonstrated that the machinery of wealth and power is inherently hierarchic and authoritarian. There are those who assure us that the happy day when the processes of modernization will spontaneously realize all social and political ideals is just over the horizon. As of the present, however, it should be noted that in those societies where these values have been realized to any extent and with any degree of solidity there have been conscious historic movements expressly devoted to their achievement and not merely a blind reliance on the "forces of modernization."

One can hardly stand in judgment on Yen Fu or the modern Chinese intelligentsia for concerning themselves with the question of state power. China has indeed been deeply humiliated, and no society can survive in the modern world without state power. However, the fact remains that where values are judged as means toward the attainment of power these values are likely to be rendered precarious, weak, and deformed.

In becoming involved with these problems, Yen Fu and China have already entered the unchartered sea of the modern world in which we all are afloat. The problem of the relation between the Faustian religion of the limitless pursuit of wealth and power and the achievement of social-political values—and even more fundamental human values—remains a problem for us as much as for them.

NOTES

CHAPTER I. The Setting.

1. All claims of this sort are never absolutely true. The doctrine of the Taiping Rebellion, as we know, embodied Christian elements. Yen Fu's contemporary, K'ang Yu-wei, had undoubtedly been influenced by Western thought in spite of his claim to have derived all his ideas from Chinese tradition. China's first ambassador to England, Kuo Sung-t'ao, had already spoken of the necessity of concerning oneself with Western ideas as well as with Western institutions.

2. This emphasis on intellectual factors in human history is quite marked in Confucian thought. It gained enormous plausibility from the fact that the intelligentsia was also the official class.

3. For a brief discussion see Liang Ch'i-ch'ao, *Intellectual Trends in the Ch'ing Period*, tr. Immanuel C. Y. Hsü (Cambridge, Mass., 1959), pp. 85–98; see also Ch'ien Mu, *Chung-kuo chin san pai nien hsüeh-shu shih* (An intellectual history of China during the last 300 years; Shanghai, 1937).

4. Ch'eng Chin-fang, "Cheng-hsüeh lun" (On correct learning) No. 3, in Ho Ch'ang-ling, *Huang-ch'ao ching-shih wen-pien* (A collection of works on statecraft; Peking, 1896), 2:3.

5. For a discussion of this school see Chiang Shu-ko, *T'ung-ch'eng wen-p'ai shu-p'ing* (A critical account of the T'ung-ch'eng school; Shanghai, 1930).

6. Mary C. Wright, *The Last Stand of Chinese Conservatism: The Tung-chih Restoration* (Stanford, 1957).

7. Teng Ssu-yü and John K. Fairbank, *China's Response to the West* (Cambridge, Mass., 1954), I, 76.

8. Wright, Chap. 8.

9. *Analects,* Bk. VIII, Chap. 9.

10. "Only men of education (*shih*) are able to maintain a fixed heart without a certain livelihood. As for the people, if they have not a certain livelihood it follows that they will not have a fixed heart"—*Mencius,* Bk. I, Chap. 7, No. 20.

11. "I do not grieve that it [the people] is poor, I grieve that it is not at peace." *Analects,* Bk. XVI, Chap. 1, No. 10.

12. Actually Confucius speaks of "enriching" the people, and this statement has often been cited to support the claim that Confucianism favored "economic development." This "enriching of the people" is, however, invariably described in orthodox Confucian literature in terms of a comfortable subsistence economy. *Analects,* Bk. XIII, Chap. 9, No. 3.

13. The word physiocratic is often used to translate the Chinese *chung-nung* (stress on agriculture). In this area also there was a marked difference between the Legalist and Confucian position. While the orthodox Confucian position stressed that agriculture was the only legitimate base of economy, the Legalists showed a more distinct interest in a systematic effort to increase agricultural production. The famous reform attributed to Lord Shang—the creation of "private" property in land—was presumably designed to increase the state's revenues.

14. Huan K'uan, "Yen t'ieh lun" (Discourses on iron and salt), in *Chu-tzu chi-ch'eng* (A collection of the writings of the philosophers; Peking, 1954), Vol. 7, Chap. 1, p. 2.

15. This is, of course, an oversimplification. The famous Sung minister Wang An-shih staunchly argued that "wealth and power" was an aim entirely compatible with the aim of popular welfare. Ssu-ma Ch'ien, the famous historian of the Han (who had no deep Confucian commitments) in his "Biographies of Money-makers" speaks in high praise of commercial entrepreneurs both for their contribution to state power and to economic progress as such (see Burton Watson, *Records of the Grand Historian of China;* New York, 1961, II, 476).

16. As often pointed out, the orthodox political-economic philosophy may also have served as rationalization of the private interests of the gentry class in its role as landed proprietor and hence opponent of centralized power.

17. Wright, p. 60.

18. *Ibid.,* pp. 167–174.

19. See Hao Yen-p'ing, *T'ung-kuang hsin cheng chung ti so-wei* (*ch'ing i*): *Chung-kuo wan-Ch'ing ti pao-shou-chu-i* (The so-called "Pure View" School of the T'ung-chih and Kuang-hsü periods: conservatism in China during the late Ch'ing period; Taipei, 1958), p. 6.

20. *Ibid.*

21. *Ibid.*

22. An excellent study of the effort is Albert Feuerwerker's *China's Early Industrialization: Sheng Hsuan-huai* (1844–1916) *and Mandarin Enterprise* (Cambridge, Mass., 1958). One of the many weaknesses of this effort may have lain precisely in the overly simple-minded understanding of the motto "wealth and power." All undertakings were thought of in terms of their immediate relevance to military aims.

23. Cited in Chao Feng-t'ien, *Wan Ch'ing wu-shih nien ching-chi ssu-hsiang shih* (Economic thought during the last fifty years of the Ch'ing dynasty); *Yen-ching hsüeh-pao ch'uan-hao* (Yenching journal of Chinese studies, special monographs), No. 18 (1939).

24. Li Hung-chang, *Li Wen-chung-kung ch'üan-chi* (Complete works of Li Hung-chang; Nanking, 1905), *Tsou-kao* (Draft memorials), 9:6.

25. Chang Chih-tung in his *Ch'üan-hsüeh p'ien* (Exhortation to Learning; Wuchang, 1898), written in June of 1898 on the very eve of the "Hundred Days Reform," attempts to define the unchanging core of Confucianism in terms of the basic norms of human relationships (*lun chi*) and the methods of personal cultivation (*hsin-shu* or *chih shen-hsin*). What must be preserved above all is a certain ideal of manhood closely associated with certain traditional moral virtues. "Filial piety, fraternal piety, loyalty, faithfulness" are the values which must be preserved. Beyond this, one finds a deep commitment to benevolent authoritarianism and a frank rejection of the concept of parliamentarianism. The *Chün-tzu* ideal of manhood includes the vocation to rule. The crucial point to note here is that the preservation of the Confucian ideal of manhood is not regarded as a means to the achievement of national power. National power must be created in order to preserve the Confucian ideal of manhood.

26. "Shang-huang ti wan-yen-shu," Yen Fu, *Yen Chi-tao shih-wen ch'ao* (A collection of Yen Fu's prose and poetry; Shanghai, 1922), ts'e 5:3.

27. Cited in Li Ting-i, *Chung-kuo chin-tai shih* (A history

of modern China; Taipei, 1956), p. 128. The word *kuo*, here
translated as "state," was occasionally used in a more restricted
sense to refer to the dynasty.
28. Professor Joseph R. Levenson has clearly developed
this distinction in his *Liang Ch'i-ch'ao and the Mind of Modern
China* (Cambridge, Mass., 1959).

CHAPTER II. The Early Years

1. His *ming* in later years was Chi-tao and his style Yu-ling.
2. Wang Shih, *Yen Fu chuan* (Biography of Yen Fu;
Shanghai, 1957), p. 1.
3. The family consisted of four children. One brother, two
years older than Yen Fu, died young. There were also two
younger sisters. See Wang Ch'ü-ch'ang, *Yen Chi-tao nien-p'u*
(Chronological biography of Yen Fu; Shanghai, 1936), p. 1.
4. *Ibid.*, p. 3.
5. For an account in English of the establishment of this
school see Wright, pp. 212–213. For a Chinese account see
Tso Tsung-t'ang *et al.*, comps., *Ch'uan cheng tsou i hui-pien*
(Collection of memorials on naval administration; Peking,
1905), Vol. 2.
6. See Yen Fu's biographical epitaph by Ch'en Pao-ch'en,
"Ch'ing ku tzu-cheng ta-fu hai-chün hsieh tu-t'ung Yen chün
mu chih-ming" (An epitaph on the tomb of Yen Fu, former
councilor and vice-admiral), in Min Erh-ch'ang, comp., *Pei-
chuan chi pu* (Supplement to a collection of epitaph biographies; Peking, 1931). Cited in Wang Ch'ü-ch'ang, p. 4.
7. Wang Ch'ü-ch'ang, p. 4.
8. See Wang Shih, p. 9.
9. Wang Ch'ü-ch'ang, p. 7.
10. Yen Fu, *Fa-i* (Spirit of the laws), *Yen i ming-chu
ts'ung-k'an*, Vol. 5 (A collection of Yen Fu's translated works;
Shanghai, 1931), Bk. XI, Chap. 6, p. 8.
11. Wang Shih, p. 12.
12. In Ch'ih Chung-hu, "Hai-chün ta shih-chi" (A record
of events in the navy), in Tso Shun-sheng, comp., *Chung-kuo
chin pai nien shih tzu-liao hsü-pien* (A supplement to materials
on Chinese history in the last 100 years; Shanghai, 1933),
pp. 323–363.
13. Quoted in Wang Ch'ü-ch'ang, p. 8, from Ch'en Pao-
ch'en's epitaph of Yen Fu.

14. Cited in Wang Shih, p. 15, from the private collection of letters (*chia-ts'ang shu-cha*) of Yen Ch'ü, Yen Fu's son and biographer.

15. See Ch'en Pao-ch'en's epitaph cited in Wang Shih, p. 15.

16. See his letter to Liang Ch'i-ch'ao, "Chih Liang Cho-ju shu," in Yen Fu, *Yen Chi-tao hsien-sheng i-chu* (Remaining works of Yen Fu; Singapore, 1959), p. 119.

17. In a footnote to the Prolegomena (*tao-yen*) of *T'ien-yen lun* (on evolution), in *Yen i ming-chu ts'ung-k'an*, I, 31 Yen Fu informs us that he had also read and translated passages in Spencer's *Social Statics*, and even in Bagehot's *Physics and Politics*, concerning the origins of human society. These translations were not to be published. The reference to Bagehot is most intriguing. Bagehot's emphasis on national communities ("the natural selection of communities") is, of course, directly relevant to Yen Fu's concerns.

18. James Legge, *Chinese Classics*, I, 357. This translation is based on Chu Hsi's philosophical interpretation of this somewhat obscure text.

19. *Ch'ang yen sheng-p'ing tu-wang p'ien-chih chih lun*.

20. "Yüan-ch'iang," *Yen Chi-tao wen-ch'ao*, Vol. 1.

21. "There can not be more good done than that of letting social progress go on unhindered" (Herbert Spencer, *A Study of Sociology;* New York, 1883, pp. 401–402).

22. See Paul Cohen, "The Anti-Christian Tradition in China," *Journal of Asian Studies*, Vol. 20, No. 2 (Feb. 1961).

23. The Chinese translation is called *Chih-na chiao-an lun*.

24. Wang Ch'ü-ch'ang, p. 12.

25. There is, of course, no evidence that he was at this time closely following Japanese developments or that his views were based on the Japanese example.

CHAPTER III. Declaration of Principles

1. "Lun shih-pien chih chi."
2. "Yüan-ch'iang,"
3. "Chiu-wang chüeh-lun,"
4. "P'i-Han." These essays are available in Yen Fu, *Yen Chi-tao shih-wen ch'ao*, and also in Ch'ien Po-tsan *et al.*, *Wu-hsü pien-fa* (The Reform Movement of 1898), Vol. 3; in *Chung-kuo chin-tai shih tzu-liao ts'ung-k'an* (A collection of

materials on modern Chinese history; Shanghai, 1953). These essays were first published in the Tientsin newspaper *Chih-pao* in 1895.

5. "Lun shih-pien chih chi" (On the speed of world change), in Ch'ien Po-tsan, III, 71.

6. *Ibid.*

7. The two characters *cheng chiao* translated inadequately as "government and philosophy" form a phrase with a deep resonance in Chinese thought. It refers to the deeply held belief that the governance of society and correct ideology are organically related. Hence the phrase refers to nothing less than basic social and intellectual transformation of society. The Chinese *chiao*, often translated "religion," means something like "true doctrine."

8. "Yüan-ch'iang" (On strength), in Ch'ien Po-tsan, III, 41.

9. *Ibid.*

10. *Ch'ün-hsüeh.*

11. "Yüan-ch'iang," p. 42.

12. Spencer's economic liberalism and his anti-statism have suffered heavily. This, however, is only one corner of his synthesis. The other elements of the synthesis are certainly very much alive—perhaps even more alive than the ideas of more celebrated nineteenth-century thinkers—e.g., his notion of the inherently pacific nature of an industrial civilization.

13. Ting Wen-chiang, *Liang Jen-kung hsien-sheng nien-p'u ch'ang-pien ch'u-kao* (First draft of a chronological biography of Liang Ch'i-ch'ao; Taipei, 1959), p. 42.

14. See the typical remark of the Hunanese Confucian scholar Yeh Teh-hui concerning K'ang Yu-wei—"In his outward appearance he is a Confucian and in his heart a barbarian"—in his *I-chiao ts'ung-pien* (Collected treatises on heretical religions; 1902), 6:17b.

15. Ting Wen-chiang, pp. 24–25.

16. "Yü *Wai-chiao-pao* chu-jen lun chiao-yü shu," in *Yen Chi-tao shih-wen ch'ao*, IV, 20–21.

17. "Some go so far as to say that their sciences all come from the East. This is, however, contrary to fact and merely serves the purposes of self-deception" ("*T'ien-yen lun* hsü," *Yen Chi-tao shih-wen ch'ao*, IV, 3).

18. *Ibid.,* p. 1.

19. *Ibid.,* p. 3.

20. *Ibid.,* p. 2.

21. Joseph Needham calls this "evolutionary naturalism in

a cyclical setting" (*Science and Civilization in China;* Cambridge, England, Vol. II, 1956, p. 485). Actually there is no indication that any of the Sung thinkers cited by him believed in the evolution of new varieties and species from old. The differentiation of the homogeneous does not involve a theory of evolution in this sense.

22. He continues to use the common features of Chinese philosophy and Western pantheism and naturalism, however, as a weapon in attacking Christianity.

23. "Lun shih-pien chih chi," p. 71.

24. *Ibid.*

25. *Ibid.*, p. 72.

26. *First Principles* (New York, 1900), p. 151.

27. "Yüan-ch'iang," p. 43.

28. Given the degree of socio-historic determinism presupposed in *Principles of Sociology*, it would appear that the quality of the individual is almost entirely determined by the quality of the social organism and is not a separate variable.

29. E.g., *Kuan-tzu*, "Chün-ch'en-pien hsia" (Treatise on lord and subject), in *Chu-tzu chi-ch'eng*, V, 177. Here the ruler in his capital is compared to the heart in the body.

30. Joseph Needham asserts the presence of the "state analogy" in China on the basis of a passage in the *Pao-p'u-tzu*. The passage as a whole is obviously, however, a case of the reverse analogy from the state to the body. One passage translated by Needham as, "Thus we see that he who can govern his body can control a kingdom," actually should be rendered (it seems to me), "The superior man can govern his body just as (*ju*) the enlightened ruler governs his state" (*Chu-tzu chi-ch'eng*, VIII, 232). The neglect of the small conjunction *ju* makes all the difference. The *Pao-p'u-tzu's* concern in this passage is obviously not with ordering the state but with "nourishing the life" of the individual. See Needham, II, 300–301.

31. Or in Marxist accounts, "bourgeois liberalism."

32. Richard Hofstadter, *Social Darwinism in American Thought* (Boston, 1955).

33. See Ernest Barker, *Political Thought in England from Spencer to the Present* (New York, 1915), pp. 84–88.

34. *Data of Ethics,* in *Select Works of Herbert Spencer* (New York, 1886), p. 499. Elsewhere Spencer describes the happy man as follows: "Bounding out of bed after an unbroken sleep, singing or whistling as he dresses, coming down with

beaming face ready to laugh on the smallest provocation, the healthy man of high powers, conscious of past successes, and by his energy, quickness, resource, made confident of the future, enters on the day's business not with repugnance but with gladness; and from hour to hour experiencing satisfactions from work effectually done, comes home with an abundant surplus of energy remaining for hours of relaxation" (*ibid.*, p. 536). Here we have the individual who has proved his fitness to survive. In his *Social Statics* (New York, 1913), p. 36, Spencer had already asserted: "Happiness signifies a gratified state of all the faculties. The gratification of a faculty is produced by its exercise. To be agreeable that exercise must be proportionate to the power of the faculty . . . Every man may have full freedom to exercise his faculties with the proviso that he shall not hurt anyone else."

35. *Data of Ethics*, p. 499.
36. "Yüan-ch'iang," p. 49.
37. *Ibid.*
38. Barker, p. 121.
39. *Ibid.*, p. 122.
40. Elsewhere he frankly states that "our sages have always profoundly feared this word [freedom]" ("Lun shih-pien chih chi," p. 73).
41. *Ibid.*
42. The same word *tzu-yu* may be translated as "liberty," and Yen Fu uses this very term to translate Mill's *On Liberty*. In most contexts, however, it seems to me that the word freedom is more apt since the connotation of the term in these essays is not strictly political—it is almost metaphysical.
43. "Yüan-ch'iang," p. 49.
44. "Lun shih-pien chih chi," p. 73.
45. "Yüan-ch'iang," p. 51.
46. *Ibid.*
47. *Ibid.*
48. "P'i-Han," in Ch'ien Po-tsan, III, 78.
49. Cited in "P'i-Han," p. 78.
50. *Ibid.*
51. "To judge from Han Yü's account the sages themselves and their ancestors and fathers could not have been human" (*Ibid.*)
52. *Ibid.*, p. 79.
53. *Ibid.*

54. It would seem that Yen Fu in recoil from Han Yü's view is here accepting Spencer's extremely restrictive conception of the role of government. Actually, however, we will find that he is full of admiration for what he regards as the immense power of the state in the modern West. This power is due precisely to the fact that in Western states the people participate in government.

55. The notion that the post-Ch'in state represented a decline from the "feudal utopia" of the ancient Three Dynasties (Hsia, Shang, and Chou) had been a common theme of Confucian discourse down through the centuries. At the end of the nineteenth century, it came to play a new role among nationalists seeking evidence of the presence of democracy in ancient China.

56. "P'i-Han," p. 80.

57. Ibid., p. 81

58. Ibid., pp. 80–81.

59. See p. 70. In "Yüan-ch'iang" Yen Fu quotes Spencer to the effect that "while there are no limits to the degree to which the people can be enlightened, this enlightenment cannot be rushed."

60. "P'i-Han," p. 80.

61. E.g., see Principles of Sociology (New York, 1884), I, 600–607.

62. Liang Ch'i-ch'ao, "Hsin-min shuo" (On the renovation of the people), in his Yin-ping-shih wen-chi (A collection of writings from the Ice-Drinker's Studio; Shanghai, 1916), 14:13.

63. "Yüan-ch'iang," p. 58.

64. Ibid., p. 57.

65. Ho chih.

66. See particularly the chapter on the "Bias of Patriotism" in his Study of Sociology. Much of this chapter is devoted to an attack on the anti-patriotic ("anti-British philistine") bias of Matthew Arnold.

67. Principles of Sociology, I, 583.

68. Particularly his translation of Jenks and his "Cheng-chih chiang-i" (Lectures on politics), Yen Chi-tao hsien-sheng i-chu, pp. 1–45.

69. Principles of Sociology, I, 479–480.

70. Barker, p. 117.

71. Those who have emphasized Spencer's "anarchic in-

dividualism" tend to overlook the fact that the citizen of his utopia is so "socialized" that there is no need for any "external" compulsion. Social discipline has been internalized by the industrial process. One might almost describe his utopia as a totalitarianism by consensus in which no one will "meddle" with the impersonal forces of the social mechanism.

72. See Lin Yüeh-hua, "Yen Fu she-hui ssu-hsiang" (Yen Fu's social thought), *She-hui hsüeh-chieh* (Sociological world), Vol. 7 (1933).

73. After the *coup d'etat* of 1898 this school was attached to Peking University.

74. The rebuttal, entitled "A Letter on the 'Refutation of Han Yü,' " was published in Liang Ch'i-ch'ao's *Shih-wu pao*. This may be found in Yeh Teh-hui, *I-chiao ts'ung-pien, chüan* 3. See also Wang Shih, p. 32.

75. Wang-Shih, pp. 57–58.

76. Wang Ch'ü-ch'ang, p. 42.

77. His patron, Wu Ju-lun, defends him against the charge and intimates that he would be willing to serve his country if invited—"Ta Chi-tao shu" (Letter in reply to Yen Fu), Jan. 28, 1898, in *T'ung-ch'eng Wu hsien-sheng ch'üan-shu* (The complete works of Wu Ju-lun; Peking, 1905), *Wu Chih-fu ch'ih-tu* (Letters of Wu Ju-lun), *chüan* 1.

78. Spencer has, of course, inoculated him against any Jeffersonian belief in any immediately available innate "good sense" of the people. The potential intellectual capacities of the people can only be actualized by a painful and prolonged process of education.

79. See Ting Wen-chiang, p. 41.

80. For a detailed discussion of these categories see "Yüan-ch'iang," pp. 41–59, *passim*.

81. "Shang-huang-ti wan-yen-shu," p. 6.

82. "Yüan-ch'iang," p. 55.

83. *Ibid.*, p. 56.

84. *Ibid.*

85. "Chiu-wang chüeh-lun" (On our salvation), in Ch'ien Po-tsan, III, 60.

86. *Ibid.*, p. 64.

87. *Ibid.*

88. He tells us nothing about the suffrage base or powers of this assembly. His later comments would indicate that at this point he merely contemplated an advisory "public-opinion" body with highly limited representation.

CHAPTER IV. Western Wisdom at its Source:
Evolution and Ethics

1. See Wang Shih, p. 33.
2. Liang Ch'i-ch'ao, in *Hsin-min ts'ung-pao,* No. 1 (Jan. 1, 1903).
3. For a Chinese treatment of this subject see Chiang Shu-ko. While the school was essentially stylistic, considerations of style and content are never totally separated within Chinese culture. By and large the leading members of the school tended to defend the philosophic concerns of the Sung against the Ch'ing scholars.
4. Wu Ju-lun (1840–1903), a *chin-shih* of the T'ung-chih period, was a protégé of Tseng Kuo-fan and a leading figure in the T'ung-ch'eng stylistic school. Later he was closely connected with Li Hung-chang.
5. See "I li-yen" (Introduction to translation), *T'ien-yen lun.*
6. *Ibid.,* p. 2.
7. *Hsin-min ts'ung-pao,* No. 7 (Apr. 1, 1903).
8. A concrete instance of his rejection of a Japanese neologism can be found in his preface to Spencer's *Study of Sociology,* where he rejects the Japanese *she-hui* (*shakai*) for "society" in favor of the classical *ch'ün,* which is much closer, in his view, to the Western concept of society as a social group rather than as a social structure.
9. Spencer, *Study of Sociology,* p. 6.
10. Yen Fu, *Ch'ün-hsüeh i-lun* (A study of sociology), *Yen i ming-chu ts'ung-k'an,* VI, 4.
11. Spencer, *Study of Sociology,* p. 6.
12. Yen Ch'ü, *Hou-kuan Yen hsien-sheng nien-p'u* (Chronological biography of Yen Fu by Yen Ch'ü), cited in Wang Shih, p. 34.
13. Wang Ch'ü-ch'ang, p. 29.
14. Hu Shih relates in his *Ssu-shih tzu-shu* (Autobiography at forty; Taipei, 1954): "Not many years after the translation of *Evolution and Ethics,* it became highly popular throughout the country and became the favorite reading of secondary school students. After China's frequent military reverses, particularly after the humiliation of the Boxer years, the slogans of 'Survival of the Fittest' (lit., 'superior victorious, inferior defeated, the fit survive') became a kind of clarion call."
15. *"T'ien-yen lun* hsü," *Yen Chi-tao shih-wen ch'ao,* IV, 2.

16. *Ibid.*, p. 3.

17. The theme of the incompatibility of human ethics and cosmic process had emerged before; see Cyril Bibby, *T. H. Huxley, Scientist, Humanist and Educator* (New York, 1960). Yen Fu remarks "that in 90 per cent of his work, he accepts the theory of natural determinism and that man is simply auxiliary. This book is the only exception" (*T'ien-yen lun,* p. 15).

18. Thomas Henry Huxley, *"Evolution and Ethics" and Other Essays* (New York, 1925), p. 6.

19. *Ibid.*, p. 81.

20. Huxley, of course, denies the existence of this "preternatural intelligence." See *Evolution and Ethics,* p. 22.

21. *Ibid.*

22. *Ibid.*, p. 82.

23. *Ibid.*

24. Darwinism, he asserts, has proven that there is no "so-called creator" (*T'ien-yen lun,* Pt. 1, p. 3).

25. Needham, Vol. II, Chaps. 10 and 15.

26. See *First Principles,* p. 317.

27. *T'ien-yen lun,* Pt. 2, p. 28.

28. *First Principles,* p. 92.

29. *T'ien-yen lun,* Pt. 2, p. 14.

30. *Ibid.*

31. The fact that the *Lao-tzu's* statement is not meant as an attack on heaven and earth is amply demonstrated by the parallel statement which follows: "The sages are not benevolent, they treat the people like straw dogs." Far from condemning the universe, Lao-tzu seems to be putting forth the Tao's sagacious indifference as a model of behavior for the sage.

32. *Evolution and Ethics,* p. 59.

33. *T'ien-yen lun,* Pt. 1, pp. 32–33.

34. Yen Fu remarks that "while Huxley maintains that one ought not to eliminate completely the element of self-interest, his conception of it is, nevertheless, narrow." Huxley grudgingly grants a certain role to self-interest in accounting for economic progress, but his attitude toward self-interest is basically negative and fearful. *T'ien-yen lun,* Pt. 1, p. 34.

35. *Evolution and Ethics,* p. 75.

36. *T'ien-yen lun,* Pt. 2, p. 47.

37. "*T'ien-yen lun* hsü," p. 2.

38. *T'ien-yen lun,* Pt. 1, p. 7.

CHAPTER V. The Wealth of Nations

1. "Yüan-ch'iang," pp. 55–56.
2. "Self-restraint, the essence of the ethical process, which is no less an essential condition of the existence of the polity, may by excess become ruinous to it" (*Evolution and Ethics*, p. 31).
3. *T'ien-yen lun*, Pt. 1, p. 34.
4. "Ssu-shih chi-hsüeh li-yen" (An introduction to Smith's economics), *Yen Chi-tao shih-wen ch'ao*, IV, 9.
5. Yen Fu, *Yüan-fu* (The wealth of nations), *Yen i ming-chu ts'ung-k'an*, Vol. 2, "I-shih li-yen" (Translator's introduction), p. 2.
6. *Yüan-Fu*, p. 26.
7. Eli Heckscher, *Mercantilism* (London, 1935), II, 15.
8. *Ibid.*, 17.
9. Smith, *Wealth of Nations*, p. 329.
10. *Ibid.*, p. 352.
11. *Ibid.*, p. 737.
12. *Ibid.*, p. 744.
13. See *Yüan-fu*, p. 959.
14. "Ssu-mi Ya-tan chuan" (Biography of Adam Smith), *Yüan-fu*, p. 2.
15. Smith, *Wealth of Nations*, p. 744.
16. *Ibid.*, p. 760. This is the last sentence in the book.
17. *Ibid.*, p. 560.
18. *Yüan-fu*, p. 707.
19. Smith, *Wealth of Nations*, p. 333.
20. *Ibid.*, p. 546.
21. *Ibid.*, p. 361.
22. *Ibid.*, p. 297. At one point (p. 560) Smith even seems to employ Yen Fu's own line of reasoning: "In modern war the great expense of firearms gives an evident advantage to the nation which can best afford that expense and consequently to an opulent and civilized over a poor and barbarous nation."
23. E.g., see the argument of the Confucian party in Huan K'uan.
24. *Yüan-fu*, Introduction, p. 2.
25. See "Ssu-mi Ya-tan chuan," *Yüan-fu*, pp. 1, 3.
26. Huxley, *Evolution and Ethics*, p. 30.
27. "I-shih li-yen," *Yüan-fu*, p. 6.
28. In the end, however, the traditional morality is more

resistant to the re-evaluation of the merchant than to the re-evaluation of the soldier. The warrior ethos is, after all, still hedged about with the aura of self-sacrifice and public service.

29. *Yüan-fu,* p. 91.

30. *Ibid.*

31. *Ibid.,* p. 790.

32. There is, however, a reference to Japan's success in procuring the abolition of legal extraterritoriality as a result of its legal reforms (*Yüan-fu,* p. 721).

33. Smith, *Wealth of Nations,* p. 558.

34. *Yüan-fu,* p. 703.

35. Smith, *Wealth of Nations,* p. 7.

36. See the abridgment of Dugald Stuart's "Life and Work of Adam Smith," in *ibid.,* p. 7.

37. *Ibid.*

38. *Ibid.,* p. 8.

CHAPTER VI. On Liberty

1. *Yen Chi-tao shih-wen ch'ao,* VI, 3.

2. Wang Ch'ü-ch'ang, p. 49.

3. *Ibid.,* p. 48.

4. Lin Yüeh-hua, p. 48.

5. Wang Shih, p. 54.

6. Yen Fu, *Ch'ün-chi ch'üan-chieh lun* (On liberty), *Yen-i ming-chu ts'ung-k'an,* Vol. 4, "I fan-li" (Translator's introduction), p. 4.

7. Barker, p. 10. Elsewhere Mill complains, "There is scarcely any outlet for energy in this country except business" (John Stuart Mill, *On Liberty;* Oxford, 1952, p. 86).

8. Mill, *On Liberty,* p. 76.

9. "I fan-li," *Ch'ün-chi ch'üan-chieh lun,* p. 2.

10. *Ibid.,* p. 4.

11. Mill, *On Liberty,* p. 24.

12. *Ibid.,* pp. 54–55.

13. *Ibid.,* p. 27.

14. *Ibid.,* p. 70.

15. *Ibid.,* p. 83. The idea of eccentricity does not translate itself easily into Yen Fu's Chinese.

16. *Ibid.,* p. 83.

17. *Ibid.,* p. 78.

18. *Ibid.,* p. 70.

19. *Ibid.,* p. 71. Yen Fu translates the word "powers" as

t'ien ping, which means something like "natural endowment."
20. Alexander Bain, *John Stuart Mill: A Criticism with Personal Recollections* (London, 1882), p. 107.
21. Paul Binswanger, *Wilhelm von Humboldt* (Frauenfeld and Leipzig, 1937), p. 189.
22. *She hsing-chi tzu-yu ming t'e-ts'ao wei min-te chih pen* (*Ch'ün-chi ch'üan-chieh lun,* p. 74).
23. Mill, *On Liberty,* p. 74.
24. *Ch'ün-chi ch'üan-chieh lun,* p. 70.
25. *Ibid.,* p. 74. It may be considered arbitrary by some to translate the work *kuo* as "state" in this passage. Actually, however, Yen Fu's text is rich in terms which refer to society in general or to the concept of "nation" (e.g., *ch'ün, she-hui, kuo-min* and *kuo-ch'un*).
26. *On Liberty,* p. 141.
27. *Ch'ün-chi ch'üan-chieh lun,* pp. 133–134.
28. "Chu-k'o p'ing-i," *Yen Chi-tao shih-wen ch'ao,* Vol. 1.
29. *Yüan-fu,* p. 795. He notes the fact that the Chinese soldier fought much more effectively in this encounter than in the Sino-Japanese war; yet the rank and file were still deprived of any training or education.
30. Lin Shu, *Chiang-t'ing ch'ien-pieh t'u-chi,* cited in Wang Ch'ü-ch'ang, p. 63.
31. See Chou Chen-fu, *Yen Fu ssu-hsiang shu-p'ing* (A critical interpretation of Yen Fu's thought; Shanghai, 1940), p. 199.
32. One will note here a subtle shift of meaning in Yen Fu's translation.
33. Yen Fu, "Yen Chi-tao yü Ch'un-ju shu-cha chieh ch'ao" (Letters of Yen Fu to Hsiung Ch'un-ju), *Hsüeh-heng* (The critical review), No. 18, letter 57.
34. Mill, *On Liberty,* p. 16. Starting out as a pure Bentham-ite, Mill had come to absorb more and more of the thought patterns of nineteenth-century historicism.
35. "I fan-li," *Ch'ün-chi ch'üan-chieh lun,* p. 2.
36. Wang Ch'ü-ch'ang, p. 74.
37. *Yen Chi-tao shih-wen ch'ao,* IV, 17–24.
38. Another impassioned attack on the revolutionaries can be found in his introduction to the translation of Spencer's *Study of Sociology.* "These shallow and hasty literati, not real-izing how long and weighty has been our past, hope, by baring their arms and rushing forward headlong, to overcome our decadent state and conquer all obstacles overnight . . . destruc-

tion is easy but what is constructed may not necessarily be of avail" (*Yen Chi-tao shih-wen ch'ao*, IV, 4).

CHAPTER VII. The Spirit of the Laws

1. Wang Ch'ü-ch'ang, p. 64. The translation is incomplete; Books XXX and XXXI remain untranslated.
2. See Book VIII, "Concerning the Corruption of the Principles of the Three Forms of Government."
3. Yen Fu, *Fa-i* (Spirit of the laws), Bk. XI, p. 8.
4. *Ibid.*, Introduction, p. 2.
5. "Other nations have made the interests of commerce yield to political interests. The latter [England] has always made its political interests yield to the interest of its commerce" (C. L. Montesquieu, *De l'esprit des lois;* Paris, 1944–1945, II, 13).
6. *Yüan-fu*, p. 720.
7. *Wealth of Nations*, Introduction, p. 6.
8. *Fa-i*, Bk. XI, p. 8.
9. *Ibid.*
10. Emile Durkheim, *Montesquieu et Rousseau, Précurseurs de la sociologie* (Paris, 1953).
11. *Fa-i*, Introduction, p. 2.
12. In his "Cheng-chih chiang-i" (Lectures on politics) of 1906, Yen Fu recommends both the methods of induction and comparative analysis as the foundation of a rigorous science of politics.
13. A whole book (XXXIX) is devoted to the question of "How Laws Should be Composed."
14. Durkheim, p. 105.
15. Durkheim is, to be sure, somewhat more ambivalent toward progress than Spencer.
16. Durkheim, p. 108.
17. *Ibid.*
18. See Chapter VIII.
19. *Fa-i*, Bk. VIII, p. 3.
20. See Chapter VIII.
21. Lenin, of course, was also profoundly exasperated with the sluggishness of the forces of history in the very heartland of capitalism itself.
22. Not all men, of course. The whole image is biased toward elitism. Only those who know the science of social evo-

lution, who clearly discern the path from the past into the future, can be the "legislators."

23. *Esprit des lois*, I, 31.

24. *Ibid.*, p. 134.

25. *Ibid.*

26. *Fa-i*, Bk. VIII, p. 24.

27. *Ibid.*, p. 28.

28. "If I were to describe the spirit of the three forms of government I would say that at the top we have democracy based on virtue. Next we have a morally-based (*yu-tao*) monarchic government, guided by the spirit of *li*. Next we have arbitrary despotism based on punishment. What is here called honor is the same as *li*, while 'fear' is [the fear] of punishments. One can see that honor is the same as *li* when one reads what Montesquieu says in this passage about 'people who have a high estimation of themselves.' When we have had a monarch guiding himself by moral principles, the behavior of the ministers has been determined by *li*" (*ibid.*, Bk. III, pp. 13–14).

29. *Ibid.*, Bk. V, p. 38.

30. *Ibid.*

31. *Ibid.*, Bk. II, p. 11.

32. *Esprit des lois*, I, 20.

33. *Fa-i*, Bk. II, p. 18.

34. *Esprit des lois*, I, 62. By many, of course, this apologia for the nobility on the part of Montesquieu is regarded as a reactionary strain in his thought. See Franklin Ford, *The Robe and the Sword* (Cambridge, Mass., 1953).

35. *Esprit des lois*, I, 288.

36. *Fa-i*, Bk. XVII, pp. 9–10.

37. *Ibid.*, p. 4.

38. *Ibid.* This passage is noteworthy for two features: (1) its tendency to acknowledge the premodern roots of Western success, (2) its favorable remarks concerning the role of Chinese culture in preserving the Chinese nation. Chou Chen-fu finds, in the latter, evidence of Yen Fu's turn to tradition. Actually this praise of the "preservative" functions of Chinese culture is the typical attitude of the modern nationalist toward the "national tradition." The implication is clear that China will transcend the culture once it is able to proceed further along the road to wealth and power.

39. *Ibid.*, Bk. XX, p. 18.

40. *Ibid.*, p. 19.

41. Montesquieu never really reconciles his flat assertion that despotism is based wholly on terror with his description of China as a state in which peace and good order are maintained among the people by the inculcation of proper customs and manners.

42. *Fa-i*, Bk. XIX, pp. 20–21.

43. *Ibid.*, p. 26.

44. *Esprit des lois*, I, 131.

45. *Ibid.*

46. *Fa-i*, Bk. VIII, pp. 23–24.

47. *Ibid.*, p. 24.

48. *Esprit des lois*, I, 27.

49. *Ibid.*, p. 46.

50. Also see Rousseau's statement that democracy suits only states which are "small and poor" (*The Social Contract;* Oxford, 1953, p. 349).

51. *Esprit des lois*, I, 162.

52. *Ibid.*

53. *Ibid.*

54. *Fa-i*, Bk. XX, p. 4.

55. *Esprit des lois*, II, 9. On the matter of commerce and democracy, Montesquieu maintains that a "commerce of economy" is not necessarily incompatible with democracy. "The spirit of commerce bears within itself the spirit of frugality, economy, moderation, work, sagacity, tranquility, good order and regularity. The evil arises when the excess of wealth destroys this spirit of commerce" (*ibid.*, I, 52).

56. *Fa-i*, Bk. IV, p. 7.

57. *Ibid.*, Bk. XVII, p. 5.

58. *Ibid.*, Bk. VIII, p. 3.

59. *Esprit des lois*, I, 162.

60. Yen Fu translates the word "individual" at this point with the deprecatory *hsiao-chi* (lit., 'small self').

61. *Fa-i*, Bk. XVII, p. 4.

62. It is interesting that the same view of antique democracy probably lies behind Hegel's conception of a truly free society. Montesquieu himself, in discussing "political liberty in its relation to the citizen," stresses the security of the individual—roughly the whole area of "civil rights."

CHAPTER VIII. A History of Politics

1. Edward Jenks, 1861–1939. An authority on English law, he became a Reader in English Law at Oxford and also taught at the newly formed London School of Economics. He wrote on English legal and constitutional history. One of his best-known works is *Law and Politics in the Middle Ages* (London, 1898).

2. Like many other generalizations about Montesquieu this one is, of course, not absolutely valid. His treatment of the evolution of Western Europe is certainly set within a historic framework and it is perhaps to this that Yen Fu alludes when, in his *Lectures on Politics* of 1906 (Cheng-chih chiang-i), p. 2, he states: "Before the eighteenth century political science was discussed without relation to history. From Plato in the Greek period right up through Rousseau . . . all political science was based on psychology or deduced from natural laws. The basing of political science on history is the approach of the nineteenth century and begins with Montesquieu."

3. Edward Jenks, *A History of Politics* (London, 1900), p. 151.

4. *Ibid.*, p. 140.

5. *Ibid.*, p. 149.

6. *Ibid.*, p. 148.

7. *Ibid.*, p. 147.

8. In his "Cheng-chih chiang-i" (p. 30) he actually states that "England may be said to represent the highest stage of the military state."

9. Yen Fu, *She-hui t'ung-ch'üan* (A history of politics), *Yen i ming-chu ts'ung-k'an*, Vol. 3, "I-che hsü" (Translator's introduction), p. 1.

10. *Ibid.*, p. 1. Like other adherents of the biological analogy who are simultaneously believers in irreversible progress, he does not linger on some of the more ominous implications of the analogy—the prospects of senescence and death.

11. This is not necessarily true of all Marxist historians. It is indeed highly doubtful whether Marx himself was committed to this view.

12. *She-hui t'ung-ch'üan*, "I-che-hsü," p. 1.

13. *Ibid.*, p. 2. In a commentary on Chap. 2 Yen Fu states that Chinese society is seven parts patriarchal and three parts military (*ibid.*, p. 15).

14. *Fa-i*, Bk. V, p. 13.
15. "Cheng-chih chiang-i," p. 80. He also continues to emphasize the revolution in the technology of communications as another factor making democracy possible.
16. "It was intensely unpopular both with 'constituencies' and representatives" (Jenks, *History of Politics*, p. 132).
17. *She-hui t'ung-ch'üan*, pp. 117–118.
18. Jenks, *History of Politics*, pp. 157–158.
19. *She-hui t'ung-ch'üan*, p. 146.
20. Jenks, *History of Politics*, p. 124.
21. Hu Han-min, "Shu Hou-kuan Yen-shih tsui-chin cheng-chien" (The recent political views of Yen Fu), *Min-pao*, No. 2 (Dec. 1906). This article is also notable for its interesting critique of Spencer's organic view of society (based on the views of the Japanese liberal Onozuka).
22. Chang Ping-lin, *"She-hui t'ung-ch'üan shang-tui"* (A discussion of *She-hui t'ung-ch'üan*), in *Chang-shih ts'ung-shu t'ai-yen wen-lu* (Collectanea of Chang Ping-lin; 1917), Vol. 20.
23. Yen Fu frequently shows an awareness (particularly in some of his commentaries on the *Esprit des lois*) of the continuing atmosphere of corruption in the state.
24. Actually, neither Sun Yet-sen nor the other revolutionaries made any broad appeal to the people as a whole. They were, however, ready to make use of the political passions of those segments of the population which were most responsive to the anti-Manchu appeal.

CHAPTER IX. Mill's *Logic*

1. Yen Fu was invited to lecture on the difference between government in China and the West as a background to the impending constitutional efforts of the Manchu government. Wang Shih, p. 72.
2. "Cheng-chih chiang-i," p. 2.
3. *Ibid.*, pp. 2–3. It is interesting to note that Mill himself in the last chapter of his *Logic* (London, 1896) (untranslated but undoubtedly read by Yen Fu) supports the notion that "laws of history" can be derived inductively. Mill succumbs up to a point to the historicism of his time in spite of his adherence to the empiricist-utilitarian tradition, which is basically not historicist in orientation.
4. "Cheng-chih chiang-i," p. 8.

MILL'S LOGIC 269

5. Yen Fu, *Ming-hsüeh* (*Logic*), *Yen i ming-chu ts'ung-k'an*, VIII, 3.
6. Yen Fu, *Ming-hsüeh ch'ien-shuo* (Logic), *Yen-i ming-chu ts'ung-k'an*, Vol. 7, "I-che tzu-hsü" (Translator's introduction), p. 1.
7. Like Hu Shih after him, Yen Fu is fully aware of the logical investigations of the ancient "logicians": Ming-chia (the School of Names), Kung-sun Lung, Hui Shih, and others. His translation of "logic" as *ming-hsüeh* is undoubtedly an allusion to their effort. He does not, however, dwell on their efforts.
8. Mill, *Logic*, p. 147.
9. "Chiu-wang chüeh-lun," *Yen Chi-tao shih-wen ch'ao*, II, 16.
10. *Ibid.* Yen Fu's hostility to Wang Yang-ming's school is most clearly expressed in a preface to an edition of Wang's works, "Wang Yang-ming hsien-sheng chi-yao san-chung" (Three collections of the important writings of Master Wang Yang-ming), *Yen Chi-tao shih-wen ch'ao*, III, 16–18. The famous translator of the classics, Legge, translates the obscure phrase *ko wu* as "investigation of things." This translation corresponds to the views of the school of Chu Hsi, who believed that the truth was to be sought in the principles lying behind the manifold of the objective world. Wang translates the term as "combating the material desires." Wang was actually very much oriented to practical activity within concrete situations: the activity which concerned him was the realization of Confucian moral values. From Yen Fu's point of view, of course, this mode of practicality has no relevance whatsoever to wealth and power.
11. "Yüan-ch'iang," p. 56.
12. Yen Fu, *Ming-hsüeh*, Bk. II, p. 33.
13. *Ibid.*, p. 66.
14. Mill, *Logic*, p. 152.
15. *Ming-hsüeh*, Bk. II, p. 80.
16. Needham, II, 322.
17. The phrase "a great instrument" is used by Yen Fu to translate Mill's word "agent" in Mill's statement, "the grand agent for transforming experimental into deductive science is the science of number" (Mill, *Logic*, p. 146).
18. *Ming-hsüeh*, Bk. II, p. 69.
19. To Yen Fu the insistence on the deductive nature of mathematics inevitably implied a derivation of truth from the human subject. He naturally regarded Chinese numerological

speculations as subjective. Whewell in arguing for the a priori necessary truth of mathematics had in a Kantian fashion spoken of this truth as fixed in the "constitution of the human mind."
    20. Morris Cohen, *Studies in Philosophy and Science* (New York, 1949), p. 135.
    21. Mill, *Logic*, p. 40.
    22. *Ming-hsüeh*, Bk. I, p. 53.
    23. *Ibid.*
    24. Whether Mill himself was able to remain consistently within the limits of his own professed philosophic premises is itself highly questionable.

CHAPTER X. Meditations on the Tao

    1. Yen Fu later wrote a most affectionate biography of this young man, whom he had met in 1900 in Shanghai. Hsiung, who had already acquired an impressive traditional education in his native city of Nanch'ang, had himself requested that Yen Fu accept him as a disciple; Yen Fu, deeply impressed with his profundity, willingly became his guide in Western learning. Like his guide and mentor, Hsiung was prepared to find all sorts of filiations and complementarities between strains of Chinese thought and the thought of the modern West. See Yen Fu, "Hsiung sheng Chi-lien chuan" (Biography of Hsiung Ch'un-ju), *Yen Chi-tao hsien-sheng i-chu*, p. 146.
    2. See Hsia Tseng-yu's introduction to Yen Fu, *Hou-kuan Yen shih p'ing-tien Lao-tzu* (*Lao-tzu* annotated by Yen Fu; Shanghai, 1931).
    3. Yen Fu, *Hou-kuan Yen-shih p'ing-tien Lao-tzu*, Pt. 1, pp. 5–6.
    4. Needham, Vol. II, sec. 10.
    5. *Tao te ching*, tr. Jan Julius Duyvendak (Wisdom of the East Series; London, 1954), p. 4.
    6. Spencer, *First Principles*, Chap. 4.
    7. Yen Fu, *Hou-kuan Yen-shih p'ing-tien Lao-tzu*, Pt. 2, p. 7.
    8. Needham (II, 87) insists that Lao-tzu's attacks on learning and knowledge only apply to the "false knowledge" of the Confucianists and not to "natural knowledge." It is also interesting to note that elsewhere Yen Fu, like Needham, sees an organic connection between "science" and "democracy." In the preface to his *Lectures on Politics* of 1906 he points out

that the Copernican theory had completely relativized the absolute notion of the "high" and "low" and had thus struck a fatal blow at all notions of status. This was one of the roots of the theory of liberty and equality. In a free and equal society, men's place is determined by their intrinsic worth proved in the crucible of natural selection and without any reference to any absolutized hierarchic social order. Lao-tzu, however, long before Copernicus, had relativized all the antitheses of the phenomenal world. See "Cheng-chih chiang-i tzu-hsü" in *Yen Chi-tao shih-wen ch'ao*, Vol. 3.

9. Yen Fu, *Hou-kuan Yen-shih p'ing-tien Lao-tzu*, Pt. 1, p. 21.

10. *Ibid.*, p. 20.

11. Yen Fu also interprets Lao-tzu's conception of the "nonactivity" (*wu-wei*) of the ruler to mean that the good ruler will make it possible for the people to act on its own behalf. Where the people's physical, intellectual, and moral powers have been developed to a maximum, wealth and power will be achieved without constant activity on the part of the ruler. See *ibid.*, Pt. 1, pp. 5–6.

12. *Tao te ching*, pp. 53–55.

13. Those terms are derived from the abstract interpretations of hexagrams No. 12 and 64 of the *Book of Changes*.

14. Yen Fu, *Hou-kuan Yen-shih p'ing-tien Lao-tzu*, Pt. 1, p. 10.

15. See Chapter III at reference to note 23.

16. Yen Fu, *Hou-kuan Yen-shih p'ing-tien Lao-tzu*, Pt. 1, p. 10.

17. *Ibid.*

18. "When the court is well purified but the fields are full of weeds and granaries empty—where the [rulers] wear decorated and embroidered robes, gird themselves with sharp swords, glut themselves with food, and have superfluous possessions— this I call robbing and arrogance" (*ibid.*, Pt. 2, p. 10).

19. *Ibid.*

20. *Ibid.*, p. 8.

21. *Ibid.*, Pt. 1, p. 1.

22. *Ibid.*, p. 14.

23. *Ibid.*, p. 7.

24. In Tantrism one may discern another—albeit entirely different—case of Buddhist mysticism linked to a life-affirming attitude.

CHAPTER XI. The Later Years

1. In 1908 appeared the last important translation—William Stanley Jevons' *Logic*.

2. En-ming was assassinated in 1907 by a revolutionary. Yen Fu immediately resigned his post.

3. Shen-ting ming-tz'u kuan. See H. S. Brunnert and V. V. Hagelstrom, *Present Day Political Organization of China*, tr. A. Beltchenko and E. E. Moran (Shanghai, 1912), p. 133; Wang Ch'ü-ch'ang, pp. 75–77.

4. Wang Ch'ü-ch'ang, p. 79.

5. *Ibid.*

6. In Yen Fu, *Yü-yeh-t'ang shih-chi* (Poems of Yü-yeh Hall), cited in Wang Ch'ü-ch'ang, p. 79.

7. Yüan had met Yen Fu in Tientsin during the 1895–1898 period and had conceived an admiration for him.

8. Hou I-shih, *Hung-hsien chiu-wen ch'ou-an t'ao-ming chi* (An account of the "theft of names" by the Peace Planning Society during Yüan Shih-k'ai's restoration attempt), cited in Wang Shih, p. 91.

9. He himself later states that he had not been opposed to revolution because of any profound love for the Aisingoro (the Manchu house) or because he was one of the inner officials of the court. See "Yen Chi-tao yü Ch'un-ju shu-cha chieh-ch'ao," *Hsüeh-heng*, No. 20 (Aug. 1923), Supplement, letter 5.

10. In Yen Fu, *Yü-yeh-t'ang shih-chi,* cited in Wang Ch'ü-ch'ang, p. 81.

11. Wang Ch'ü-ch'ang, pp. 82–83. A letter of later years to Hsiung indicates a conflict over the question of curriculum.

12. *Ibid.,* p. 88.

13. *Ibid.,* p. 110.

14. "Yen Chi-tao yü Ch'un-ju shu-cha chieh-ch'ao," *Hsüeh-heng*, No. 10 (Oct. 1922).

15. Wang Shih, p. 99.

16. This remark is not meant to deprecate the importance of conscious intellectual attitudes. One might say that in the case of Hu Shih and Ch'en Tu-hsiu—and a fortiori in the case of the May Fourth generation—the new intellectual attitude had finally penetrated down to the existential level.

17. See "Chia-shu pa t'ung" (Eight letters to the family), *Yen Chi-tao hsien-sheng i-chu*, pp. 154–162.

18. Wang Shih, p. 87.

19. Chou Chen-fu, *Yen Fu ssu-hsiang shu-p'ing,* pp. 251–310.

20. "Yen Chi-tao yü Ch'un-ju shu-cha chieh-ch'ao," *Hsüeh-heng,* No. 20 (Aug. 1923), Supplement, letter 5. Written after the assassination of Sung (hiao-jen in 1913.

21. *Ibid.,* Supplement, letter 3. Written shortly before Sung Chiao-jen's assassination.

22. *Ibid.,* No. 6 (June 1922), letter 1.

23. *Ibid.,* letter 2.

24. "Min-yüeh p'ing-i" (A critique of *The Social Contract*), *Yung-yen* (Justice), Vol. 2, Nos. 1 and 2 (Feb. 1914).

25. Chou Chen-fu, *Yen Fu ssu-hsiang shu-p'ing,* p. 272.

26. See Chapter III at references to notes 38 and 39.

27. Mill, *On Liberty,* p. 16.

28. Rousseau's *Social Contract* is, to put it mildly, by no means an easy text to interpret. What we are dealing with here is what might be called vulgar Rousseauism.

29. *Chün-chi ch'üan-chieh lun,* "I-fan-li," p. 2.

30. "Cheng-chih chiang-i," p. 2.

31. "Min-yüeh p'ing i," p. 6.

32. Yen Fu is not aware of Marxism. The "socialism" of Sun Yat-sen and others was, of course, not Marxist.

33. "Min-yüeh p'ing-i," p. 6.

34. "Yen Chi-tao yü Ch'un-ju shu-cha chieh-ch'ao," *Hsüeh-heng,* No. 20 (Aug. 1923), Supplement, letter 1.

35. E.g., his response to the assassination of Sung Chiao-jen. See *ibid.,* Supplement, letter 5.

36. *Ibid., Hsüeh-heng,* No. 12 (Dec. 1922), letter 25, probably written in 1916 after Yüan's death.

37. *Ibid.,* No. 7 (July 1922), letter 12.

38. *Ibid.,* No. 8 (Aug. 1922), letter 18.

39. *Ibid.,* letter 18.

40. Chou Chen-fu, *Yen Fu ssu-hsiang shu-p'ing,* p. 256.

41. Hou I-shih, *Hung-hsien chiu-wen ch'ou-an t'ao-ming chi,* cited in Chou Chen-fu, *Yen Fu ssu-hsiang shu-p'ing,* pp. 254–258.

42. Lit., 'Yours is the horse's head we must follow'—an allusion to a story in the *Tso chuan.*

43. See Liang Ch'i-ch'ao, "I-tsai so-wei kuo-t'i ti wen-t'i che" (How strange the so-called question of state structure!), in his *Yin-ping shih wen-chi,* Vol. 55.

44. *Yüan-fu,* p. 790.

45. *Ibid.,* p. 703.

46. Yen Fu, "Jih-pen hsien-fa i-chieh-hsü" (An introduction to Ito's *Commentaries on the Japanese Constitution*), *Yen Chi-tao shih-wen ch'ao*, III, 28.

47. Wang Shih (p. 43) points, however, to an interesting exception to this attitude in 1897 when Yen Fu wrote an article supporting the idea of a Sino-Russian alliance, "Chung-Ngo chiao i lun" (Views on Russian-Chinese relations). Yen Fu actually states that China should model itself on Russia. While both are unlimited monarchies, Russia has already made some progress toward modernization. It is interesting to note, however, his statement that "the degree of power of monarchy is in direct proportion to the degree of enlightenment among the people."

48. *Wealth of Nations,* p. 558.

49. *Yüan-fu,* pp. 702–703.

50. "Yen Chi-tao yü Ch'un-ju shu-cha chieh-ch'ao," *Hsüeh-heng,* No. 6 (June 1922), letter 5.

51. *Ibid.*

52. *Ibid.*

53. *Ibid.*

54. Yüan Shih-k'ai had asked Yen Fu to be a sort of official reporter on the course of the war.

55. "Yen Chi-tao yü Ch'un-ju shu-cha chieh-ch'ao," *Hsüeh-heng,* No. 7 (July 1922), letter 13.

56. *Ibid.,* No. 13 (Jan. 1923), letter 34.

57. Ever since the beginning of the war, Yen Fu points out, the British government has entrusted ministerial posts to experts without regard to party.

58. *Ibid.,* letter 39.

59. The students of the May Fourth generation probably arouse no hope in his breast. How can callow, untrained youths save China? *Ibid., Hsüeh-heng,* No. 20 (Aug. 1923), letters 21 and 22.

60. "All I can do," he states at one point, "is sit and watch the sinking boat. I have no power and even if I did I could do nothing to save it." *Ibid.,* No. 20 (Aug. 1933).

61. Yen Fu *et al.,* "K'ung-chiao hui chang-ch'eng" (The program of the Confucian Society), *Yung-yen,* Vol. 1, No. 14 (June 1913).

62. *Ibid.,* "Fu-lu" (Supplement), p. 3, and *passim.*

63. "Yen Chi-tao yü Ch'un-ju shu-cha chieh-ch'ao," *Hsüeh-heng,* No. 7 (July 1922), letter 4. In 1914 Yen Fu translated Dr. Alfred Westharp's "View on Chinese Education" ("Chung-

kuo chiao-yü i," *Yung-yen*, 2:3 and 4:1). Westharp supported the notion of a Chinese education based on Confucian values which would be in keeping with China's national character. Yen Fu was struck by this foreigner's advocacy of traditional Chinese values.

64. "Yen Chi-tao yü Ch'un-ju shu-cha chieh-ch'ao," *Hsüeh-heng*, No. 12 (Dec. 1922), letter 24.

65. *Ibid.*, No. 18 (June 1923), letter 59.

66. Elsewhere he states, "The four books and five classics are a rich mine. We must, however, use new tools to dig out and refine the ore." *Ibid.*, No. 13 (Jan. 1923), letter 39. An epitome of Yen Fu's final formulation of his worldly philosophy can be found in his testament to his children where he charges them to know that: (1) China will not be destroyed; its old tradition (*chiu fa*) may be diminished or increased but must not be overthrown; (2) If a man wishes to enjoy life he must give primary attention to his physical health; (3) One must be diligent in one's undertakings; lost opportunities will not return; (4) Think carefully and logically; (5) Increase your intellectual capacities; it is not easy to achieve high human capacities; (6) In conflicts between the society and the individual, one must think lightly of the individual and emphasize the interests of society.

67. *Ibid.*, No. 12 (Dec. 1922), letter 26.

68. A quotation from *Chuang-tzu*, this is a description of the Taoist adept finally free of desires.

69. "Yen Chi-tao yü Ch'un-ju shu-cha chieh-ch'ao," *Hsüeh, heng*, No. 20 (Aug. 1923), letter 74.

CHAPTER XII. Some Implications

1. He uses this kind of vocabulary only in his embittered old age, when it had already become common currency.

2. Again, one need not deny the claim that the "ultimate end" is economic welfare. The proximate end is, however, decidedly not less important than the professed ultimate end.

3. Chiang Kai-shek has, with indifferent success, attempted to bend Confucius to the goals of state power.

4. *The Growth of Philosophic Radicalism* (Boston, 1955), pp. 120–150.

5. Max Weber tends to credit the nation-state with an im-

portant role in the very genesis of "capitalism." "The constant struggle for power—in peace and war—of competing nation-states created the greatest opportunities for modern Western capitalism." Max Weber, *Wirtschaft und Gesellschaft* (Tübingen, 1956), II, 823.

6. Some nineteenth- and twentieth-century thinkers not so exclusively economic in orientation have indeed argued a functional relationship between the process of democratization and the growth of the nation-state, of military conscription, and of nationalism in general.

SELECTED BIBLIOGRAPHY

Bagehot, Walter. Physics and Politics. New York, 1881.

Bain, Alexander. John Stuart Mill: A Criticism with Personal
Recollections. London, 1882.

Barker, Ernest. Political Thought in England from Spencer to the
Present. New York, 1915.

Bibby, Cyril. T. H. Huxley, Scientist, Humanist and Educator.
New York, 1960.

Binswanger, Paul. Wilhelm von Humboldt. Frauenfeld and Leipzig,
1937.

Brunnert, H. S. and V. V. Hagelstrom. Present Day Political
Organization of China, tr. A. Beltchenko and E. E. Moran.
Shanghai, 1912.

Chao Feng-t'ien趙豐田. Wan Ch'ing wu-shih nien ching-chi ssu-
hsiang shih 晚清五十年經濟思想史(Economic thought
during the last fifty years of the Ch'ing dynasty); Yen-ching
hsüch-pao chuan-hao 燕京學報專號(Yenching journal
of Chinese studies, special monographs), No. 18. 1939.

Ch'en Pao-ch'en陳寶琛 "Ch'ing ku tzu-cheng ta-fu hai-chün hsieh
tu-t'ung Yen chün mu chih-ming" 清故資政大夫海軍協都
統嚴君墓誌銘(An epitaph on the tomb of Yen Fu, former
councilor and vice-admiral); in Min Erh-ch'ang閔爾昌,
comp., Pei-chuan chi pu碑傳集補(Supplement to a collection
of epitaph biographies). Peking, 1931.

277

Chiang Shu-ko 美書閣 . T'ung-ch'eng wen-p'ai shu-p'ing 桐城
文派述評 (A critical account of the T'ung-ch'eng school).
Shanghai, 1930.

Ch'ien Mu 錢穆. Chung-kuo chin san pai nien hsüeh-shu shih
中國近三百年學術史 (An intellectual history of China
during the last 300 years). Shanghai, 1937.

Ch'ien Po-tsan 剪伯贊 et al. Wu-hsü pien-fa 戊戌變法
(The Reform Movement of 1898); in Chung-kuo chin-tai shih
tzu-liao ts'ung-k'an 中國近代史資料叢刊 (A
collection of materials on modern Chinese history). 4 vols.;
Shanghai, 1953.

Ch'ih Chung-hu 池仲祜 . "Hai-chün ta shih-chi" 海軍大事記
(A record of events in the navy); in Tso Shun-sheng 左舜
生 , comp., Chung-kuo chin pai nien shih tzu-liao hsü-pien
中國近百年史資料續編 (A supplement to
materials on Chinese history in the last 100 years), pp. 323-
363. Shanghai, 1933.

Chou Chen-fu 周振甫 . Yen Fu ssu-hsiang shu-p'ing 嚴復思想
述評 (A critical interpretation of Yen Fu's thought).
Shanghai, 1940.

------Yen Fu shih-wen hsüan 严复詩文选 (A selection of Yen
Fu's poetry and essays). Peking, 1959.

Cohen, Morris. Studies in Philosophy and Science. New York, 1949.

Cohen, Paul. "The Anti-Christian Tradition in China," Journal of
Asian Studies, 20.2:169-180 (Feb. 1961).

Durkheim, Émile. Montesquieu et Rousseau, Précurseurs de la
sociologie. Paris, 1953.

Ford, Franklin. The Robe and the Sword. Cambridge, Mass., 1953.

Halévy, Élie. The Growth of Philosophic Radicalism. Boston, 1955.

Hao Yen-p'ing 郝延平 . T'ung-kuang hsin cheng chung ti so-wei
(ch'ing i): Chung-kuo wan-Ch'ing ti pao-shou-chu-i 同光
新政中的所謂（清義）中國晚清的保守主義
(The so-called "Pure View" School of the T'ung-chih and
Kuang-hsü periods: conservatism in China during the late
Ch'ing period). Taipei, 1958.

Heckscher, Eli. Mercantilism. 2 vols.; London, 1935.

Ho Ch'ang-ling賀長齡 . Huang-ch'ao ching-shih wen-pien皇朝
經世文編 (A collection of works on statecraft). 24 ts'e;
Peking, 1896.

Ho Lin 賀麟 . "Yen Fu ti fan-i"嚴復的翻譯(The translations
of Yen Fu); Tung-fang tsa-chih 東方雜誌 (Eastern
miscellany), 22.21:75-87 (Nov. 1925).

Hofstadter, Richard. Social Darwinism in American Thought.
Boston, 1955.

Huan K'uan桓寬 . "Yen t'ieh lun"鹽鐵論 (Discourses on
iron and salt); in Chu-tzu chi-ch'eng 諸子集成 (A
collection of the writings of the philosophers), Vol. 7. Peking,
1954.

Huxley, Thomas Henry. "Evolution and Ethics" and Other Essays.
New York, 1925.

------Science and the Hebrew Tradition. New York, 1897.

Jenks, Edward. A History of Politics. London, 1900.

Jevons, William Stanley. Logic. New York, 1879.

Legge, James. The Chinese Classics. 5 vols.; Hong Kong, 1960.

Levenson, Joseph R. Liang Ch'i-ch'ao and the Mind of Modern China. Cambridge, Mass., 1959.

Li Ting-i 李定一 . Chung-kuo chin-tai shih 中國近代史 (A history of modern China). Taipei, 1956.

Liang Ch'i-ch'ao 梁啟超 . "I-tsai so wei kuo-t'i ti wen-t'i che 異哉所謂國體的問題者 (How strange the so-called question of state structure); in his Yin-ping shih wen-chi 飲冰室文集 (A collection of writings from the Ice-Drinker's Studio), Vol. 55. Shanghai, 1916.

------Intellectual Trends in the Ch'ing Period, tr. Immanuel C.Y. Hsü. Cambridge, Mass., 1959.

Lin Yüeh-hua 林耀華 . "Yen Fu she-hui ssu-hsiang" 嚴復社會思想 (Yen Fu's social thought); She-hui hsüeh-chieh 社會學界 (Sociological world), 7:1-81 (June 1933).

Mill, John Stuart. Logic. London, 1896.

------On Liberty. Oxford, 1952.

Montesquieu, C.L. De l'esprit des lois. 2 vols.; Paris, 1944, 1945.

Needham, Joseph. Science and Civilization in China. 4 vols.; Cambridge, England, 1954-1962.

Rousseau, Jean-Jacques. The Social Contract. Oxford, 1953.

Smith, Adam. The Theory of Moral Sentiments. Boston, 1817.

------An Inquiry into the Nature and Causes of the Wealth of Nations. London, 1875.

Spencer, Herbert. A Study of Sociology. New York, 1883.

------Principles of Sociology. New York, 1884.

------Data of Ethics; in Select Works of Herbert Spencer.
New York, 1886.

Teng Ssu-yü and John K. Fairbank. China's Response to the West.
Cambridge, Mass., 1954.

Ting Wen-chiang 丁文江 . Liang Jen-kung hsien-sheng nien-p'u
ch'ang-pien ch'u-kao 梁任公先生年譜長編初稿
(First draft of a chronological biography of Liang Ch'i-ch'ao).
Taipei, 1959.

Ts'ai Yüan-p'ei 蔡元培 . "Wu-shih nien lai Chung-kuo chih
che-hsüeh" 五十年來中國之哲學 (Chinese
philosophy in the last fifty years); in Shen-pao kuan pien-chi
tsui-chin wu-shih nien 申報館編輯最近之五十年
(The last fifty years), comp. The Shen-pao Co. Shanghai,
1923.

Tso Tsung-t'ang 左宗棠 et al., comps. Ch'uan cheng tsou i
hui-pien 船政奏議彙篇 (Collection of memorials on
naval administration). Peking, 1905.

Wang Ch'ü-ch'ang 王遽常 . Yen Chi-tao nien-p'u 嚴幾道年
譜 (Chronological biography of Yen Fu). Shanghai, 1936.

Wang Shih 王栻 . Yen Fu chuan 嚴復傳 (Biography of Yen Fu).
Shanghai, 1957.

Weber, Max. Wirtschaft und Gesellschaft. 2 vols.; Tübingen, 1956.

Wright, Mary C. The Last Stand of Chinese Conservatism: The
Tung-chih Restoration. Stanford, 1957.

Yen Fu 嚴復. "Chung-kuo chiao-yü i" 中國教育議 (A
discussion of Chinese education); Yung-yen 庸言 (Justice),

2. 3-4:1-19 (Mar. 1914). A translation of an article by

Dr. Alfred Westharp (Wei Hsi-chin 偉西琴).

------"Min-yüeh p'ing-i" 民約平議 (A critique of The Social

Contract); Yung-yen, 2. 25-26:1-11 (Feb. 1914).

------Yen Chi-tao shih-wen ch'ao 嚴幾道詩文鈔 (A collection

of Yen Fu's prose and poetry). 6 ts'e; Shanghai, 1922.

------"Yen Chi-tao yü Ch'un-ju shu-cha chieh-ch'ao" 嚴幾道與

純如書扎節鈔 (Letters of Yen Fu to Hsiung Ch'un-ju);

Hsüeh-heng, wen-lu 學衡文錄 (The critical review,

literary section), No. 6:1-5 (June 1922), No. 7:1-8 (July

1922), No. 8:1-8 (Aug. 1922), No. 10:1-9 (Oct. 1922), No. 12:

1-10 (Dec. 1922), No. 13:1-13 (Jan. 1923), No. 15:1-8 (Mar.

1923), No. 16:1-6 (Apr. 1923), No. 18:1-8 (June 1923),

No. 20:1-6 (Aug. 1923).

------Yen i ming-chu ts'ung-k'an 嚴譯名著叢刊 (A collection

of Yen Fu's translated works). Shanghai, 1931.

------T'ien-yen lun 天演論 (On evolution); Yen i ming-chu ts'ung-

k'an, Vol. 1. A translation of ThomasHenry Huxley (Ho-hsü-

li 赫胥黎), Evolution and Ethics.

------Yüan-fu 原富 (The wealth of nations); Yen i ming-chu ts'ung-

k'an, Vol. 2. A translation of Adam Smith (Ya-tan-ssu-mi 亞

當斯密), The Wealth of Nations.

------She-hui t'ung-ch'üan 社會通銓 (A history of politics);

Yen i ming-chu ts'ung-k'an, Vol. 3. A translation of

Edward Jenks (Chen-k'o-ssu 甄克思), A History of Politics.

------Ch'ün-chi ch'üan-chieh lun 群己權界論 (On liberty); Yen i

ming-chu ts'ung-k'an, Vol. 4. A translation of John Stuart

Mill (Mu-lo 穆勒), On Liberty.

------Fa-i 法意 (Spirit of the laws); Yen i ming-chu ts'ung-k'an,
    Vol. 5. A translation of C. L. Montesquieu (Meng-te-ssu-
    chiu 孟德斯鳩), De l'esprit des lois.

------Ch'ün-hsüeh i-lun 羣學肄論 (A study of sociology);
    Yen i ming-chu ts'ung-k'an, Vol. 6. A translation of
    Herbert Spencer (Ssu-pin-sai erh 斯賓塞爾), A Study
    of Sociology.

------Ming hsüeh ch'ien-shuo 名學淺說 (Logic); Yen i ming-chu
    ts'ung-k'an, Vol. 7. A translation of William Stanley Jevons
    (Yeh-fang-ssu 耶芳斯), Logic.

------Ming-hsüeh 名學 (Logic); Yen i ming-chu ts'ung-k'an, Vol. 8.
    A translation of John Stuart Mill, Logic.

------Hou-kuan Yen-shih p'ing-tien Lao-tzu 侯官嚴氏評點
    老子 (Lao-tzu annotated by Yen Fu). Shanghai, 1931.

------Chuang-tzu p'ing-tien 莊子評點 (Chuang-tzu with
    commentary and punctuation). Hong Kong, 1953.

------Yen Chi-tao hsien-sheng i-chu 嚴幾道先生遺著
    (Remaining works of Yen Fu). Singapore, 1959.

------"Cheng-chih chiang-i" 政治講議 (Lectures on politics);
    Yen Chi-tao hsien-sheng i-chu, pp. 1-45.

Yen Fu et al. "K'ung-chiao hui chang-ch'eng" 孔教會章程
    (The program of the Confucian Society); Yung-yen, fu-lu
    (supplement), 1.14:1-8 (June 1913).

------ "K'ung-chiao hui ch'ing yuan shu" 孔教會請願
      書 (A petition of the Confucian Society); Yung-yen, fu-lu,
      1.16:1-5 (July 1913).

Chang Chih-tung 張之洞

Chang Chü-cheng 章居正

Chang I 張翼

Chang Ping-lin 章炳麟

Chang Shih-chao 章士釗

Chang-shih ts'ung-shu t'ai-yen
  wen-lu 章氏叢書太炎
  文錄

Chang T'ai-yen 章太炎
  (Chang Ping-lin)

Chang Yüan-chi 張元濟

ch'ang yen sheng-p'ing tu-wang
  p'ien-chih chih lun 嘗言生
  平獨往偏至之論

Ch'en Tu-hsiu 陳獨秀

cheng chiao 政教

"Cheng-chih chiang-i, tzu-hsü"
  政治講義自序

"Cheng-hsüeh lun" 政學論

Cheng Kuan-ying 鄭觀應

Ch'eng Chin-fang 程晉芳

ch'eng i 誠意

Ch'i 齊

Chia-ch'ing 嘉慶

"Chia-shu pa t'ung" 家書八通

chia-ts'ang shu-cha 家藏書札

Chiang-t'ing ch'ien-pieh t'u-chi
  江亭餞別圖圖

ch'iang-jou 強肉

chieh-chü 絜矩

Chien-wei 建威

ch'ien-k'un 乾坤

Ch'ien-lung 乾隆

chih 質

chih kuo p'ing t'ien-hsia 治國
  平天下

chih-li 質力

"Chih Liang Cho-ju shu"
  至梁卓如書

Chih-na chiao-an lun 支那
  教案論

Chih-pao 直報

chih-p'ing 治平

chih shen-hsin 治身心

chih-tsu 知足

chin-shih 進士

chin-shih ch'u-shen 進士
  出身

ching shih 經世

ching-shih wei yung 經世為用

ch'ing i 清議

284

chiu fa 舊法
"Chiu-wang chüeh-lun" 救亡
　決論
Chu Ko-liang 諸葛亮
"Chu-k'o p'ing-i" 主客評議
Chu Yuan-chang 朱元章
ch'u li 出力
"Chung-Ngo chiao i lun" 中俄
　交誼論
chung-nung 重農
chü-jen 舉人
Ch'üan-hsüeh p'ien 勸學篇
"Chün-ch'en-pien hsia" 君臣
　篇下
ch'ün 羣
ch'ün-hsüeh 羣學
ch'ün tao 羣道
En-ming 恩銘
fa chih 法治
fa-tu 法廣

Han-fei-tzu 韓非子
Han Wu-ti 漢武帝
Han Yü 韓愈
Ho Ch'ang-ling 賀長齡
ho chih 合志
hou hsien 後賢
Hou I 侯毅 (Hou I-shih)

Hou I-shih 侯疑始
Hou Kuan 侯官
Hou-kuan Yen hsien-sheng nien-p'u
　侯官嚴先生年譜
hsi 翁
Hsia Tseng-yu 夏曾佑
Hsiang Yü 項羽
hsiao-chi 小己
hsiao-chi chih tzu-yu 小己
　之自由
hsiao jen 小人
hsin 信
Hsin ch'ing-nien 新青年
"Hsin-min shuo" 新民説
Hsin-min ts'ung-pao 新民
　叢報
hsin-shu 心術
hsing chi 行己
hsing-ch'i 形氣
Hsiung Chi-lien 熊季廉 (Hsiung
　Ch'un-ju)
Hsiung Ch'un-ju 熊純如
　(Hsiung Chi-lien)
"Hsiung sheng Chi-lien chuan"
　熊生季廉傳
hsü-chün 虛君
Hsü T'ung 徐彤
Hsüeh Fu-ch'eng 薛福成

Hsün-tzu 荀子
Hu Han-min 胡漢民
hu shang 護商
Huang Shao-yen 黃少岩
Huang Tsung-hsi 黃宗羲
hui 諱
Hui Shih 惠施
Hung-hsien chiu-wen ch'ou-an
   t'ao-ming chi 洪憲舊聞
籌安盜民記

i 義
"I-che hsü" 譯者序
"I-che tzu-hsü" 譯者自序
I-chiao ts'ung-pien 翼教叢編
"I fan-li" 譯凡例
i li 義利
"I li-yen" 譯例言
"I-shih li-yen" 譯氏例言
i wu 一物

jen 仁
jen chih 人治
jen hsin 人心
jen-li 人力
jen shih 人事
jen t'ien wei chih 任天為治
"Jih-pen hsien-fa i-chieh-hsü"
   日本憲法義解序

ju 如
Jung-lu 榮祿

k'ao-cheng p'ai 考證派
ko wu 格物
Ku Hung-ming 辜鴻銘
ku wen 古文
Ku Yen-wu 顧炎武
Kuan Chung 管仲
kuan, ping, kung, shang, fa, chih
   官兵工商法制
Kuan-tzu 管子
Kuang-hsü 光緒
kung 公
kung-ch'an 共產
kung-hsin 公心
kung li 公理
kung li 功利
Kung-sun Lung 公孫龍
Kung-yang 公洋
kuo 國
kuo-ch'ün 國羣
kuo-ch'ün chih tzu-yu 國羣
   之自由
kuo-min 國民
Kuo Sung-t'ao 郭嵩燾
Kuo-wen hui-pien 國聞彙編
Kuo-wen-pao 國聞報

286

Lao-tzu 老子

li 利

li 禮

Li Hung-chang 李鴻章

Li Wen-chung-kung ch'üan-chi
李文忠公全集

Li Yüan-hung 黎元洪

liang-chih 良知

Lin Hsü 林旭

Lin Shu 林紓

Lin Tse-hsü 林則徐

Liu Pang 劉邦

Liu Tsung-yüan 柳宗元

Liu Yü-hsi 劉禹錫

Lu Hsiang-shan 陸象山

Lu Hsün 魯迅

lun chi 倫紀

"Lun shih-pien chih chi" 論世
變之亟

Ma Chien-chung 馬建忠

min chih 民質

Min-pao 民報

min sheng 民生

min-te 民德

min-tsu-chu-i 民族主義

ming 名

Ming-chia 名家

ming-hsüeh 名學

mo 末

pai-hua 白話

pao chiao 保教

pao kuo 保國

Pao-p'u-tzu 保樸子

pen 本

pen-t'i 本體

p'i 闢

"P'i-Han" 闢韓

pien fa 變法

p'ien t'i 駢體

pu jen 不仁

pu k'o ssu-i 不可思議

pu-lu 補錄

pu pei 不備

pu-ssu-tieh-ni-chiao 卜斯
迭尼教

p'u 樸

san-kang 三綱

shakai 社會

"Shang-huang-ti wan-yen-shu"
上皇帝萬言書

shang ti 上帝

Shanghai ch'ing-mien hui 上海
青年會

she hsing-chi tzu-yu ming t'e-ts'ao

wei min-te chih pen 釋行己
自繇明特操為民德之本

287

she-hui 社會

"She-hui t'ung-ch'üan shang-tui"
社會通詮商兌

Shen Chia-pen 沈家本

Shen Pao-chen 沈葆楨

Shen Pu-hai 申不害

Shen-ting ming-tz'u kuan 審定
名詞館

sheng 生

shih 士

shih-shih ch'iu shih 實事
求是

Shih-wu pao 時務報

shu 術

shu 恕

"Shu Hou-kuan Yen-shih tsui-chin
cheng-chien" 述侯官嚴
氏最近政見

Shuo-wen 說文

Ssu-ma Ch'ien 司馬遷

"Ssu-shih chi-hsüeh li-yen"
其氏計學例言

Ssu-shih tzu-shu 四十自述

su 素

Sun-tzu 孫子

Sung Chiao-jen 宋教仁

ta 達

"Ta Chi-tao shu" 答幾道書

ta li 大利

ta-wei 大偽

T'an Ssu-t'ung 譚嗣同

T'ang Shao-i 唐紹儀

T'ang T'ai-tsung 唐太宗

tao 道

Tao te ching 道德經

tao-yen 導言

Teng Cheng-hsiu 鄧承修

t'i 體

t'i-yung 體用

t'ien hsia 天下

t'ien-hsia kuo-chia 天下國家

t'ien hsing 天行

t'ien-ping 天稟

"T'ien-yen lun hsü" 天演論序

tsa 雜

tsa niu 雜糅

Tsai-hsün 載洵

Ts'ai Yüan-p'ei 蔡元培

Ts'ao Ts'ao 曹操

Tseng Kuo-fan 曾國藩

Tso chuan 左傳

tsou-kao 奏稿

tsung chiao-hsi 總教習

tsung-pan 總辦

T'u Jen-shou 屠仁守

Tung Chung-shu 董仲舒

288

tung-lai 東來
t'ung 通
T'ung-ch'eng 桐城
T'ung-ch'eng Wu hsien-sheng
　ch'üan-shu 桐城吳
　先生全書
T'ung-chih 同治
T'ung-i hsüeh-t'ang 通藝
　學堂
T'ung-wen kuan 通文館
Tzu-cheng yüan 資政院
tzu-yu 自繇
Tzu-yu lun 自由論
tz'u 詞

Wai-chiao-pao 外交報
Wang An-shih 王安石
Wang Chia-pi 王家璧
Wang Fu-chih 王夫之
Wang Hsi-fan 王錫藩
Wang Kuo-wei 王國為
Wang Shou-yun 王綬云
Wang T'ao 王韜
Wang Wen-shao 王文韶
Wang Yang-ming 王陽明
"Wang Yang-ming hsien-sheng
　chi-yao san-chung" 王陽明
　先生集要三種
wei 偽

wei chi 未濟
wei yen 威嚴
Wei Yüan 魏源
wen 文
Wen-hsiang 文祥
Wo Jen 倭仁
Wu Chih-fu ch'ih-tu 吳摯父尺牘
Wu Ju-lun 吳汝綸
wu tao 無道
wu wei 無為

ya 雅
Yang-ch'i-hsiang 陽崎鄉
Yang Tu 楊度
yang wu 洋務
Yang-wu 揚武
Yeh Teh-hui 葉德輝
Yen Chen-hsien 嚴振先
Yen Ch'ü 嚴璩
Yen Hsiu 嚴修
Yen Po-yü 嚴伯玉 (Yen Ch'ü)
Yu-ling 又陵
yu tao 有道
yuan-tao 原道
Yung-cheng 雍正
yü chü 予豦據
"Yü Wai-chiao-pao chu-jen lun
　chiao-yü shu" 與外交報
　主人論教育書

289

Yü-yeh-t'ang shih-chi 瘉樊堂
  詩集
"Yüan-ch'iang" 原強
Yüan Pao-heng 袁保恆

Yüan Shih-k'ai 袁世凱
Yüeh Fei 岳飛
yün-hui 運會

INDEX

M

A